Quinoa
The Everyday Superfood

The Everyday Superfood

Quinoa

150

Gluten-Free Recipes
to Delight Every Kind
of Eater

SONOMA
PRESS

Quinoa for Every Day

5 Unexpected Ways to Enjoy Quinoa

Quinoa is a superfood in more ways than one: Not only is it a gluten-free health-booster packed with nutrients, it's a delicious everyday grain (actually, the edible seed of a grain) that can please anyone, from dedicated vegans to die-hard carnivores. Here are just a few of the unexpected ways you'll learn to enjoy quinoa.

Blended in a smoothie: You can blend raw quinoa into a smoothie for a high-protein, high-fiber snack or meal any time of the day. You'll find a whole chapter on quinoa smoothies in these pages, but the Frozen Super-Berry Smoothie (page 79) is a great place to start.

As a movie night treat: Popped quinoa (page 125) makes a delicious and healthy snack, perfect for movie night in place of popcorn. You can also sprinkle popped quinoa on yogurt or oatmeal for texture and crunch.

In granola: Quinoa granola bars? Yes, please. Raw quinoa adds great texture to granola. Take this combination one step further with Super-Powered Granola Bars (page 124) and enjoy a high-protein snack great for a hike or a lazy day outside.

In dessert: Quinoa is a satisfying way to make your favorite desserts gluten-free. Sweet treats and quinoa are a winning pair, and these amazing Double-Chocolate Brownies (page 258) are a good place to start.

In sushi: Quinoa makes a satisfying and nutritious rice substitute, as evidenced in these delicious Quinoa California Rolls (page 206).

Contents

7 Soups, Stews & Chilis

8 Main Dishes

9 Treats

Introduction

When it comes to good food, there's nothing quite like home cooking. Creating enticing, healthy foods as part of an everyday diet, whether for your family, yourself, friends, or guests, makes cooking a true pleasure, and the dishes that come out of your kitchen become especially wonderful. The 150+ nutritious, mouthwatering recipes in this book can make quinoa—the tasty, gluten-free superfood—an enjoyable addition to any meal you cook. These dishes will satisfy not just health-conscious folks, but the pickiest of eaters—including you!

The tiny, grain-like seed known as quinoa has been grown in South America since ancient times. So why has the rest of the world only now gotten excited about it? Until very recently, you probably couldn't even pronounce quinoa (KEEN-wah), and you would have been hard-pressed to find it, other than in hard-core health food stores. Today, every national supermarket chain carries quinoa, and you can buy it from bulk bins and in every form from breakfast cereal to beverages.

Quinoa, cooked and eaten much like grain, is tasty, with a slightly nutty flavor and a delicate texture. It's versatile, taking on the flavor of other ingredients in a dish and adapting well to most grain-based recipes. And it's terrifically simple and quick to prepare, cooking in just 20 minutes. Even after a long day at work or school, you can easily whip up a quinoa dish that pleases every member of your household. Save the leftovers for tomorrow's lunch.

Quinoa is considered a superfood. It's as nutrient-dense and ultra-good for you as it is high in fiber and heart-healthy "good fats." It's a complete protein, making it an excellent food choice for vegetarians, vegans, and anyone who simply wants to eat less meat. It's packed with antioxidants that may reduce inflammation in your body and boost your immune function, as well as perhaps help reduce your risk of some forms of cancer, heart disease, diabetes, and obesity.

Anyone can enjoy quinoa and benefit from its nutritional advantages, but if you're on a gluten-free diet, you're among the biggest winners in the quinoa game. Although the quinoa plant is a grain, its edible part is a seed, making it 100 percent gluten-free. Every one of the recipes in this book is gluten-free, giving you more than 150 scrumptious new options for healthy eating.

Let's cook!

1

Go Against the Grain

You know quinoa is good for you. There's a lot of interesting stuff to know about this superfood, but you don't have to learn everything about quinoa to know it's delicious, versatile, and easy to make. In fact, you can cook and eat quinoa like just about any grain, even though it's not a grain at all. That's why it's an ideal addition to anyone's menu, whether you're including more superfoods in your diet, eating healthier in general, or just broadening your culinary horizons. To delight your palate and please everyone who eats at your table, make quinoa the star—not just an understudy—of the meal.

A Superfood for Every Day

Adding superfoods to your diet is always an excellent idea. As a superfood, quinoa is especially rich in certain vitamins, minerals, and other nutrients that can make you healthier. Superfoods range from the very familiar, such as spinach, salmon, black beans, cinnamon, and blueberries, to the exotic, such as algae, kombucha, goji berries, hempseed, and noni. Over the past several years, quinoa has moved from the exotic category to the familiar, becoming widely available in stores and widely used in everyday recipes.

What makes quinoa a superfood?

- **Quinoa is mega-nutritious.** A cup of cooked quinoa contains 222 calories, 39 grams of carbs, 8 grams of protein, and 4 grams of fat and delivers 58 percent of the RDA (recommended daily allowance) of manganese, 30 percent of the magnesium, 28 percent of the phosphorus, 19 percent of the folate, 18 percent of the copper, 15 percent of the iron, and 13 percent of the zinc.

- **Quinoa is a fantastic source of antioxidants.** Antioxidant molecules do their work by slowing down or blocking a chemical reaction in the body called oxidation, which affects the components in the food you eat: fat, protein, and carbohydrates. Oxidation can damage or kill cells in your body. Antioxidants stop this process, which means they help prevent cellular damage and, say many nutrition experts, a lot of the disorders related to it. Antioxidants also fight disease by supporting immune function.

- **Quinoa has powerful anti-inflammatory capabilities.** Its antioxidants fight chronic inflammation caused by persistent injuries, toxins, or viruses in the body, or by autoimmune reactions. Lasting weeks, months, or even years, chronic inflammation can lead to fibrosis (as in Crohn's disease), tissue destruction (as in gum disease), and wounds that don't heal. It has been implicated in disorders from allergies to rheumatoid arthritis, and scientific evidence now suggests that inflammation can play a part in depression.

- **Quinoa is said to be a cancer-fighter.** By helping reduce oxidation and prevent cellular damage—especially damage to DNA—quinoa's antioxidant punch could help reduce your risk of cancer. Similarly, the anti-inflammatory power of quinoa may protect you against various cancers related to chronic inflammation.

Quinoa is heart-healthy. A great delivery system for "good fats," quinoa has monounsaturated fat oleic acid and the omega-3 fat alpha-linolenic acid (ALA). ALA is an anti-inflammatory, which suggests it could reduce inflammatory damage to your blood vessels and your risk of various cardiovascular diseases, including atherosclerosis and angina.

Quinoa combats obesity. An unhealthy diet high in calories and saturated fat not only adds to your waistline, it can also cause chronic inflammation. This is especially true for habitual overeaters, who consistently trigger acute (short-term) inflammation that over time becomes chronic.

Quinoa may reduce your risk of diabetes. Studies have shown that eating high-fiber, high-protein foods like quinoa decreases your risk of developing type 2 diabetes. Quinoa also has a low glycemic index of 53, so it doesn't cause the blood sugar spikes that can send insulin levels haywire. Quinoa's anti-inflammatory properties also come into play, reducing the chronic inflammation that's a type 2 diabetes risk factor.

Quinoa may help delay the aging process. It can help reduce the chronic inflammation that some scientists think contributes to the muscle loss that comes with aging. Researchers are also studying anti-inflammatories in the treatment of stroke and neurodegenerative problems such as memory loss.

Quinoa is much higher in fiber than most grains. It gives you more of the benefits of fiber, such as improved digestive health and lower cholesterol levels. All that fiber makes you feel full without eating a whole lot of quinoa, and feeling satisfied longer means you eat less of the fattening stuff.

Quinoa is a complete protein. This is extremely rare in the plant world and a boon for vegetarians, vegans, and anyone else hoping to cut some of the meat out of their diet. High in all nine of the essential amino acids—the components of protein—quinoa is an outstanding source of this vital nutrient.

Quinoa is one very super food indeed.

All About Quinoa

TYPES OF QUINOA

While there are hundreds of varieties of quinoa, you're likely to come across only three: white, red, and black. In nutritional terms they're virtually identical, and the other differences among them are pretty subtle. Color is the main thing that sets them apart from each other; for that reason, many cooks choose which to use according to the colors they want in their dish.

White quinoa: The most widely available kind of quinoa, white quinoa is often simply called quinoa. It's a bit tan in color, so you might also see it labeled ivory, golden, yellow, or blond. White quinoa has the mildest flavor and most delicate texture among the three major varieties, with just a hint of nuttiness on the palate. About 10 to 15 minutes of cooking yields a fluffy result. White quinoa works well as a stand-in for rice in many dishes.

Red quinoa: Somewhat nuttier and crunchier than white quinoa, red quinoa holds its shape a bit better and sticks together less. This makes it ideal for salads and dishes that call for a distinct grainy texture. Taking 3 or 4 minutes longer to cook than white quinoa, red quinoa can add striking color to a dish.

Black quinoa: A little crunchier still, black quinoa has a flavor that some call earthier and others call sweeter than white quinoa. Like red quinoa, it holds its shape well when cooked and works nicely in dishes that call for separate grains. Its color makes a dramatic contrast to the greens, reds, and other hues of accompanying ingredients. Black quinoa needs about 5 minutes more cooking than white.

Rainbow quinoa: This is not an actual variety but a blend of white, red, and black quinoa. You might see it labeled tricolor quinoa or quinoa blend. Some cooks love its confetti-like appearance, but others prefer to stick with one color at a time, because of the differences in cooking times.

QUINOA ON A BUDGET

Quinoa is an amazing "new" find for a food that's been around for thousands of years. But with its newfound popularity comes its high price. The price of white quinoa now ranges from $4.50 to $8.50 per pound, compared with $2.00 or less for brown rice and 70 cents or less for white rice. The rainbow ($7.00 to $12.00 per pound), red ($7.50 to $14.00 per pound), and black ($9.00 to $19.00 per pound) varieties cost even more. But balance this superfood's monetary value with its outstanding nutritional value, offering, for instance, 8 grams of protein for each cooked cup—about twice that of brown or white rice. Savvy shopping can keep your quinoa costs to a minimum.

SHOP AROUND. White quinoa that costs $5 per pound at Trader Joe's runs 67 cents per pound more at Walmart and $2 more per pound at Whole Foods.

BUY IN BULK. Supermarkets as well as natural food stores sell many dry goods from bulk bins. Get your quinoa there instead of the packaged goods aisle and you're likely to save 60 percent or more.

CHECK OUT LESS EXPENSIVE STORE BRAND PRODUCTS. You probably won't be able to tell the difference between it and brand-name quinoa.

HIT A WHOLESALE CLUB SUCH AS COSTCO OR SAM'S CLUB, where you can buy quinoa in large quantities and score low prices.

GO ONLINE. Manufacturers and discount retailers sell a wide selection of quinoa without the overhead costs of brick-and-mortar stores. And they deliver, sometimes for free.

USE WHITE QUINOA. It's easiest to find and significantly less expensive than other varieties.

TRY QUINOA/RICE BLENDS. The nutritional benefits will be reduced, but so will your costs.

THE NUTRITIONAL FACTS

Recognized by the United Nations as a superfood and proposed by NASA as an ideal food for astronauts on long space flights, quinoa is an established nutritional powerhouse. See what just one cup of cooked quinoa (about 6.5 ounces or 185 grams) offers:

- **Packed with antioxidants to eat yourself healthy.** The amazing antioxidants in quinoa act as an anti-inflammatory, and "good fats" make it heart-healthy.

- **8 grams of protein per cooked cup.** This is significantly more than almost any grain. By weight, quinoa is a whopping 14 percent protein, and it's a complete, high-quality protein that contains all the amino acids you need—and that you won't get from rice or wheat.

- **Half the carbs of pasta.** One cup of cooked quinoa has half the carbs as the same amount of cooked pasta—39 grams to pasta's 78 grams—and about 10 percent fewer carbs than rice, corn, or wheat.

- **More fiber than one cup of spinach.** Healthy *and* you don't have to worry about anything caught in your teeth! Quinoa's 5 grams of fiber is more than twice as much as you'll find in most other grains.

- **Quinoa is all about the good fat.** Its 4 grams of fat per one-cup serving is about the same as in corn and 2.5 times more than in wheat and rice. Half of its fat consists of omega-3 and omega-6 fatty acids, making it a healthy no-brainer.

- **442 milligrams of lysine—significantly more than any grain.** Lysine is an essential amino acid. Not only does lysine help make quinoa a complete protein, it's an important nutrient on its own, key to calcium absorption and other functions.

- **58 percent of the RDA (recommended daily allowance) of manganese.** You may not be very familiar with manganese, but it's important for nutrient absorption, wound healing, and bone development—and it's just one of quinoa's many antioxidants. The antioxidants vitamin E, zinc, and copper are also abundant in quinoa.

- **30 percent of the RDA of magnesium.** Magnesium regulates your blood pressure, helps with blood sugar levels, and alleviates migraines.

- 15 percent of the RDA of iron. Iron deficiency is the most common nutrient deficiency, and iron is essential to blood oxygenation. Quinoa has about 3.5 times more iron than wheat, 6.3 times more than corn, and 18 times more than rice.

- 20 percent of the RDA of folic acid (folate), a B vitamin. Quinoa is also rich in riboflavin (B_2), niacin (B_3), and pyridoxine (B_6).

SWAP IT!

It's easy to give your diet a healthy, exciting makeover with quinoa. It's a very adaptable ingredient that can stand in for many starches (especially grains, which can sabotage your efforts to eliminate gluten) and boost the nutrition in your meals. Make the switch to quinoa, and you'll transform your diet into fuel for a healthy lifestyle. Try quinoa:

- **Instead of oats in breakfast cereal.** Oats are gluten-free, but they can nevertheless cause adverse digestive reactions in gluten-intolerant people. Quinoa does great for breakfast, as a hot or cold cereal. Cook up a creamy, fruit-studded pot of hot quinoa, or fill your bowl with Toasty Quinoa Granola (page 52).

- **As an alternative to rice in side dishes.** Quinoa packs about twice the protein of brown or white rice, so pilafs, fried rice, and rice and beans—among hundreds of other dishes—step up a nutritional rung or two when you make them with quinoa.

- **To stand in for pasta in salad.** Whether as the main ingredient in an orzo salad or as an accent in a composed veggie salad, quinoa delivers not only beautiful texture but 2 to 9 times the various B vitamins of wheat pasta.

- **Instead of barley in soups.** Hearty winter soups such as beef-barley and mushroom-barley are just as warming and toothsome when you use quinoa. Plus, quinoa soundly beats barley in most vitamin and mineral categories.

- **As a substitute for potatoes in casseroles.** With 3 times the fiber of potatoes, quinoa can make your casseroles more nourishing. It also gives an entirely new texture to old favorites.

- **To replace wheat flour in baked treats.** If a recipe doesn't need gluten to work, you can probably make it with quinoa flour. Think gluten-free chocolate-chip cookies, blueberry muffins, carrot cake, and more.

Quinoa
a timeline

3000 BC:
In the high plains region of the Andes Mountains of Bolivia and Peru, the Incas begin to cultivate Quinoa. It is among the Incas' most important foods; they consider it sacred and called it *chisaya mama*: "the mother of all grains."

16th Century:
Spanish conquistador Francisco Pizarro and his soldiers arrive in the *altiplano* searching for riches. They set about crushing the Inca Empire and raiding for treasure. To cripple the Incas, Pizarro has the quinoa fields destroyed and bans its cultivation. The Spaniards hold quinoa in contempt as a "dirty" Indian food.

17th Century: Almost 90 percent of the Incas die of disease or as overworked slaves, and quinoa has all but disappeared. The survivors turn to other food sources, such as potatoes and corn.

19th Century: Quinoa remains virtually unknown outside South America.

1970s: Health food advocates discover quinoa, prompting a renewed demand for the superfood.

1990s: Demand for quinoa grows as superfood advocates embrace quinoa.

2012: The United States imports 57.6 million pounds of quinoa, speaking to the current boom in the superfood's popularity.

1984: Bolivia—which produces 70 percent of the world's quinoa—begins to export it to the United States.

2007: The United States imports 7.3 million pounds of quinoa.

2013: The United Nations General Assembly declares an International Year of Quinoa to draw awareness to the role quinoa can play in improving food security and nutrition.

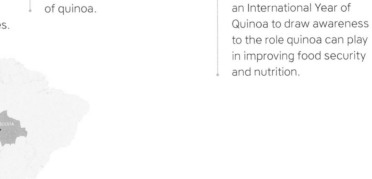

QUINOA MYTHS

There's no denying that quinoa's gone big-time, but misconceptions about the superfood still swirl through kitchens across the country.

- **Quinoa is a grain:** Wrong. Quinoa is a "pseudograin" or "pseudocereal." Unlike true grain, also called cereal, quinoa seeds don't come from any species of grass. It's used like a grain and can be ground into flour, but it comes from a shrub that's related to spinach, beets, and chard. Other pseudograins include amaranth, buckwheat, and chia. Next time you hear someone refer to quinoa as a supergrain, you'll know the truth.

- **Quinoa is exotic and hard to find:** Wrong. Major supermarket chains, discount retailers, and wholesale clubs sell quinoa. You can also buy the superfood online from major shopping websites. It comes packaged and in bulk, dried and parboiled, as breakfast cereal and in gluten-free baked goods, in boxed side dishes and frozen entrées, and as flakes and flour.

- **Quinoa is bland and unappetizing:** Wrong. Quinoa has a subtle nutty flavor and delicate crunchiness, and it cooks up nice and fluffy. It lends a pleasant texture to all kinds of dishes and soaks up the flavors of sauces and other ingredients. The specialty shades—rainbow, red, and black—add color and fun to sides and main dishes.

- **Quinoa is bitter:** Wrong. Quinoa isn't bitter if you rinse it before cooking, even if the packaging indicates it already has been washed. When harvested, quinoa is naturally coated with bitter-tasting substances called *saponins* that repel hungry birds and are disagreeable to humans. Quinoa is processed to remove the saponins before being sold.

That leaves one more interesting bit of quinoa lore: Quinoa is politically correct. This one is complicated. True, the United Nations proclaimed 2013 the International Year of Quinoa, declaring: "Faced with the challenge of increasing the production of quality food to feed the world's population in the context of climate change, quinoa offers an alternative for those countries suffering from food insecurity." The case of Bolivia, however, may bring that statement into question.

On the plus side, quinoa is mostly grown by small farmers rather than corporations, which helps maximize the superfood boom's economic benefits to the communities where it's grown. In Bolivia, which produces most of the world's quinoa, the income of quinoa farmers has gone up, but quinoa's success has not been undisputed.

According to some analysts, many farmers have come to see quinoa as too valuable to eat. They sell their entire crop for profit rather than saving some for themselves, instead eating cheaper, less-nourishing processed foods. Bolivians who aren't profiting from quinoa's international popularity are also turning to commercial foods because they can no longer afford the increasingly expensive superfood.

Some researchers raise another concern: Farmers have dedicated more and more land to quinoa, reducing the land available for other crops that have traditionally been a significant part of the local diet. In addition, land that should be allowed to rest between quinoa crops stays in cultivation, leading to soil depletion that threatens quinoa's sustainability. With experts arguing all sides of the situation, the jury remains out on the ultimate implications of quinoa's success.

QUINOA FOR EVERYONE

The recipes in this book are designed to please all kinds of eaters. Because quinoa can be incorporated into a wide variety of dishes, it is a welcome part of any diet, from carnivorous to vegan. The superfood works well in everything from fried chicken and birthday cake to health shakes and vegan entrées.

All the recipes are clearly labeled to help you choose dishes that suit you and your family's needs and diets, as well as your available time and energy. Tips throughout teach you how you can adapt the recipes for even the pickiest eater in your household. Use the following recipe labels to quickly identify meals that will suit your household's taste buds every day of the week:

MEAT LOVERS: Quinoa will please even the most strident meat-and-potatoes fan. It can replace the mashed potatoes you might have with a steak dinner or go in your grandma's pork chop–potato bake. It can stand in for rice in *carne asada* burritos or a homey chicken-and-rice stew, be used instead of wheat in the crust on juicy fried pork chops, or replace the pasta under chicken parmesan. Of course, you can add meat to many quinoa dishes. Try thick-cut bacon next to quinoa pancakes or grilled, sliced sirloin atop a quinoa-avocado salad. Or you can sneak in quinoa in place of meat in carnivore-friendly dishes such as sloppy joes and turkey burgers.

VEGANS AND VEGETARIANS: As a complete protein, quinoa makes an excellent addition to vegan and vegetarian diets. Instead of brown rice, barley, or other grains, which are not complete proteins, use this superfood to create hunger-beating, muscle-building meals. Cooking for a mixed audience of vegans and non-vegans isn't a problem, since quinoa dishes can satisfy everyone at the table. Think tofu fried rice, barley risotto, and whole-wheat baked ziti, and then swap out the grain for quinoa. Delicious!

KIDS: Researchers have found that most kids don't mind—and many don't even notice—when healthy foods are substituted for less healthy ones. This is a boon if you want to introduce superfoods into your child's diet. With a trip to the supermarket, you can bring more protein, good fat, vitamins, and minerals into your pantry without causing a ripple. Wheat pasta can be replaced with quinoa pasta in dishes such as macaroni and cheese, spaghetti and meatballs, buttered noodles, and chicken-and-stars soup. Quinoa can take the place of rice in California rolls, and quinoa flour can substitute for wheat in breaded chicken fingers. When it's time for milk and cookies, quinoa flour can step up to the baking plate, and quinoa milk can wash down the sweet treats.

LARGE GROUPS: Headed to a party or potluck, or hosting an event of your own? Instead of contributing a potato, rice, or pasta dish, bring a pan of quinoa. For a Cinco de Mayo party, whip up some spicy quinoa chili, quinoa and beans, and jalapeño "cornbread." At that school fundraiser, show up with a quinoa lasagna or chocolate quinoa cake. On New Year's Eve, delight your guests with hors d'oeuvres such as mushroom-quinoa tartlets, quinoa canapés with smoked salmon, and quinoa blinis to go with that caviar.

SINGLETONS: Cooking for one? Quinoa is your friend. It's great as a leftover. You can prepare a large batch of the superfood and refrigerate or freeze part of it, either on its own or in a premade dish. Pop it in the fridge, and it will last several days, reemerging with the same great flavor and texture it had when made fresh. One session in the kitchen can yield three days' worth of quinoa–sweet potato salad for lunch, a mushroom-quinoa soup that you can portion and freeze for a rainy day, a shepherd's pie that will greet you after working late, or quinoa energy bars to pack in your gym bag.

MAKE AHEAD: Recipes that freeze well are perfect to make ahead for a quick dinner when you're short on time. Recipes with this label can be prepared during a batch cooking session, such as when making a casserole, soup, or stew. These recipes can also be prepared ahead and put in the oven the next day.

ONE POT: Convenient options when you don't want to make a big mess in the kitchen, these flavor-packed meals are created in a single skillet, saucepan, bowl, baking dish, Dutch oven, or stockpot. Kitchen clean up doesn't get any easier.

30-MINUTE: In today's fast-paced world, it can be hard to find time to prepare a homemade meal with everything else that needs to fit into your day. These recipes can be made in 30-minutes or less from start to finish, making your day a little easier.

One label you will not need in this book is gluten-free. This is because every recipe in this book was designed to take advantage of quinoa's role as a satisfying substitute for gluten in your diet.

The Very Basics

COOKING WITH QUINOA

In only 15 to 20 minutes, you can cook a batch of perfect, fluffy quinoa. It's as easy to prepare as white rice and takes about the same amount of time, and it's easier and much quicker to cook than brown rice. You can make it on the stovetop or in your steamer, rice cooker, or slow cooker. In a pinch, you can even cook quinoa in your microwave.

How to Prepare Quinoa

There are many different opinions on how much water to use to cook quinoa and on how much quinoa a given combination will yield. Most recipes call for a ratio of 1 part quinoa to 2 parts water, others for more water. Do a little experimenting. If the quinoa turns out too crunchy, you need to use more water. Too mushy? You need less. Red and black versions may require more water. Your ratios will depend partly on the age of your dry quinoa: The older the seeds (make sure they're not stale!), the more water you'll need. The recipes in this book use a ratio of 1:2 dry quinoa to water and assume that the yield will be about 3 cups.

To ensure no trace of bitterness shows up in your food, give the quinoa a rinse before you cook it, even if the packaging states it has already been washed. Pour the dry quinoa into a fine-mesh sieve and run cold water over it until the water runs clear; then shake it to drain. Now you're ready to go!

HOW MUCH TO USE?

DRY QUINOA	WATER	COOKED YIELD	SERVES
1 cup	2 cups	3 cups	4 to 6, depending on dish
¼ to ⅓ cup	½ to ⅔ cup	¾ to 1 cup	1 to 2, depending on dish

COOKING TIMES FOR DIFFERENT TYPES OF QUINOA

QUINOA COLOR	COOKING TIME
White	15 minutes
Red	18 minutes
Black	20 minutes
Rainbow	15 to 20 minutes

Stovetop Quinoa

VEGANS, ONE POT, 30-MINUTE

MAKES 3 CUPS / PREP: 5 MINUTES / COOK: 15 TO 20 MINUTES

Like rice, quinoa is typically prepared on the stove. It's generally boiled in water, with a little salt, but you can use vegetable, mushroom, or chicken stock to add a lot of flavor to quinoa's inherent nuttiness. Give the quinoa extra flair by substituting ½ to 1 cup of dry white wine for the same amount of stock.

1 cup dry quinoa
2 cups water or stock
½ teaspoon salt

Step 1: Measure Measure the dry quinoa into a fine-mesh sieve.

Step 2: Rinse Put the quinoa in a fine-mesh strainer. Rinse it with cold water until the water runs clear. Drain the quinoa.

Step 3: Cook In a medium saucepan over high heat, bring the liquid to a boil. Add the salt and the quinoa to the water. Give the mixture a stir and bring it back to a boil. Turn the heat to low, and cover the pan. Simmer the quinoa for 15 minutes.

Step 4: Check After 15 minutes, check the quinoa for doneness. The grains should be translucent, and a little white tail should spiral out from each. To ensure fluffy quinoa, check that the grains aren't stuck together. They should be slightly firm (but not crunchy), because the quinoa continues cooking and softening for a few minutes after being removed from the heat.

Red and black quinoa generally require a few minutes more to cook than white quinoa (see the Cooking Times chart, page 30). Whatever the color, if the quinoa isn't done at 15 minutes, cover the pan, cook a minute longer, and test again.

Step 5: Rest When the quinoa is ready, remove it from the heat and check to see if any excess liquid remains in the pan. If so, drain the quinoa through a fine-mesh sieve and return it to the pan. Cover the pan with a clean dish towel (to keep condensation from dripping back into the pan), cover with the lid, and let the quinoa stand for 5 to 10 minutes.

Step 6: Fluff Like couscous, cooked quinoa should be fluffed just before going into a recipe or onto the table. Uncover the pan and use a fork to fluff and separate the grains. When done, the quinoa should look light and delicate.

Tip **Quinoa makes great leftovers. To maintain freshness between cooking and eating, put the quinoa in an airtight container or plastic zip-top bag and pop it into the refrigerator. It will keep for 3 or 4 days; if necessary, reheat it in a microwave or steamer when you're ready to eat. Alternatively, you can freeze it and then defrost it in the fridge before using.**

Steamer / Rice Cooker Quinoa

VEGANS, ONE POT, 30-MINUTE

MAKES 3 CUPS / PREP: 5 MINUTES / COOK: 15 TO 20 MINUTES

Your steamer or rice cooker is a very handy tool for cooking quinoa and even makes the process a little easier than cooking on the stovetop. All you need to do is prep the quinoa, push a button, and walk away until it's done—your device may even turn off automatically. The quinoa undergoes essentially the same process that it does on the stovetop, so refer to the Stovetop Quinoa recipe (page 31) for more details about each step.

1 cup dry quinoa
2 cups water or stock
½ teaspoon salt

Rinse and drain the quinoa, and put it in the steamer or rice cooker. Stir in the water and salt.

Turn on your steamer or rice cooker. If your device has several settings, choose the "white rice" option or whatever setting you use to cook white rice. For devices that require a time setting, turn the timer to 15 to 20 minutes, depending on the color of the quinoa (see Cooking Times chart, page 30).

When your steamer or rice cooker completes its cycle, test the quinoa for doneness. Cook for another minute or two if necessary. Once the quinoa is cooked, unplug and open your device and drain off any excess liquid in the quinoa. Return the cooking container to the steamer or rice cooker, and lay a clean dish towel across the inner rim. Close the lid over the towel, and let the quinoa stand for 10 to 15 minutes.

Fluff the quinoa with a fork, and serve with desired toppings or use in a recipe.

Per cup: Calories 223; Fat 4g; Saturated fat 0g; Sodium 395mg; Protein 8.6g; Fiber 4g

Slow Cooker Quinoa

VEGANS, ONE POT

MAKES 3 CUPS / PREP: 5 MINUTES / COOK: 2 TO 6 HOURS

If you're a slow cooker fan, you already know how convenient it can be to wake up or come home to a fresh, piping hot meal that seems almost to have cooked itself. Luckily, you can enjoy the same results with quinoa. What's more, your slow cooker can marry quinoa with all kinds of ingredients and flavors to produce delicious, healthy dishes.

1 cup dry quinoa
2 cups water or stock
½ teaspoon salt

Rinse and drain the quinoa, and pour it into the slow cooker. Stir in the water and salt.

Cover the slow cooker and turn it on. Cook, undisturbed, for 4 to 6 hours on low or 2 to 3 hours on high.

Test the quinoa for doneness. All of the water should be absorbed. If not, drain the quinoa through a fine-mesh sieve.

Fluff the quinoa with a fork, and serve with desired toppings or use in a recipe.

Tip **If you do lift the slow cooker's lid during its cycle to peek, replace it as quickly as you can. Your cooker might take as long as 20 minutes to recover the heat that's lost when the cover is removed.**

Per cup: Calories 223; Fat 4g; Saturated fat 0g; Sodium 395mg; Protein 8.6g; Fiber 4g

Microwave Quinoa

VEGANS, ONE POT, 30-MINUTE

MAKES 3 CUPS / PREP: 5 MINUTES / COOK: 6 TO 10 MINUTES

Quinoa cooked in a microwave is a little less fluffy than quinoa cooked on a stovetop, but it's perfectly serviceable in most recipes. The two processes differ, and it's debatable whether the microwave makes the job easier. But if you don't have access to a stove or steamer—say, when you're at work or staying in a hotel—you can prepare quinoa in a microwave.

1 cup dry quinoa
2 to 3 cups water
½ teaspoon salt

Rinse and drain the quinoa, and pour it into a microwave-safe dish. Stir in the water and salt. Loosely cover the dish with a lid or plastic wrap.

Microwave on high for 4 minutes. Stir, then re-cover the dish and microwave for another 2 minutes.

Check the quinoa for doneness. If it's not ready, stir the quinoa again, re-cover, and microwave for another minute. You may need to add more water to keep the quinoa from drying out. If so, stir in about a tablespoon. Continue cooking and stirring until the quinoa is done. Total cooking time could be 10 minutes or more.

When the quinoa is ready, let it stand for at least 1 minute, covered. Drain off any excess water through a fine-mesh sieve.

Fluff the quinoa with a fork, and serve with desired toppings or use in a recipe.

Tip Select a cooking dish that can hold at least 1 quart, with at least 2 inches of space above the surface of the quinoa. The water will boil up during cooking and overflow if using a smaller dish.

Per cup: Calories 223; Fat 4g; Saturated fat 0g; Sodium 395mg; Protein 8.6g; Fiber 4g

Toasted Quinoa

Enhance quinoa's naturally nutty, subtle flavor and remove any last traces of bitterness by toasting it. Whether you're going to use it in a salad or main course or process it into flour for baking, toasted quinoa turns any dish into an entirely new experience. A quick session in a skillet before cooking is all it takes.

1 cup dry quinoa

Rinse the quinoa, and drain it well. While it's still wet, put it in a large, dry, nonstick sauté pan. Turn the heat on to medium.

Stir the quinoa constantly until the grains are dry, about 2 minutes. Turn up the heat to medium-high and continue stirring. The grains will start to pop and turn golden. Remove the pan from the heat when the quinoa is lightly browned and smells nutty, about 6 minutes.

Spread the toasted quinoa on a baking sheet or large plate to cool. Once it has cooled thoroughly, use it immediately or store it in a tightly sealed jar in a dark closet or in the refrigerator.

Per cup: Calories 223; Fat 4g; Saturated fat 0g; Sodium 9mg; Protein 8.6g; Fiber 4g

ABOUT QUINOA FLAKES

Quinoa seeds rolled thin, quinoa flakes can do almost anything rolled oats can do. They look like rolled oats and have a similar mild taste that supports other flavors in sweet or savory dishes. You might find quinoa flakes in the cereal aisle or the baking aisle, or both, because you can use them for anything from a creamy, hot breakfast cereal to a crispy fried-food coating or a gooey cookie. Use quinoa flakes anywhere you might use rolled oats to add a gluten-free kick of protein and antioxidants to your meals.

Quinoa Flour

VEGANS, MAKE AHEAD

MAKES ABOUT 3 CUPS (1 POUND) / PREP: 1 TO 35 MINUTES / COOK: 2 HOURS, 30 MINUTES

You can use gluten-free quinoa flour in place of all-purpose wheat-based flours in recipes for many non-yeast baked goods, as well as in myriad other ways that you might use wheat flour. Quinoa flour is very easy—and more nutritious—to make fresh at home. (Try making your flour from toasted quinoa to give it a nuttier spin.) Before using raw quinoa flour, you must heat-process it to maximize its flavor, texture, and nutrition. A little hassle-free time in the oven turns quinoa flour's somewhat earthy, grassy notes into mild sweetness and refines its slightly coarse texture for softer, more consistent baking results.

2½ cups (1 pound) dry quinoa, divided
(If you prefer to use store-bought flour, measure out 3 cups [1 pound] and skip to the next page.)

Rinse the quinoa, and drain it well. If you don't plan to toast it, spread it out on baking sheets and leave it in a warm, dry place until all the water has evaporated. If you wish to toast the grains, use the Toasted Quinoa recipe on page 36.

Preheat the oven to 220°F.

For grinding into flour, a coffee/spice grinder is by far the best choice. A food processor on maximum power will work, but it won't produce the very fine, even flour you can get from a grinder. Pour ¼ cup of dry quinoa into a clean grinder; any more, and the grind won't be fine enough. Grind in 15-second pulses, shaking the grinder up and down for best results. Continue grinding until the flour is very fine, about 1½ minutes in all. Empty the grinder into a medium mixing bowl, and repeat until you have ground all the seeds.

Loosely and evenly spread out the flour on a rimmed baking sheet to a depth of no more than ¼ inch. Use more than one pan if necessary.

Heat the flour in the oven for 2½ hours without stirring or turning. Remove it from the oven, and allow it to cool completely.

Use the flour immediately, or store it in an airtight container or zip-top bag and keep in the refrigerator for up to 6 months, or in the freezer for up to 1 year.

Per cup: Calories 557; Fat 9g; Saturated fat 1g; Sodium 8mg; Protein 21g; Fiber 11g

ABOUT QUINOA PASTA

Gluten-free pasta is everywhere. Dozens of companies make noodles of brown rice, white rice, corn, and other grains, including quinoa. Spaghetti, macaroni, fusilli, and many more shapes are available in boxes, bags, and bulk bins. But despite the huge market, gluten-free pasta still gets a bad rap as a noodle that's prone to fall apart, clump, or go mushy during cooking, or to deliver a gritty, gummy, or cardboard-y eating experience.

Quinoa pasta is not immune to such criticism. Manufactured and prepared correctly, though, quinoa pasta holds its shape, takes on a springy texture when cooked, and tastes like wheat pasta with a nutty twist. It can be both flexible and firm, with a good al dente bite.

Shop around and experiment with different brands and shapes to find your favorite. Quinoa pasta usually combines quinoa with rice, Khorasan wheat, or corn. In fact, some pasta labeled "quinoa"—including the best-selling organic brand—is in fact made mostly of corn. Check the ingredients carefully to select the brand that best suits your dietary needs, keeping in mind that some added ingredients may include gluten if gluten-free is not specified.

If you know how to cook regular pasta, you'll have no problem cooking quinoa pasta. As the saying goes, simply "cook according to package directions." It's best cooked al dente, so check for doneness a minute or so before the time given on the package. Note that there's less wiggle room in quinoa pasta's cooking time: It's a little easier to overcook it so it breaks apart. Tinker with cooking times and tweak to find out what works best for you.

Sprouted Quinoa

VEGANS, MAKE AHEAD

MAKES ABOUT 3 CUPS / PREP: 10 MINUTES / COOK: 24 HOURS

Germinated quinoa seeds, aka sprouted quinoa, are the pumped-up version of quinoa. Sprouting makes quinoa even more digestible than it already is, generates even more vitamins and minerals, and gives a big boost to its amino acids. When sprouted, quinoa is pretty to look at as well as delicious to eat. Its nutty flavor profile is enhanced by subtle hints of its relative, the beet. You can eat sprouted quinoa just as you would bean sprouts—raw or cooked in salads, sandwiches, and stir fries—or regular quinoa, prepared on the stovetop with about half as much water. Sprouted quinoa is difficult to find in stores, but it's very easy to sprout at home. You can set it up to sprout and leave it to do its thing, tending to it every 6 to 8 hours.

1 cup dry quinoa

Thoroughly rinse the dry quinoa. Soak it in tepid water for 30 minutes, drain it through a sieve, and put it in a quart jar.

Cover the jar with a sprouting lid or perforate the jar's regular lid 8 to 10 times (you can do that with a hammer and nail). Set the jar upside down over a bowl, taking care not to block the holes in the lid.

Every 6 hours or so, rinse the quinoa by filling the jar with water and draining it through the lid. Put the jar back in the bowl. In just a day or two, the quinoa will sprout—you'll see its spiral tail curling from the grains. Give the sprouts a final rinse.

Leave the sprouts in the jar over the bowl, and let the water evaporate completely. You may need to stand the jar upright to finish the process. Do not allow the sprouts to dry out.

Use them immediately, or put them in a sealed zip-top bag or glass container and store them in the refrigerator for up to 3 days.

Per cup: Calories 223; Fat 4g; Saturated fat 0g; Sodium 9mg; Protein 8.6g; Fiber 4g

Chicken Stock

MAKES 3 QUARTS / PREP: 15 MINUTES / COOK: 1 HOUR, 30 MINUTES / TOTAL: 7 HOURS, 30 MINUTES

Many savory quinoa recipes can be enriched by cooking the dry quinoa with stock instead of water. Homemade stock is so much more flavorful and nutritious that it's worth taking a little extra time to prepare your own. The exact ingredients are up to you—feel free to make substitutions for any of the vegetables or herbs, keeping in mind that the flavor of the final product has to work with many different quinoa dishes. Resist the urge to add salt or other seasonings: A plain stock allows you precise control over the seasoning of your dishes.

4 pounds chicken wings

1 pound chicken breast, cut into 1-inch cubes (optional, for added chicken flavor)

2 large yellow onions, diced

3 large carrots, diced

4 celery stalks, diced

5 garlic cloves, crushed

2 tablespoons coarsely chopped fresh parsley

2 bay leaves

2 packets unflavored gelatin dissolved in ½ cup cold water (optional, for thickening)

In a large stockpot over medium-low heat, bring the chicken wings, chicken breast (if using), onions, carrots, celery, garlic, parsley, bay leaves, and 4 quarts water to a boil. Immediately turn the heat down to low.

Cook for 1½ hours at a very gentle simmer. A light scum will form on the surface of the stock, and gentle simmering will keep it from mixing back into the liquid. Using a spoon, remove the scum from the stock.

Remove the stock from the heat, and allow it to cool enough that it's safe to handle. Carefully pour it through a fine-mesh sieve into a large bowl to remove any solids and clarify the liquid.

Let the stock cool completely; then transfer it to sealed containers (not zip-top bags) and refrigerate until it is chilled, about 6 hours. The fat in the stock will congeal on the surface; skim it off along with any scum.

If the stock is too thin, add the dissolved gelatin and return the stock to the stove. Bring it to a boil, and cook until the gelatin is fully dissolved in the stock.

Use immediately, or refrigerate or freeze in airtight containers or zip-top bags. Before freezing, portion the stock out into pints so you can easily grab the desired amount when cooking. The stock will keep in the refrigerator for up to 5 days and in the freezer for up to 6 months.

Tip **Make Vegetable Stock the same way, leaving out the chicken and gelatin and increasing the vegetables by one-third. To bring out more vegetable flavor, sauté them in a tablespoon or two of oil for a few minutes before putting them in the pot. Be careful that they don't brown. For a richer stock, add 1 cup of chopped mushrooms.**

Per serving (1 cup): Calories 10; Fat 1g; Saturated fat 0g; Sodium 764mg; Protein 1g; Fiber 1g

Marinara Sauce

KIDS, LARGE GROUPS, VEGANS, MAKE AHEAD, 30-MINUTE

MAKES 3½ CUPS / PREP: 5 MINUTES / COOK: 25 MINUTES

Marinara is a simple preparation of tomatoes and basil: no oregano, no onions, no nothing. The full flavor of the tomatoes is center stage, so your sauce will be best when made from the finest canned tomatoes you can find. Seek out San Marzanos from Italy or a good organic brand, and complement them with extra-virgin olive oil and the freshest basil.

2 tablespoons extra-virgin olive oil
3 garlic cloves, minced
1 (28-ounce) can diced tomatoes, undrained
Salt
Freshly ground black pepper
3 tablespoons minced fresh basil

In a large saucepan over medium heat, heat the olive oil. Add the garlic and cook until it starts to sizzle; do not brown it. Add the tomatoes, including the juice, and turn up the heat to medium-high.

Bring the sauce to a boil; then turn the heat down to low. Simmer the sauce, uncovered, stirring occasionally until the sauce thickens, about 15 minutes. Season with the salt and pepper. Add the basil and cook for another 2 to 3 minutes. Remove from the heat.

Use immediately, or refrigerate or freeze in airtight containers or zip-top bags. The marinara will keep in the refrigerator for up to 4 days and in the freezer for up to 4 months.

Tip **This recipe is well suited to doubling, so you can make enough for leftovers that you can freeze for another day. Simply double the amounts of all the ingredients.**

Per serving (1/2 cup): Calories 57; Fat 4g; Saturated fat 1g; Sodium 29mg; Protein 1g; Fiber 1g

Balsamic Vinaigrette

VEGANS, MAKE AHEAD, ONE POT, 30-MINUTE

MAKES 1 CUP / PREP: 3 MINUTES

The sweet piquancy of this basic vinaigrette is a lovely complement to quinoa's mild nuttiness. It's also a great foundation for any number of variations: Switch out regular balsamic for white balsamic or olive oil for avocado or another oil. Or add in a few additional ingredients like 2 tablespoons of Dijon mustard along with a tablespoon of honey, 1½ teaspoons of minced fresh marjoram or other herbs, or ¼ cup of puréed fresh or frozen raspberries.

¾ cup extra-virgin olive oil
¼ cup balsamic vinegar
2 garlic cloves, cut lengthwise into thin slices
½ teaspoon salt
½ teaspoon freshly ground black pepper

In a medium bowl or quart jar, whisk or shake together the olive oil, vinegar, garlic, salt, and pepper thoroughly to emulsify the oil and vinegar (the dressing will thicken and become opaque).

Use immediately, or refrigerate in a tightly sealed container. The vinaigrette will keep for 1 week.

Per serving (2 tablespoons): Calories 166; Fat 18g; Saturated fat 2g; Sodium 148mg; Protein 0g; Fiber 0g

Lemon–Thyme Vinaigrette

VEGANS, MAKE AHEAD, ONE POT, 30-MINUTE

MAKES 1 CUP / PREP: 5 MINUTES

Fresh and zingy, this dressing is perfect for cold quinoa salads or hot sides served with fish. The addition of zest makes it a treat for the nose as well as the tongue. Add a tablespoon of honey to make it more kid-friendly.

¾ cup extra-virgin olive oil
¼ cup freshly squeezed lemon juice
1 tablespoon minced fresh thyme
1 garlic clove, cut lengthwise into thin slices
½ teaspoon fresh lemon zest
½ teaspoon salt
¼ teaspoon freshly ground black pepper

In a medium bowl or quart jar, whisk or shake together the olive oil, lemon juice, thyme, garlic, lemon zest, salt, and pepper thoroughly to emulsify the oil and lemon juice (the dressing will thicken and become opaque).

Use immediately, or refrigerate in a tightly sealed container. The vinaigrette will keep for 3 to 4 days.

Per serving (2 tablespoons): Calories 166; Fat 18g; Saturated fat 2g; Sodium 148mg; Protein 0g; Fiber 0g

Tarragon–Dijon Vinaigrette

VEGANS, MAKE AHEAD, ONE POT, 30-MINUTE

MAKES 1 CUP / PREP: 4 MINUTES

The sophisticated flavors of this vinaigrette can upgrade a quinoa salad or a chicken or fish dish. Its aromatic notes of tarragon and spicy Dijon presence bring a French style to your table. Add 2 tablespoons of gluten-free mayonnaise to make a creamy version.

¾ cup extra-virgin olive oil

¼ cup white wine vinegar or rice vinegar

1 tablespoon minced fresh tarragon

2 teaspoons Dijon mustard, plus more if desired

1 garlic clove, cut lengthwise into thin slices

½ teaspoon salt

¼ teaspoon freshly ground black pepper

In a medium bowl or quart jar, whisk or shake together the olive oil, vinegar, tarragon, mustard, garlic, salt, and pepper thoroughly to emulsify the oil and vinegar (the dressing will thicken and become opaque).

Use immediately, or refrigerate in a tightly sealed container. The vinaigrette will keep for 1 week.

Per serving (2 tablespoons): Calories 166; Fat 19g; Saturated fat 3g; Sodium 162mg; Protein 0g; Fiber 0g

Citrus Dressing

KIDS, VEGANS, MAKE AHEAD, ONE POT, 30-MINUTE

MAKES 1 CUP / PREP: 15 MINUTES

This recipe gets its acid from citrus instead of vinegar, so it's as tasty for breakfast as it is for dinner. It's excellent with chicken and shrimp, or tossed with a bowl of cold quinoa topped with strawberries. You can save time by using store-bought juice, but fresh is much, much tastier.

½ cup extra-virgin olive oil

3 tablespoons freshly squeezed clementine, mandarin orange, or tangerine juice

3 tablespoons freshly squeezed blood orange juice

1 tablespoon freshly squeezed lime juice

1 tablespoon agave nectar, plus more if desired

½ teaspoon salt

¼ teaspoon freshly ground black pepper

In a medium bowl or quart jar, whisk or shake together the olive oil, clementine juice, orange juice, lime juice, agave, salt, and pepper thoroughly to emulsify the oil and juices (the dressing will thicken and become opaque).

Use immediately, or refrigerate in a tightly sealed container. The dressing will keep for 3 or 4 days.

Per serving (2 tablespoons): Calories 122; Fat 13g; Saturated fat 2g; Sodium 148mg; Protein 0g; Fiber 0g

Cilantro–Lime Dressing

VEGANS, MAKE AHEAD, ONE POT, 30-MINUTE

MAKES 1 CUP / PREP: 10 MINUTES

Depending on which direction your taste buds face, this dressing will evoke either Southeast Asia or the American Southwest. It pairs well with many spicy quinoa dishes—especially if you go non-vegan, non-paleo and add a couple tablespoons of plain, gluten-free Greek yogurt—and is excellent on grilled seafood. For cool-as-a-cucumber salads, give the dressing a little heat of its own with a few dashes of sriracha or cayenne pepper.

⅔ cup extra-virgin olive oil
⅓ cup freshly squeezed lime juice
½ cup chopped fresh cilantro
2 garlic cloves, minced
2 teaspoons sugar
2 teaspoons salt
Dash ground coriander

In a medium bowl or quart jar, whisk or shake together the olive oil, lime juice, cilantro, garlic, sugar, salt, and coriander thoroughly to emulsify the oil and juices (the dressing will thicken and become opaque).

Use immediately, or refrigerate in a tightly sealed container. The dressing will keep for 3 or 4 days.

Per serving (2 tablespoons): Calories 151; Fat 17g; Saturated fat 2g; Sodium 582mg; Protein 0g; Fiber 0g

Harissa–Cinnamon Dressing

VEGANS, MAKE AHEAD, ONE POT, 30-MINUTE

MAKES 1 CUP / PREP: 4 MINUTES

Laced with the flavors of North Africa, this marvelous dressing lends an exotic twist to quinoa salads and main courses alike. Harissa, its main flavoring, is a hot chili paste from Tunisia that's becoming widely available in tubes and jars, as well as in powdered form (read labels carefully to find one that's gluten-free). The dressing will impress your family and guests and keep them guessing while they savor a delicious meal.

¾ cup extra-virgin olive oil

¼ cup freshly squeezed lemon juice

2 tablespoons harissa paste, more or less according to desired heat

1 tablespoon honey

1 teaspoon ground cinnamon

½ teaspoon salt

In a medium bowl or quart jar, whisk or shake together the olive oil, lemon juice, harissa paste, honey, cinnamon, and salt thoroughly to emulsify the oil and juices (the dressing will thicken and become opaque).

Use immediately, or refrigerate in a tightly sealed container. The dressing will keep for 1 week.

Per serving (2 tablespoons): Calories 185; Fat 20g; Saturated fat 3g; Sodium 194mg; Protein 0g; Fiber 0g

Sesame–Ginger Dressing

VEGANS, MAKE AHEAD, ONE POT, 30-MINUTE

MAKES 1 CUP / PREP: 7 MINUTES

Flavors from Japan, China, and Korea make this dressing a perfect match for most any Asian-style quinoa dish. Prepare it with half the amount of canola oil to create a great dipping sauce for raw or steamed veggies. Add a dash of sesame oil to give the dressing a hint of smokiness.

⅔ cup canola oil

2 tablespoons plus 2 teaspoons sesame tahini

2 tablespoons plus 2 teaspoons low-sodium tamari

2 tablespoons freshly squeezed lemon juice

1 tablespoon freshly grated ginger

2 teaspoons rice vinegar

2 teaspoons honey

2 garlic cloves, minced

½ teaspoon sriracha (optional)

In a medium bowl or quart jar, whisk or shake together the canola oil, tahini, tamari, lemon juice, ginger, vinegar, honey, garlic, and sriracha (if using) thoroughly to emulsify the oil and juices (the dressing will thicken and become opaque).

Use immediately, or refrigerate in a tightly sealed container. The dressing will keep for 1 week.

Per serving (2 tablespoons): Calories 204; Fat 21g; Saturated fat 2g; Sodium 302mg; Protein 1g; Fiber 1g

3

Breakfast

Toasty Quinoa Granola

SINGLETONS, VEGETARIANS, MAKE AHEAD

MAKES 6 CUPS / PREP: 20 MINUTES / COOK: 25 MINUTES

Packed with filling nuts and seeds, this granola makes a high-energy start to the day or a great pick-me-up afternoon snack. The recipe is easy and endlessly adaptable, and you can change ingredient proportions to suit your taste. Mix it into plain Greek yogurt, pour some quinoa or almond milk over it, or heat it in the microwave with some milk to turn it into hot cereal.

½ cup butter, melted

½ cup honey

3 cups quinoa flakes

2 teaspoons ground cinnamon

⅓ cup raw almonds

⅓ cup raw pecans

⅓ cup raw pepitas (pumpkin seeds)

⅓ cup raw sunflower seeds

¾ cup unsweetened coconut flakes or shredded coconut

½ cup raisins

½ cup dried cranberries

Tip Substitute canola oil for the butter to create vegan granola. Use your imagination to make different granola each time: cashews, dried cherries, diced dried dates, and unsweetened banana chips are just a few fun additions.

Preheat the oven to 350°F.

In a small mixing bowl, whisk together the butter and honey. Put the quinoa flakes in a large mixing bowl, and pour the butter-honey mixture over the flakes. Stir to coat the flakes evenly. Sprinkle on the cinnamon, and mix to distribute it evenly.

Add the almonds, pecans, pepitas, sunflower seeds, and coconut to the bowl. Stir and toss to combine thoroughly.

On a rimmed baking sheet, spread the granola out. Bake for 10 minutes; then stir. Bake for another 6 or 7 minutes, and stir again. Continue baking and stirring in progressively shorter increments until the granola turns golden.

Remove the granola from the oven, and add the raisins and cranberries. Allow it to cool completely.

Store in airtight containers. The granola will keep for 2 weeks in the pantry, 3 weeks in the refrigerator, and 2 months in the freezer.

Per serving (1 cup): Calories 660; Fat 33g; Saturated fat 15g; Sodium 123mg; Protein 13g; Fiber 9g

Crispy Quinoa-Maple Cold Cereal

KIDS, SINGLETONS, VEGANS, MAKE AHEAD

MAKES 6 CUPS / PREP: 15 MINUTES / COOK: 30 TO 50 MINUTES

Sometimes when you can't quite wake up in the morning, you need a really crunchy breakfast to open your eyes. This cereal will do the trick, not just with its crunch but with the sweetness of maple syrup. Leave off the milk, and it makes a satisfying snack.

6 cups cooked quinoa, cooled
⅓ cup chia seeds
1 tablespoon plus 1 teaspoon ground cinnamon
¼ teaspoon salt
⅓ cup pure maple syrup
1 tablespoon vanilla extract

Preheat the oven to 325°F.

In a large mixing bowl, stir together the quinoa, chia seeds, cinnamon, and salt.

In a small mixing bowl, stir together the maple syrup and vanilla extract. Pour the maple-vanilla mixture over the dry ingredients, and toss to combine thoroughly.

Transfer the cereal to a rimmed baking sheet lined with parchment paper. Flatten it into an even layer with your hand.

Bake the cereal for 30 minutes. Using the edge of a large spoon, break the cereal into bite-size chunks. If the cereal is not yet golden brown, bake for another 6 or 7 minutes; then check the color. If necessary, stir the cereal and return it to the oven to continue baking, checking it every few minutes and stirring to ensure it bakes evenly, until the cereal is done.

Remove from the oven and allow the cereal to cool completely. Store in airtight containers. The cereal will keep for 2 weeks in the pantry, 3 weeks in the refrigerator, and 2 months in the freezer.

Per serving (1 cup): Calories 288; Fat 4g; Saturated Fat 1g; Sodium 107mg; Protein 9g; Fiber 7g

Quinoa with Mango, Strawberries, Green Grapes & Yogurt

SINGLETONS, VEGETARIANS, 30-MINUTE

SERVES 4 / PREP: 25 MINUTES

Are you rushed in the mornings, thinking you don't have time for a healthy, nutritious breakfast? Preparation of this quinoa breakfast is as easy as can be and will help you start your morning on the right side of the bed. Change it up a bit by chilling the quinoa, using plain yogurt, or switching in whatever fresh fruits you desire.

3 cups cooked red quinoa, cooled
1 mango, cut into ½-inch cubes
1 cup halved seedless green grapes
1 cup quartered strawberries
1 cup vanilla Greek yogurt
3 tablespoons chopped pistachios (optional)

Portion out the quinoa into 4 cereal bowls. Evenly distribute the mango, grapes, and strawberries into each bowl. Spoon a ¼-cup dollop of yogurt on top of the fruit in each bowl. Top each serving with 2 teaspoons of pistachios (if using), and serve immediately.

Tip **Turn this dish into a vegan treat by leaving off the yogurt and pouring on some almond milk or another nondairy milk.**

Per serving: Calories 285; Fat 2g; Saturated Fat 1g; Sodium 28mg; Protein 13g; Fiber 6g

Hot Apple–Cinnamon Quinoa with Pecans

KIDS, SINGLETONS, VEGANS, MAKE AHEAD, ONE POT

SERVES 4 / PREP: 35 MINUTES / COOK: 15 MINUTES

Like a blast of mom love from your childhood, this hot cereal is comforting on cold mornings, especially when you're not feeling your best. Cooking the apples with the quinoa softens them for a nice contrast with the slightly chewy cereal. Add a pat of butter or a couple tablespoons of milk for a decadent twist.

2 cups water

1 cup dry quinoa, rinsed

½ teaspoon salt

1½ cups peeled and diced apples

½ teaspoon ground cinnamon

½ cup toasted, chopped pecans

1 tablespoon plus 1 teaspoon maple syrup

¼ cup raisins

In a medium saucepan over high heat, bring the water to a boil. Add the quinoa, salt, and apples and cook as described in the Stovetop Quinoa recipe on page 31.

Once the quinoa is cooked, add the cinnamon, pecans, and maple syrup and stir to combine thoroughly.

Portion the cereal into 4 bowls, and sprinkle each with 1 tablespoon of raisins. Serve immediately.

To store, refrigerate in airtight containers. The cereal will keep for 2 days.

Per serving: Calories 360; Fat 18g; Saturated fat 2g; Sodium 298mg; Protein 8g; Fiber 7g

Quinoa Pudding
with Strawberries & Pistachios

KIDS, VEGETARIANS, MAKE AHEAD, ONE POT

SERVES 4 / PREP: 10 MINUTES / COOK: 30 MINUTES

Pudding fans, rejoice. Quinoa makes great pudding that's a lot like a rice or tapioca pudding. What a treat for breakfast. Of course, quinoa pudding is fantastic for dessert, too.

3 cups whole milk
2 tablespoons vanilla extract
⅓ cup sugar
⅛ teaspoon salt
1 cup quinoa
1 cup quartered strawberries
3 tablespoons chopped pistachios (optional)

In a medium saucepan over medium heat, stir together the milk, vanilla extract, sugar, and salt until the sugar has dissolved. Bring the liquid to a boil, and add the quinoa. Give the mixture a stir, and bring it back to a boil. Turn the heat to low and simmer for 30 minutes, stirring frequently.

Once the pudding has thickened, remove it from the heat and allow it to cool. If desired, move it to the refrigerator to chill.

Portion the pudding into 4 glasses or bowls, and top each with an equal amount of the strawberries. Sprinkle each serving with 2 teaspoons of the pistachios (if using) and serve.

To store, refrigerate the pudding, strawberries, and pistachios (if using) in separate airtight containers. The pudding will keep for 2 days.

Tip **The chocolate version of this dish is equally delicious (and sinful for breakfast). Just add ⅓ cup cocoa powder along with the milk.**

Per serving: Calories 383; Fat 11g; Saturated Fat 4g; Sodium 146mg; Protein 13g; Fiber 4g

Creamy Chai-Spiced Quinoa

SINGLETONS, VEGETARIANS, MAKE AHEAD, ONE POT, 30-MINUTE

SERVES 4 / PREP: 5 MINUTES / COOK: 5 MINUTES

Native to India, masala chai (spiced tea) can include many different ingredients. The three foundational spices in chai are cardamom, cinnamon, and ginger, which flavor this dish. If you love chai beverages, you'll love this quinoa cereal.

2 cups milk of your choice
2 cups water
1⅓ cups quinoa flakes
¾ teaspoon ground cardamom
¾ teaspoon ground cinnamon, plus more for sprinkling
¼ teaspoon ground ginger
2 tablespoons maple syrup
⅛ teaspoon salt

In a medium saucepan over medium-high heat, bring the water and milk to a boil. Add the quinoa flakes to the boiling liquid, and stir to combine.

Remove the saucepan from the heat, and mix in the cardamom, cinnamon, ginger, maple syrup, and salt. Cover the pot, and let the cereal stand until it has thickened to the desired consistency, usually 3 or 4 minutes.

Portion the cereal into 4 bowls. Sprinkle each with the additional cinnamon, and serve immediately.

To store, refrigerate in airtight containers. The cereal will keep for 2 days.

Tip In India, there are as many versions of masala chai as there are people who brew it. Explore the many flavors of chai by mixing and matching the basic three spices with other traditional ingredients: ground fennel, coriander, nutmeg, cloves, star anise, and black pepper.

Per serving: Calories 239; Fat 4g; Saturated fat 2g; Sodium 137mg; Protein 9g; Fiber 3g

Quinoa–Yogurt Parfait
with Peaches & Blueberries

KIDS, VEGETARIANS, 30-MINUTE

SERVES 4 / PREP: 25 MINUTES

This pretty parfait celebrates the bounty of summer. It's an excellent brunch dish, and its flexible ingredient proportions make it easy to multiply the recipe to serve more than four. But its quick preparation time means you can enjoy this breakfast any day of the week; it's also lovely for lunch.

2 cups vanilla Greek yogurt
3 cups cooked red quinoa
1 cup diced peaches
1 cup blueberries
4 sprigs fresh basil

Scoop 3 tablespoons of yogurt into the bottom of each of 4 tall glasses. Top each with ⅓ cup of quinoa; then layer on 2 tablespoons each of peaches and blueberries. Repeat the layers. Complete the parfaits by topping each with the remaining ¼ cup yogurt. Garnish each glass with a basil sprig and serve.

Per serving: Calories 317; Fat 5g; Saturated Fat 1g; Sodium 43mg; Protein 16g; Fiber 5g

Quinoa-Blueberry Buttermilk Pancakes

KIDS, VEGETARIANS

MAKES 12 TO 16 PANCAKES / PREP: 10 MINUTES / COOK: 25 MINUTES

This is a wonderful dish to serve your family on a Saturday morning before they head out to their various activities. The sweetness of the blueberries sets off the tanginess of the quinoa-buttermilk combination. Bonus: Quinoa plus blueberries equals an antioxidant blast.

2 cups Quinoa Flour (page 37) or store bought
2 tablespoons light brown sugar
2 teaspoons ground cinnamon
1 teaspoon baking soda
¾ teaspoon salt
2 eggs
2 cups buttermilk
2 tablespoons canola oil, plus more for the griddle
1 teaspoon vanilla extract
1 cup fresh or frozen blueberries
Maple syrup, for drizzling

Tip **If you're using frozen berries and are left with some thawed juice, combine** it with your maple syrup in a 1:3 ratio. Heat the syrup for a minute or so in the microwave for hot blueberry syrup.

In a large mixing bowl, whisk together the Quinoa Flour, sugar, cinnamon, baking soda, and salt. In a medium mixing bowl, lightly beat the eggs. Whisk in the buttermilk, canola oil, and vanilla extract.

Pour the wet ingredients over the dry ingredients, and mix until just combined. Quickly stir in the blueberries. It's okay if the batter is a little lumpy.

Heat a large skillet or griddle over medium heat, and drizzle on just enough oil to keep the pancakes from sticking. When the pan is hot but not smoking, pour on ¼ cup of batter for each pancake. Let the pancakes cook until small bubbles begin to form on their surface. Flip the pancakes, and cook for another minute or two. Transfer the finished pancakes to a warm platter, and cover with a clean dish towel to keep warm. Continue cooking until all the batter is gone.

Serve immediately with a cruet of maple syrup. To store any leftovers, layer them with waxed paper in an airtight container and refrigerate. The pancakes will keep for 2 days.

Per serving (1 pancake): Calories 233; Fat 4g; Saturated Fat 1g; Sodium 266mg; Protein 4g; Fiber 2g

Ecuadorian Quinoa–Banana Cakes

KIDS, SINGLETONS, VEGANS

MAKES 4 OR 8 CAKES / PREP: 15 MINUTES / COOK: 16 TO 28 MINUTES

Ecuador is the third largest quinoa producer. Quinoa farms dot the uplands of the Andes Mountains, while the low-lying coastal plain is the world's largest producer of bananas. These little cakes marry the two in a treat that might remind you of banana bread. Go ahead, add some walnuts if you wish.

1 large, ripe banana in its skin
1½ cups cooked quinoa
¼ cup sugar
½ teaspoon vanilla extract
3 tablespoons Quinoa Flour (page 37) or store bought
¾ cup canola oil

In a medium saucepan over medium-high heat, boil the unpeeled banana for 10 minutes in 1½ quarts of water. Remove it from the pot, and allow it to cool until it's safe to handle. In a medium mixing bowl, peel and mash the banana.

Mix the quinoa with the mashed banana. Add the sugar, vanilla extract, and Quinoa Flour and stir to combine thoroughly.

In a large sauté pan over medium heat, heat the canola oil until hot but not smoking. Divide the dough into 4 or 8 equal portions, depending on whether you want smaller or larger cakes. Using your hands, shape each portion into a flat cake.

Place the cakes in the hot oil. Don't crowd the pan, as it will cool down the oil and make your cakes greasy. Fry the cakes on both sides until golden brown, 4 to 7 minutes per side. Drain on paper towels.

It's best to eat the cakes while they are still warm, but you can save them for later in the day. Layer the cakes with waxed paper, and store them in an airtight container in a cool, dry place.

Per serving (4 cakes): Calories 682; Fat 45g; Saturated Fat 4g; Sodium 4mg; Protein 10g; Fiber 5g

Quinoa Waffles
with Cherries, Strawberries & Almond Butter

KIDS, VEGETARIANS

MAKES 8 TO 12 WAFFLES / PREP: 10 MINUTES / COOK: 40 MINUTES

These waffles get a little extra crunch and a lot of extra nutrition from the chia seeds that speckle their nooks and crannies. More importantly, they're delicious. Wouldn't they be even tastier with a side of bacon?

2¼ cups Quinoa Flour (page 37) or store bought
2 tablespoons chia seeds
2 tablespoons sugar
1 tablespoon baking powder
¾ teaspoon salt
2 eggs
1 cup water
1¼ cups milk of your choice
½ cup canola oil, plus more for brushing
1 teaspoon pure vanilla extract
¼ cup almond butter
1 cup halved strawberries
1 cup cherries
Maple syrup, for drizzling

In a large mixing bowl, whisk together the Quinoa Flour, chia seeds, sugar, baking powder, and salt.

In a medium mixing bowl, lightly beat the eggs. Whisk in the water, milk, canola oil, and vanilla. Pour the wet ingredients over the dry ingredients, and mix until just combined.

Preheat the waffle iron.

Brush the waffle iron with a little canola oil. Pour a portion of the batter onto the iron, and close the lid. The waffles are ready when the lid lifts easily; time depends on the waffle iron. When each waffle is done, transfer it to a warm platter and cover with a clean dish towel to keep warm. Continue making waffles until the batter is gone.

Divide the warm waffles among 4 plates, and top each serving with 1 tablespoon of almond butter. Scatter equal amounts of the strawberries and cherries across each plate, and serve with a cruet of maple syrup on the table.

To store any leftovers, layer the waffles with waxed paper in an airtight container. The waffles will keep for 2 days in the refrigerator. Alternatively, you can freeze them for up to a month and pop them in the toaster whenever you want a quick breakfast.

Per serving (1 waffle): Calories 478; Fat 18g; Saturated Fat 2g; Sodium 220mg; Protein 8g; Fiber 3g

Savory Quinoa–Zucchini Egg Muffins with Mushrooms & Feta

LARGE GROUPS, SINGLETONS, VEGETARIANS, MAKE AHEAD

MAKES 12 MUFFINS / PREP: 20 MINUTES / COOK: 30 MINUTES

A satisfying grab-and-go breakfast, these muffins are like omelets on wheels. They're just as good at snack time, and when made as mini-muffins, they're a tempting hors d'oeuvre. Make a double batch and freeze half: You can eat them one by one, reheated in the microwave.

Cooking spray
2 teaspoons extra-virgin olive oil
2 medium zucchini, shredded
1 cup sliced white or button mushrooms
½ teaspoon freshly ground black pepper
1 teaspoon garlic powder
1 teaspoon salt, divided
3 eggs
1 cup egg whites
1½ cups cooked quinoa, cooled
1½ cups crumbled feta, divided

Preheat the oven to 350°F.

Place cupcake liners in a 12-cup muffin tin, and spray generously with cooking spray.

In a large sauté pan over medium heat, heat the olive oil. Add the zucchini, mushrooms, pepper, garlic powder, and ½ teaspoon of salt. Sauté, stirring frequently, until the vegetables are tender but not mushy, about 5 minutes. Transfer to a paper towel-lined bowl, leaving any liquid behind in the pan. Set aside to cool.

In a large mixing bowl, whisk together the eggs and egg whites for 30 seconds. Add the quinoa, 1 cup of feta, the cooled vegetables, and the remaining ½ teaspoon of salt. Mix well.

Divide the batter among the 12 muffin cups, filling each cup about ¾ full. If there's extra batter, do not overfill the cups. Line another muffin tin or some ramekins with greased cupcake liners, and fill each ¾ of the way. Sprinkle the remaining ½ cup of feta over the muffins.

Bake for 20 minutes, or until a toothpick comes out clean when inserted into a muffin. Remove the muffins from the oven, and let them cool for about 10 minutes before removing them from the tin. They're best served hot.

To store, refrigerate the muffins in an airtight container; they'll keep for 4 days. In the freezer, they'll keep for up to 3 months.

Tip **These muffins will stick to most muffin tins, even greased nonstick ones. Cupcake liners generously coated with cooking spray are your best bet.**

Per serving (1 muffin): Calories 163; Fat 7g; Saturated Fat 3g; Sodium 444mg; Protein 10g; Fiber 2g

Quinoa Crust Quiche
with Pancetta & Melted Onions

MEAT LOVERS, MAKE AHEAD

SERVES 4 TO 6 / PREP: 1½ HOURS / COOK: 50 MINUTES

Like a cookie-crumb pie crust, the quinoa crust in this recipe is pressed into the pie pan and baked before it's filled. Flaky and buttery, it's a versatile match for any filling, whether savory or sweet. Even pie crust snobs give the thumbs-up to the quinoa version.

For the crust

1 cup Quinoa Flour (page 37) or
    store bought
¼ teaspoon baking powder
¼ teaspoon salt
¼ cup butter, plus more for greasing, at
    room temperature
2 tablespoons cold water

For the filling

1½ cups diced pancetta
1 large onion, very thinly sliced
6 eggs
1½ cups heavy cream
¼ cup grated Parmesan cheese
2 tablespoons minced fresh thyme
¾ teaspoon salt
¼ teaspoon freshly ground black pepper
⅓ cup diced Gorgonzola (optional)
2 tablespoons minced fresh chives

To make the crust Preheat the oven to 350°F.

Grease the bottom and sides of a 9-inch pie plate.

In a medium bowl, whisk together the Quinoa Flour, baking powder, and salt. Add the butter and, using a fork, cut it into the dry ingredients until the resulting dough is uniform and crumbly. Sprinkle on the cold water, and stir it evenly throughout the dough. To test the dough, press a pinch of crumbs between your fingers; they should stick together but not go mushy. If the dough is too dry, add a bit more water; if it's too wet, add a bit more flour.

Transfer the dough to the pie pan, and press it evenly across the bottom and up the sides. Refrigerate the pie crust for 10 minutes.

Place a sheet of parchment paper over the top of the pie pan, and fill it with about 1 pound of dry beans or rice, to hold down the bottom of the crust so it doesn't puff up while it bakes. Bake the crust in the oven for 15 minutes, or until lightly golden, watching that the sides don't get too dark.

Remove the crust from the oven and set aside to cool.

To make the quiche Preheat the oven to 375°F.

In a large sauté pan over medium-high heat, cook the pancetta, stirring occasionally, until it's crisp and lightly golden. Transfer the pancetta to a plate covered with a paper towel and set aside. Leave the rendered pancetta fat in the pan.

Add the onion to the fat in the pan, and cook until it softens and begins to brown, about 10 minutes. Remove the pan from the heat and allow the onion to cool.

In a large mixing bowl, beat together the eggs and cream. Stir in the Parmesan, thyme, salt, and pepper. Set aside.

Scatter the pancetta across the bottom of the pie crust, and cover the pancetta evenly with the onion. Gently pour the egg-cream mixture into the pie crust. Sprinkle the Gorgonzola (if using) over the top of the quiche.

Put the quiche on a baking sheet and bake for 35 minutes. If it has not set in the center, bake for another 10 minutes. The quiche is done when it has set (a toothpick comes out clean) and the top is golden. If the rim of the pie crust starts getting too brown, squeeze some foil around the edges of the pan to cover it.

Remove the quiche from the oven, and allow it to set for 10 minutes.

Slice into wedges and serve, garnished with the chives.

To store, cover the pie pan tightly with plastic wrap, or cut the quiche into wedges and put them into airtight containers. The quiche will keep for 3 days in the refrigerator or 2 weeks in the freezer.

Tip Pancetta is an Italian specialty similar to bacon. Pancetta, however, may be flavored with black pepper or other spices, while bacon is always smoked after curing. Pancetta is salt-cured pork belly, and it needs to be cooked before eating. If you can't find pancetta, you can substitute bacon or ham.

Per serving: Calories 550; Fat 42g; Saturated Fat 22g; Sodium 1,233mg; Protein 19g; Fiber 3g

Quinoa with Asparagus, Snow Peas, Fried Egg & Ajvar

SERVES 4 / PREP: 20 MINUTES / COOK: 15 MINUTES

This recipe calls for *ajvar* (AY-var), a Serbian condiment made of roasted red bell peppers and, depending on the cook, any combination of roasted eggplant, garlic, hot chile peppers, and lemon. It's sold by the jar in the condiment or specialty foods section of supermarkets and may be mild or spicy. If you can't find *ajvar*, substitute some minced, roasted red bell peppers.

3 cups cooked quinoa, kept warm in a baking dish

2 tablespoons tomato paste

1 teaspoon salt, divided

¼ teaspoon freshly ground black pepper

8 asparagus spears, bases removed, cut into 1-inch pieces

1 cup snow peas, strings removed

2 scallions, bulb discarded, cut on the bias

½ teaspoon freshly squeezed lemon juice

2 cups water

4 eggs

½ teaspoon grated dried lemon peel (optional)

¼ cup *ajvar*

Preheat the oven to 200°F.

To the dish of quinoa, add the tomato paste, ½ teaspoon of salt, and the pepper. Stir to combine thoroughly. Put the dish in the oven and cover with a clean, damp dish towel to keep warm.

In a large sauté pan over medium heat, bring the asparagus, snow peas, scallions, remaining salt, lemon juice, and water to a simmer, and turn the heat down to medium-low. Tightly cover the pan and cook the vegetables until crisp-tender, about 4 minutes. Drain thoroughly.

Portion the quinoa into 4 oven-safe bowls, and top each with ¼ of the vegetables. Place the bowls in the oven, and cover with the re-dampened dish towel.

In a small sauté pan over medium-high heat, fry each egg separately. Remove them to a warmed platter as they are done.

Take the bowls out of the oven, and top each with one of the fried eggs. Dust with the lemon peel if desired, and serve with a tablespoon of *ajvar* in a small ramekin at each place setting. The finished dish is not suitable for leftovers.

Per serving: Calories 300; Fat 10g; Saturated Fat 2g; Sodium 164mg; Protein 16g; Fiber 7g

Low-Country Quinoa "Grits" with Shrimp

SERVES 4 / PREP: 20 MINUTES / COOK: 30 MINUTES

South Carolina's coastal Low Country, arguably the buckle of the so-called "grits belt" that stretches from Texas to Virginia, is famous for its shrimp fisheries. The two ingredients come together in this classic dish, a longtime breakfast staple among shrimpers and now a highlight on the menus of high-end restaurants. Standing in for the grits, quinoa gives the dish a little extra texture—and a whole lot more nutritional value.

For the quinoa

4 tablespoons butter

1 cup dry quinoa, rinsed

1 clove garlic, peeled

1½ cups Chicken Stock (page 40) or store bought

1½ cups whole milk

½ teaspoon salt

¾ cup shredded cheddar cheese (added later)

For the shrimp

3 slices thick-cut bacon

1 green bell pepper, chopped

½ cup chopped onion

2 garlic cloves, minced

¼ teaspoon cayenne pepper

16 raw medium shrimp, shelled and deveined

2 tablespoons dry sherry or 1 tablespoon Worcestershire sauce

2 tablespoons freshly squeezed lemon juice

Salt

Freshly ground black pepper

2 scallions, bulbs removed and green portions chopped, for garnish

To make the quinoa In a medium saucepan over medium heat, melt the butter. Add the quinoa and garlic clove, and stir to coat. Pour in the stock, milk, and salt, and give the mixture a stir. Increase the heat to medium-high, and bring to a boil. Turn the heat to low, and cover.

Simmer the quinoa for 15 minutes, until the quinoa is tender and the liquid in the pot is like a thin porridge. Remove the garlic clove and discard. Take the pot off the heat, keeping it covered.

To make the shrimp While the quinoa cooks, in a sauté pan over medium heat, fry the bacon until crisp. Remove it from the pan and drain on paper towels. Once cool, crumble the bacon. Set aside.

Add the green pepper, onion, garlic, and cayenne to the bacon grease. Cook and stir until the onion is translucent, about 8 minutes. Add the shrimp and sherry. Cook, stirring constantly, until the shrimp just turns pink and opaque, about 3 minutes. Do not overcook the shrimp.

Remove the pan from the heat, and stir in the lemon juice. Season with salt and pepper.

Stir the cheese into the quinoa until melted. If necessary, put the pot over low heat for a few minutes. Season with salt and pepper.

Portion the quinoa among 4 bowls. Lay 4 shrimp on top of the quinoa in each, and spoon any sauce from the pan into the bowls. Garnish with the crumbled bacon and scallions and serve.

To store, refrigerate the quinoa and shrimp in separate airtight containers. They will keep for 3 days in the refrigerator and 1 month in the freezer.

Per serving: Calories 576; Fat 28g; Saturated Fat 15g; Sodium 1,198mg; Protein 37g; Fiber 4g

Vegetable Omelet
with Quinoa & Goat Cheese

SINGLETONS, VEGETARIANS

SERVES 4 / PREP: 20 MINUTES / COOK: 35 MINUTES

This vegetarian omelet has real stick-to-your ribs staying power, thanks to the quinoa. If you're an incorrigible carnivore, you can add bacon or chicken to the filling. If you're an incurable lazybones, you can prepare the recipe as a scramble instead of an omelet.

For the filling
1½ cups fresh cauliflower florets
2 tablespoons extra-virgin olive oil, divided
2 garlic cloves, minced
2 tightly packed cups fresh spinach, torn
1½ cups cooked quinoa
1 tablespoon balsamic vinegar
¼ teaspoon red chili flakes (optional)
Salt
Freshly ground black pepper

For the omelet
1 dozen eggs
½ teaspoon salt
¼ teaspoon freshly ground black pepper
4 teaspoons butter, divided
4 ounces fresh, young goat cheese, divided
2 tablespoons minced parsley

To make the filling Preheat the oven to 400°F.

In a medium mixing bowl, toss the cauliflower with 1 tablespoon of olive oil. Spread the cauliflower out on a baking sheet, and roast it until it starts to brown, about 7 minutes. It should be tender but not soft. Remove from the oven and set aside.

In a large sauté pan over medium-high heat, heat the remaining 1 tablespoon of olive oil. Add the garlic and spinach, and cook until the spinach is fully wilted. Drain off any fluid.

Add the cauliflower and quinoa to the sauté pan, and stir to combine. Drizzle on the vinegar, and sprinkle on the chili flakes (if using). Stir and season with salt and pepper. Cover and set aside.

Turn off the oven, and leave the door partially open so it cools down to about 200°F.

To make the omelet In a large mixing bowl, beat the eggs. Stir in the salt and pepper. Portion the eggs evenly into four cups or bowls.

In a medium, nonstick sauté pan over medium heat, heat 1 teaspoon of butter. Pour one portion of the eggs into the pan, and tilt the pan to spread the egg evenly. When the bottom of the omelet has set, lift the edge and allow any liquid egg to run under to cook. Do not allow the egg to brown.

When the omelet is almost set on top, spoon ¼ of the quinoa-vegetable mixture onto ½ of the omelet. Dot the filling with 1 ounce of goat cheese, then flip the other half of the omelet over the filling.

Slide the omelet onto a plate, and put the plate in the warm oven. Repeat the process for the remaining 3 omelets. Sprinkle the parsley over the omelets and serve. The finished dish is not suitable for leftovers.

Per serving: Calories 458; Fat 31g; Saturated Fat 12g; Sodium 847mg; Protein 25g; Fiber 3g

4

Smoothies

Homemade Quinoa Milk

KIDS, SINGLETONS, VEGANS, MAKE AHEAD, 30-MINUTE

MAKES ABOUT 1 QUART / PREP: 20 MINUTES

You've seen nondairy soy, rice, and almond milk in your supermarket, but have you seen quinoa milk? Protein- and nutrient-rich, creamy, and slightly nutty-tasting, it's great not only in smoothies but to drink on its own, to pour on cereal, and as a substitute for cow's milk in all kinds of recipes. Quinoa milk is super-easy to make at home; you'll just need a reusable nut-milk bag or some cheesecloth and a fine-mesh sieve.

3 cups cooked quinoa
3 cups water, divided

In a blender, blend the quinoa and 2 cups of water on high until smooth, 1 to 3 minutes.

Pour the milk into a nut-milk bag or a cheesecloth-lined fine-mesh sieve. Holding the bag over a large bowl, gently massage or press the bag to speed up the draining of the liquid. When all the milk has filtered into the bowl, discard the pulp left in the bag.

Return the milk to the blender, add the remaining 1 cup of water, and blend for about 30 seconds. Check the consistency of the milk. If it's thicker than you wish, add more water and blend again. Repeat until the milk reaches the desired consistency.

Refrigerate the quinoa milk in an airtight container. It will keep 3 to 4 days. Shake before using. Do not freeze.

Tip **Looking for some variety? After the milk reaches the consistency you want, try adding sweeteners such as agave nectar or honey, or flavorings such as vanilla extract, ground cinnamon, or cocoa powder.**

Per cup: Calories 70; Fat 1g; Saturated Fat 0g; Sodium 0mg; Protein 2g; Fiber 0g

Frozen Super-Berry Smoothie

KIDS, SINGLETONS, VEGANS, 30-MINUTE

SERVES 2 / PREP: 10 MINUTES

Like a nondairy milkshake, this icy blend of quinoa milk and frozen fruit is a treat any time of day. It's especially delicious in summer, when berries are in season. Just pop some fresh ones in a zip-top bag and put them in the freezer. The quinoa-berry combo makes this smoothie an antioxidant dynamo.

2 cups cold Quinoa Milk (page 78)
1 cup frozen blueberries
1 cup frozen raspberries
1 teaspoon agave nectar (optional)
2 sprigs fresh mint for garnish

In a blender, blend the Quinoa Milk, blueberries, raspberries, and agave nectar (if using) on medium-high until mostly smooth. Divide the smoothie between 2 glasses, and garnish each with a sprig of mint.

Per serving: Calories 270; Fat 2g; Saturated Fat 0g; Sodium 2mg; Protein 3g; Fiber 8g

Tropical Fruit Shake

KIDS, SINGLETONS, VEGANS, 30-MINUTE

SERVES 2 / PREP: 10 MINUTES

Welcome to the tropics, where juicy, nutrition-laden fruit weighs down the lush foliage. The purple passion fruit may be new to you. Its tough rind hides an aromatic mass of pods filled with orange, pulpy juice and small, black seeds. The fruit has a sweet-tart flavor that crosses guava with citrus, and it's high in fiber and antioxidants.

2 cups cold Quinoa Milk (page 78)

½ cup unsweetened coconut milk

3 purple passion fruit, pulp scooped out of the rind

½ peeled, pitted, and cubed mango

1 teaspoon agave nectar (optional)

In a blender, blend the Quinoa Milk, coconut milk, passion fruit pulp, mango, and agave (if using) on high until smooth. Divide the smoothie between 2 glasses and serve.

To store, pour the shake into an airtight container. It will keep for 2 days in the refrigerator. Before serving, run it through the blender.

Per serving: Calories 300; Fat 15g; Saturated Fat 13g; Sodium 18mg; Protein 2g; Fiber 6g

Classic Strawberry–Banana Smoothie

KIDS, SINGLETONS, VEGANS, 30-MINUTE

SERVES 2 / PREP: 10 MINUTES

A time-honored smoothie flavor combination, strawberries and bananas are sweetened here with succulent peaches. For more creaminess, toss in a cup of vanilla Greek yogurt; for more frostiness, freeze the bananas. This smoothie is packed with potassium, vitamin C, and antioxidants.

2 cups cold Quinoa Milk (page 78)
1 ripe banana, sliced
2 peaches, peeled and diced
1 cup sliced strawberries, plus 2 more
    strawberries, sliced, for garnish
Ice (optional)
1 teaspoon honey (optional)

In a blender, blend the Quinoa Milk, banana, peaches, strawberries, ice (if using), and honey (if using) on high until smooth. Divide the smoothie between 2 glasses, and garnish each with 1 sliced strawberry.

To store, pour the smoothies into an airtight container. The smoothies will keep for 2 days in the refrigerator. Before serving, run it through the blender and top with sliced strawberries.

Per serving: Calories 194; Fat 2g; Saturated Fat 0g; Sodium 1mg; Protein 3g; Fiber 4g

Green Smoothie Supreme

SINGLETONS, VEGANS, 30-MINUTE

SERVES 2 / PREP: 20 MINUTES / COOK: 2 MINUTES

Don't let the idea of a smoothie stuffed with veggies turn you off. Your taste buds and your body will thank you. Here, sweet, fresh pineapple and the zing of fresh ginger shine over the kale and spinach flavors, but you'll get all the antioxidants, fiber, vitamins, and iron of the greens—almost without knowing it.

2 cups cold Quinoa Milk (page 78)

¾ cup deribbed, parboiled, and chopped fresh kale (see tip)

¾ packed cup fresh baby spinach

¾ cup diced fresh pineapple

2 tablespoons chia seeds

1½ teaspoons grated fresh ginger

2 teaspoons agave nectar (optional)

In a blender, blend the Quinoa Milk, kale, spinach, pineapple, chia seeds, ginger, and agave (if using) on high until smooth. Divide the smoothie between 2 glasses and serve.

To store, pour the smoothie into an airtight container. It will keep for 2 days in the refrigerator. Before serving, run it through the blender.

Tip To parboil the kale, bring a large pot of water, about ⅔ full, to a boil. Prepare an ice bath by putting 2 or 3 trays of ice in a large mixing bowl and filling it about ⅔ of the way with cold water. Plunge the kale leaves into the boiling water and cook for 2 minutes. Transfer the kale to the ice bath and cool thoroughly. Dry the kale before using.

Per serving: Calories 179; Fat 4g; Saturated Fat 0g; Sodium 21mg; Protein 5g; Fiber 5g

Carrot-Orange Immune Infusion

KIDS, SINGLETONS, VEGANS, 30-MINUTE

SERVES 2 / PREP: 15 MINUTES

This sunny, bright orange smoothie is a real pick-me-up when you're sick—and when you're not. Turmeric has been used medicinally for centuries in India and China; it is an anti-inflammatory as well as an antioxidant. It is also used as a spice in many cuisines. With a warm, slightly spicy flavor and a sharp-sweet aroma, turmeric is sold fresh or dried. Start out with a small amount if using it for the first time until you find the amount best suited to your palate.

2 cups cold Quinoa Milk (page 78)

¼ cup quinoa flakes

¾ cup shredded carrot

1 seedless orange, peeled and separated into segments

1 large apple, peeled, cored, and chopped

¾ teaspoon grated fresh ginger

½ teaspoon grated fresh turmeric or ¼ teaspoon ground turmeric

2 teaspoons honey (optional)

Ice (optional)

In a blender, blend the Quinoa Milk, quinoa flakes, carrot, orange, apple, ginger, turmeric, honey (if using), and ice (if using) on high until smooth. Divide the smoothie between 2 glasses and serve.

To store, pour the smoothie into an airtight container. The smoothie will keep for 2 days in the refrigerator. Before serving, run it through the blender.

Per serving: Calories 259; Fat 2g; Saturated Fat 0g; Sodium 32mg; Protein 5g; Fiber 7g

Green Tea–Avocado Antioxidant Shake

SINGLETONS, VEGANS, 30-MINUTE

SERVES 2 / PREP: 15 MINUTES

Who can resist this creamy, pale green smoothie? It's enjoyably energizing thanks to the green tea, and hunger-quenching thanks to the avocado. And, of course, it packs an antioxidant wallop that amplifies the benefits of quinoa.

2 cups cold Quinoa Milk (page 78)
½ cup very strong green tea, chilled
½ apple, peeled, cored, and chopped
½ cup seedless green grapes
½ avocado, peeled, pitted, and diced
1 tablespoon freshly squeezed lemon juice
2 tablespoons minced fresh cilantro (optional)
2 teaspoons agave nectar (optional)
Ice (optional)

In a blender, blend the Quinoa Milk, green tea, apple, grapes, avocado, lemon juice, cilantro (if using), agave (if using), and ice (if using) on high until smooth. Divide the shake between 2 glasses and serve.

To store, pour the shake into an air-tight container. It will keep for 2 days in the refrigerator. Before serving, run it through the blender.

Per serving: Calories 274; Fat 11g; Saturated Fat 2g; Sodium 6mg; Protein 1g; Fiber 6g

Blueberry-Kiwifruit Smoothie

KIDS, SINGLETONS, VEGANS, 30-MINUTE

SERVES 2 / PREP: 10 MINUTES

Quinoa flakes thicken this smoothie into a hearty, satisfying breakfast or snack. Blended together, the quinoa milk and flakes yield a drink that knocks protein, fiber, antioxidants, and a host of other nutrients out of the ballpark. Throw in some blueberries and kiwifruit, and you're talking antioxidant insanity!

2 cups cold Quinoa Milk (page 78)
⅓ cup quinoa flakes
1½ cups blueberries
2 kiwifruits, peeled and diced
1 teaspoon agave nectar (optional)
Ice (optional)

In a blender, blend the Quinoa Milk, quinoa flakes, blueberries, kiwifruits, agave (if using), and ice (if using) on high until smooth. Divide the smoothie between 2 glasses and serve.

To store, pour the smoothie into an airtight container. It will keep for 2 days in the refrigerator. Before serving, run it through the blender.

Per serving: Calories 283; Fat 2g; Saturated Fat 0g; Sodium 6mg; Protein 4g; Fiber 7g

Chocolate–Cherry Protein Shake

KIDS, SINGLETONS, VEGANS, 30-MINUTE

SERVES 2 / PREP: 10 MINUTES

Chocolate makes everything okay. Glazed donuts, filled croissants, and crazy coffee drinks have their place, but if you want to skip the carbs and midmorning cravings, this shake is for you. Switch out the cherries for strawberries, raspberries, or blueberries if they're in season.

2 cups cold Quinoa Milk (page 78)
1 cup pitted cherries, fresh or frozen
½ cup coconut milk
2 scoops protein powder of your choice
2 tablespoons unsweetened cocoa powder
2 teaspoons agave nectar (optional)
Ice (optional)

In a blender, blend the Quinoa Milk, cherries, coconut milk, protein powder, cocoa powder, agave (if using), and ice (if using) on high until smooth. Divide the shake between 2 glasses and serve.

To store, pour the shake into an airtight container. It will keep for 2 days in the refrigerator. Before serving, run it through the blender.

Per serving: Calories 430; Fat 17g; Saturated Fat 14g; Sodium 65mg; Protein 26g; Fiber 5g

Banana—Almond Energy Shake

KIDS, SINGLETONS, VEGANS, 30-MINUTE

SERVES 4 / PREP: 10 MINUTES

This smoothie will power you up and keep you going strong for hours. Try it before you work out or go for that run, and see what a difference it makes in your performance. For an extra treat, add some cocoa powder or unsweetened coconut flakes.

2 cups cold Quinoa Milk (page 78)
2 ripe bananas, sliced
⅓ cup almond butter
½ teaspoon ground cinnamon
½ teaspoon vanilla extract
1 teaspoon agave nectar (optional)
Ice (optional)

In a blender, blend the Quinoa Milk, bananas, almond butter, cinnamon, vanilla, agave (if using), and ice (if using) on high until smooth. Divide the shake between 2 glasses and serve.

To store, pour the shake into an airtight container. It will keep for 2 days in the refrigerator. Before serving, run it through the blender.

Per serving: Calories 471; Fat 24g; Saturated Fat 2g; Sodium 1mg; Protein 12g; Fiber 5g

5

Snacks & Sides

Simple Quinoa Pilaf

SINGLETONS, VEGANS, MAKE AHEAD, ONE POT, 30-MINUTE

SERVES 4 / PREP: 5 MINUTES / COOK: 10 MINUTES

Easy as can be, this deceptively plain dish is loaded with flavor. It's also a great vehicle for other flavors. Try adding sautéed vegetables such as diced carrots and celery, fresh herbs such as thyme and marjoram, lemon juice, and spices such as curry and *za'atar*.

2 tablespoons extra-virgin olive oil

1 small onion, finely chopped

¼ teaspoon salt, plus more for seasoning

3 cups cooked quinoa, prepared with Vegetable Stock (Chicken Stock substitution tip, page 41)

Salt

Freshly ground black pepper

¼ cup chopped fresh flat-leaf parsley

In a large sauté pan over medium-high heat, heat the olive oil. Add the onion and salt and sauté until the onion softens and turns translucent, 5 to 6 minutes. Fluff the quinoa, and add it to the pan, tossing to combine with the onion. Season with salt and pepper, and sprinkle in the parsley. Serve immediately.

To store, refrigerate it in an airtight container. The dish will keep for 4 days in the refrigerator and 1 month in the freezer.

Per serving: Calories 242; Fat 10g; Saturated Fat 2g; Sodium 169mg; Protein 9g; Fiber 5g

Creamy Parmesan—Garlic Quinoa

KIDS, SINGLETONS, MAKE AHEAD, ONE POT, 30-MINUTE

SERVES 4 / PREP: 20 MINUTES / COOK: 10 MINUTES

Sweet, nutty roasted garlic, squeezed out of its skin and spread on a thick slice of ciabatta, is a thing of beauty—but also a gluten nightmare. Replace the bread with quinoa, and you've got a side dish full of antioxidants, Vitamin C, Vitamin B$_6$, and manganese. And, of course, it's full of gorgeous cheesy garlic flavor.

2 tablespoons unsalted butter

4 large garlic cloves, roasted (see the Quinoa and Roasted Vegetable Bowl recipe, page 200) and mashed

1 recipe Simple Quinoa Pilaf (page 92)

⅔ cup grated fresh Parmesan cheese

½ cup toasted pine nuts (optional)

Salt

Freshly ground black pepper

In a large sauté pan over medium heat, melt the butter. Add the garlic and sauté, mashing and chopping, to form a uniform paste, 3 to 4 minutes.

Fluff the Simple Quinoa Pilaf, and add it to the pan, tossing to mix in the garlic paste. Remove the pan from the heat, and stir in the Parmesan. Add the pine nuts (if using). Season with salt and pepper, and serve immediately.

To store, refrigerate in an airtight container. The quinoa will keep for 3 days. Do not freeze.

Per serving: Calories 461; Fat 31g; Saturated Fat 8g; Sodium 1,102mg; Protein 15g; Fiber 5g

Quinoa Pilaf
with Wild Rice & Mushrooms

SINGLETONS, VEGETARIANS, MAKE AHEAD

SERVES 4 / PREP: 10 MINUTES / COOK: 1 HOUR

A little different from the other pilaf recipes in this chapter, this one more or less adapts the traditional rice pilaf method. The rice—quinoa, that is—goes into the pan with the cooking vegetables, herbs, or other ingredients in the pilaf; then you pour the water or stock in, and the rice cooks with the lid closed. The process makes a deeply flavored, satisfying dish.

1 tablespoon unsalted butter

1 ½ cups sliced cremini mushrooms

⅓ cup dry white wine

1 tablespoon extra-virgin olive oil

¾ cup finely chopped onion

1 ½ teaspoons minced fresh thyme

1 ½ teaspoons minced fresh sage

½ teaspoon salt, plus more for seasoning

2 cups Vegetable Stock (Chicken Stock substitution tip, page 41)

½ cup uncooked wild rice

½ cup dry quinoa, rinsed

¼ cup chopped fresh flat-leaf parsley, plus 2 tablespoons for garnish

Freshly ground black pepper

In a small sauté pan over medium-high heat, melt the butter. When it starts to foam, add the mushrooms and sauté for 2 minutes. Pour in the wine and cook until the liquid has evaporated, about 4 minutes. Remove the pan from the heat and set aside.

In a large saucepan over medium heat, heat the olive oil. Add the onion and sauté until soft and translucent, about 5 minutes. Add the thyme, sage, and salt and cook, stirring frequently, for 1 minute.

Stir in the Vegetable Stock, turn the heat up to medium-high, and bring the liquid to a boil. Add the wild rice, and turn the heat down to medium-low. Cover the pot, and without lifting the cover, simmer until the rice is tender, about 35 minutes.

Add the quinoa and mushrooms to the pot with the wild rice. Bring to a boil; then reduce the heat to low and cook until the quinoa is tender, about 15 minutes. Mix in ¼ cup of parsley. Remove from the heat and season with salt and pepper.

Garnish the pilaf with the remaining 2 tablespoons of parsley and serve.

To store, refrigerate in an airtight container. The pilaf will keep for 4 days; it will keep for 1 month in the freezer.

Tip **Feeling indulgent? Stir ½ cup heavy cream into the pilaf about 5 minutes before it's done cooking.**

Per serving: Calories 253; Fat 9g; Saturated Fat 3g; Sodium 701mg; Protein 10g; Fiber 4g

Red Quinoa
with Toasted Pecans & Rosemary

SINGLETONS, MAKE AHEAD, ONE POT

SERVES 4 / PREP: 15 MINUTES / COOK: 5 MINUTES

Visually elegant, with rich colors and a smart rosemary-sprig garnish, this side will upgrade any dish. The nutty, delicately sweet flavor of the red quinoa lends a sophistication to just about any poultry dish, as does its multi-textured mouthfeel. If you're feeling decadent, toss with a couple tablespoons of unsalted butter when you're ready to serve.

1 tablespoon extra-virgin olive oil

3 cups cooked red quinoa, prepared with Chicken Stock (page 40) or store bought

¾ cup whole pecans

1 teaspoon minced fresh rosemary, plus 4 sprigs for garnish

Salt

Freshly ground black pepper

In a medium sauté pan over medium-high heat, heat the olive oil. When the oil is hot but not smoking, add the quinoa and pecans and sauté until they just start to sizzle, about 2 minutes. Turn the heat down to medium, add the minced rosemary, and season with salt and pepper. Cover and cook for 1 minute.

Remove the pan from the heat and serve immediately, garnishing each dish with a sprig of rosemary.

To store, refrigerate in an airtight container. The nuts will lose some of their crunch, but the quinoa will keep for 3 days. In the freezer, it will keep for 1 month.

Per serving: Calories 397; Fat 16g; Saturated Fat 3g; Sodium 236mg; Protein 10g; Fiber 5g

Quinoa Superfood Bites

KIDS, VEGETARIAN, MAKE AHEAD

YIELD 24 BITES / PREP TIME: 10 MINUTES / COOK TIME: 25 MINUTES

These small bites are more than delicious. They are also packed with healthy superfoods, including edamame, kale, and, of course, quinoa. They freeze well, too, so you can keep some stored in a zipper bag in the freezer and just thaw and reheat them when you want a healthy but tasty snack.

2½ cups cooked and cooled quinoa
½ cup quinoa flakes
4 eggs, beaten
6 green onions, finely chopped
1 cup finely chopped kale
⅔ cup shelled edamame
2 garlic cloves, minced
¼ cup feta cheese, crumbled
¼ cup grated Parmesan cheese
1 tablespoon chopped fresh thyme
½ teaspoon sea salt
¼ teaspoon freshly cracked black pepper

Preheat the oven to 375°F. Spray two mini muffin tins with cooking spray.

In a small bowl, mix all the ingredients until well combined.

Roll the batter into 24 balls and put them in the mini muffin tins.

Bake in the preheated oven until golden brown, 25 to 30 minutes.

Cool on a wire rack for 10 minutes. Serve hot or cold.

To store, refrigerate or freeze in an airtight container. They keep for five days in the fridge and 6 months in the freezer.

Per serving (2 bites): Calories: 210; Fat: 6g; Saturated Fat: 2g; Sodium: 184mg; Protein: 11g; Fiber: 4g

Quinoa "Mashed Potatoes"

SINGLETONS, VEGANS, KIDS, MAKE AHEAD

SERVES 4 / PREP: 20 MINUTES / COOK: 45 MINUTES

At an altitude of 13,000 chilly feet, the Ecuadoreans of the Andes still eat many of the foods that kept their ancient ancestors warm and nourished. Two such foods, quinoa and potatoes, go into this traditional recipe, which is typically served with meat or eggs. Serve it with your favorite carnivore's steak.

3 cups water
½ teaspoon salt, plus more for seasoning
1 cup dry quinoa, rinsed
Quinoa Milk (page 78), as needed
1 large potato, peeled and chopped

Tip Punch up your mashed quinoa by adding some roasted garlic, cream cheese, or shredded cheddar to the mash.

In a medium saucepan over high heat, bring the water to a boil. Add the salt and quinoa. Give the mixture a stir, and bring it back to a boil. Turn the heat to low, and cover the pan. Simmer the quinoa for 30 minutes, until it's very soft; during cooking, you may need to spoon some additional boiling water into the pot, a little at a time, to keep the quinoa from drying out.

Add the quinoa to a large mixing bowl and mash it. Add Quinoa Milk as necessary to achieve the consistency you prefer.

While the quinoa is simmering, boil the potato until it is fork tender. Turn off the stove, and drain the water from the pot. Mash the potato right in the cooking pot, adding Quinoa Milk as necessary to achieve the consistency you prefer in your mashed potatoes.

Mix the quinoa and potato. Turn the heat to medium and cook until the mash resembles mashed potatoes, about 5 minutes. Remove from the heat and season with salt. Serve immediately.

To store, refrigerate in an airtight container. The mash will keep for 5 days; it will keep for 1 month in the freezer.

Per serving: Calories 218; Fat 2g; Saturated Fat 0g; Sodium 304mg; Protein 8g; Fiber 5g

Quinoa with Roasted Brussels Sprouts & Bacon

MEAT LOVERS, SINGLETONS

SERVES 4 / PREP: 15 MINUTES / COOK: 30 MINUTES

Brussels sprouts are a fantastic winter dish, even more so when you caramelize them in the oven and add savory crumbled bacon. Throw in some toothsome, nutty quinoa, and you have an elegant side for a meat-and-potatoes meal.

3 cups halved small, fresh Brussels sprouts

⅓ cup extra-virgin olive oil, plus more if desired

1 teaspoon kosher or coarse sea salt

3 cups cooked quinoa

6 slices thick-cut bacon, fried crisp and crumbled

Salt

Freshly ground black pepper

 Tip **Substitute walnut oil for the olive oil to bring quinoa's nutty hints to the fore.**

Preheat the oven to 375°F.

In a large mixing bowl, toss the Brussels sprouts, olive oil, and salt until the sprouts are thoroughly coated. Spread out the sprouts on a rimmed baking sheet. Leave the excess oil and salt in the bowl and set it aside.

Roast the sprouts, stirring occasionally, until they are tender and partially crispy and brown, 10 to 15 minutes depending on the size of the sprouts. Remove the sprouts from the oven, and turn the heat down to 325°F.

Transfer the sprouts to the reserved bowl, and add the quinoa and crumbled bacon. Toss to combine, adding additional olive oil if necessary. Season with salt and pepper and serve hot.

To store, refrigerate in an airtight container. The bacon will lose its crispness, but the quinoa will keep for 3 days. Do not freeze.

Per serving: Calories 385; Fat 24g; Saturated Fat 4g; Sodium 792mg; Protein 12g; Fiber 6g

Quinoa Curry
with Lentils & Cauliflower

SINGLETONS, VEGANS

SERVES 6 AS A SIDE, 4 AS A MAIN / PREP: 20 MINUTES / COOK: 50 MINUTES

Inspired by the curries of India, this aromatic dish is a medley of textures. Cooking the quinoa with turmeric turns it a vivid yellow that looks beautiful next to chicken breasts. For variety, add or substitute other vegetables, such as potatoes, peas, or green beans.

For the quinoa

1 teaspoon extra-virgin olive oil
½ cup diced carrot
¼ teaspoon ground turmeric
¼ teaspoon ground cumin
½ teaspoon salt
2 cups water
1 cup dry quinoa, rinsed

For the lentils

2 tablespoons extra-virgin olive oil
1 medium onion, finely chopped
2 garlic cloves, minced
2 whole, small, dried red chile peppers (optional)
1 tablespoon curry powder
1 teaspoon salt, plus more for seasoning
2½ cups water
1½ cups dry lentils
1 cup parboiled cauliflower florets

To make the quinoa In a medium saucepan over high heat, heat the olive oil. Add the carrot and sauté until it just starts to brown. Stir in the turmeric, cumin, and salt. Sauté for 1 minute.

Add the water to the pot, and bring it to a boil. Stir in the quinoa, and bring the water back to a boil. Turn the heat to low, and cover the pan. Simmer the quinoa until it is tender, about 15 minutes. Remove the pan from the heat and set it aside, covered, for at least 5 minutes.

To make the lentils In a large saucepan over medium heat, heat the olive oil. Add the onion and cook, stirring occasionally, until the edges are golden, about 5 minutes. Add the garlic and chile (if using), and stir for 2 minutes. Add the curry powder and salt, and stir for 1 minute.

Add the water and lentils to the pan, cover, and simmer, stirring occasionally, for 5 minutes. Add the cauliflower, cover, and simmer until the lentils and cauliflower are tender, about 15 minutes. Season with salt.

Place a mound of quinoa in the middle of each plate, and spoon the lentils over the quinoa. Garnish each serving with a sprig of cilantro and serve.

To store, refrigerate in an airtight container for 4 days; it will keep in the freezer for 1 month.

Tip If you choose to use the chile, watch the heat in your curry and remove the pepper when the lentils are as spicy as you want them to be.

Per serving: Calories 336; Fat 8g; Saturated Fat 1g; Sodium 649mg; Protein 17g; Fiber 18g

Quinoa Loaf
with Chard & Broccoli

LARGE GROUPS, MAKE AHEAD

SERVES 8 AS A SIDE, 4 AS A MAIN / PREP: 30 MINUTES / COOK: 45 TO 50 MINUTES

Essentially a crustless quiche, this loaf delivers vegetables under the radar. The colorful sun-dried tomato pesto brightens up the looks and flavor of the side. You can turn the loaf into an entrée by serving 2 slices instead of 1, and if you're expecting company or heading to a potluck, make several loaves.

For the pesto

½ cup drained, chopped sun-dried tomatoes

½ cup extra-virgin olive oil

¼ cup tightly packed fresh basil leaves

2 garlic cloves

½ cup toasted pine nuts

⅓ cup grated Parmesan cheese

½ teaspoon salt

¼ teaspoon freshly ground black pepper

For the loaf

1 teaspoon unsalted butter

1 cup Quinoa Flour (page 37) or store bought

1 teaspoon baking powder

1 cup water

⅔ cup extra-virgin olive oil

½ cup half-and-half

6 eggs, lightly beaten

1 cup cooked quinoa, cooled

1 cup steamed broccoli florets

1 cup chopped, steamed chard

½ cup chopped onion, sautéed

1½ cups shredded Swiss or Gruyère cheese, divided

¾ teaspoon salt

½ teaspoon ground nutmeg

¼ teaspoon freshly ground black pepper

To make the pesto In a blender or food processor, purée the tomatoes, olive oil, basil, garlic, pine nuts, Parmesan, salt, and pepper until smooth.

▸——→

To make the loaf Preheat the oven to 350°F.

Grease a 9-by-5-inch loaf pan with the butter.

In a large mixing bowl, whisk together the Quinoa Flour and baking powder. Mix in the water, olive oil, half-and-half, and eggs and combine well. Add the cooked quinoa, broccoli, chard, onion, 1 cup of cheese, salt, nutmeg, and pepper and mix to combine well.

Pour the vegetable mixture into the loaf pan, making sure the vegetables are evenly distributed. Sprinkle the remaining ½ cup of cheese over the top.

Bake until set and a toothpick inserted in the center comes out clean, 45 to 50 minutes.

Allow the loaf to cool slightly before cutting it into 1-inch-thick slices. Top each slice with 1 tablespoon of pesto. Serve hot or warm.

To store, refrigerate the pesto and loaf in separate airtight containers. The loaf will keep for 4 to 5 days. Do not freeze.

Per serving: Calories 558; Fat 48g; Saturated Fat 10g; Sodium 538mg; Protein 16g; Fiber 4g

Black Quinoa
with Peas & Mint

SINGLETONS, VEGANS, MAKE AHEAD, ONE POT, 30-MINUTE

SERVES 4 / PREP: 10 MINUTES / COOK: 15 MINUTES

The springtime green of baby peas creates a vivid contrast to the drama of the black quinoa. Gorgeous next to salmon, this side can be served hot or cold; try topping it with crumbled feta to make the colors really pop.

¼ cup plus 1 teaspoon extra-virgin olive oil, divided

2 teaspoons minced garlic

1 cup fresh baby peas

½ teaspoon salt, plus more for seasoning

2 tablespoons water

3 cups cooked black quinoa

¼ cup coarsely chopped fresh mint, plus 4 sprigs for garnish

1 lemon, zested

In a large sauté pan over medium-high heat, heat 1 teaspoon of olive oil. Add the garlic, and sauté for 1 minute. Stir in the peas, salt, and water. Cook for 1 minute; then turn the heat down to low, cover the pan, and steam the peas until they are crisp-tender, about 2 minutes.

Remove the pan from the heat, and drain off any remaining liquid through a fine-mesh sieve. Return the peas to the pan, and turn the heat to medium. Add the quinoa, chopped mint, lemon zest, and remaining ¼ cup of olive oil. Toss to combine well and heat through. Season with salt.

Serve, garnishing each portion with a mint sprig.

To store, refrigerate or freeze in an airtight container. The quinoa will keep for 3 days in the refrigerator and 1 month in the freezer.

Per serving: Calories 231; Fat 17g; Saturated Fat 3g; Sodium 301mg; Protein 9g; Fiber 6g

Quinoa Thanksgiving Stuffing

LARGE GROUPS, VEGANS, MAKE AHEAD

SERVES 8 / PREP: 20 MINUTES / COOK: 1 HOUR

It's hardly a secret that stuffing is most people's favorite part of the turkey day feast. This gluten-free recipe, healthier on all counts than the traditional bread-based ambrosia, allows for a little more indulgence. You can cook it inside the bird or in a baking dish on the side, as described here.

1½ teaspoons unsalted butter or cooking oil

3 tablespoons extra-virgin olive oil

2 cups diced celery

2 medium onions, diced

1½ cups Vegetable Stock (Chicken Stock substitution tip, page 41), plus more if needed

3 tablespoons chopped fresh sage

3 tablespoons chopped fresh thyme

½ teaspoon salt, plus more for seasoning

6 cups cooked quinoa (white or red), prepared with Chicken or Vegetable Stock (page 40)

Freshly ground black pepper

Preheat the oven to 375°F.

Grease a 9-by-13-inch baking dish with the butter.

In a large saucepan over medium heat, heat the olive oil. Add the celery and onions, and sauté until they soften and become translucent, 5 to 10 minutes. Increase the heat to medium-high and add the Vegetable Stock, sage, thyme, and salt. Simmer for 5 minutes. Add the quinoa to the pot, and mix all ingredients together well. If necessary, add more stock and adjust the seasoning with salt and pepper.

Transfer the stuffing into the baking dish, and spread it out evenly. Cover with foil, and bake for 30 minutes. Uncover and bake for 15 more minutes.

Serve warm.

Tip   Almost endless variations are possible with this stuffing. You can adapt this recipe to your taste by adding almost anything you like: cranberries or raisins, pecans or hazelnuts, giblets or sausage, mushrooms or sweet potatoes . . . you name it.

Per serving: Calories 257; Fat 10g; Saturated Fat 2g; Sodium 515mg; Protein 10g; Fiber 5g

Quinoa–Jalapeño Cornbread

KIDS, LARGE GROUPS, MAKE AHEAD

MAKES 9 (3-BY-3-INCH) SQUARES / PREP: 10 MINUTES / COOK: 25 MINUTES

Historians trace the origins of cornbread to the pre-colonial Native North Americans, but this version throws in ancient South American quinoa. It's a delicious spinoff with a slightly chewy texture and some mild heat added by the jalapeño (which you may leave out if you prefer). Warm and slathered with butter, this is a perfect side for Southern or Mexican food.

1 teaspoon butter
2 cups Quinoa Flour (page 37) or store bought
1 cup cornmeal
¼ cup sugar
1½ tablespoons baking powder
2 eggs, lightly beaten
1½ cups milk
6 tablespoons melted butter
¾ cup cooked quinoa, cooled
1 deribbed, seeded, minced jalapeño (optional)

Preheat the oven to 375°F.

Grease a 9-by-9-inch baking dish with the butter.

In a large mixing bowl, whisk together the Quinoa Flour, cornmeal, sugar, and baking powder.

In a small mixing bowl, mix together the eggs, milk, and melted butter. Gradually add the dry ingredients to the wet ingredients, and stir until just combined. Stir in the cooked quinoa and the jalapeño (if using), breaking up any lumps.

Pour the batter into the baking dish. Bake until a toothpick inserted in the center comes out clean and the bread is light brown around the edges, about 25 minutes.

Cut the bread into 9 even squares. Serve warm or cool.

To store, refrigerate in an airtight container. To freeze, wrap each square in plastic wrap or waxed paper and place in an airtight container. The cornbread will keep 5 days in the refrigerator and 1 month in the freezer.

Per serving: Calories 345; Fat 13g; Saturated Fat 6g; Sodium 101mg; Protein 9g; Fiber 4g

Lemon-Spinach Quinoa Linguine

VEGANS, ONE POT, 30-MINUTE

SERVES 4 / PREP: 10 MINUTES / COOK: 10 MINUTES

Delicate and elegant, this simple side works beautifully with fish. Quinoa pasta is surprisingly tasty and cooks up to a nice al dente texture. As when cooking any type of pasta, do not overcook it. Mushy pasta is never a pleasant texture.

2 tablespoons extra-virgin olive oil
3 garlic cloves, very thinly sliced
1½ pounds fresh spinach, chopped
1 tablespoon freshly squeezed lemon juice, plus more for seasoning
½ teaspoon salt, plus more for seasoning
¼ teaspoon freshly ground black pepper
4 cups cooked quinoa linguine, al dente, tossed in olive oil to prevent sticking
¼ cup grated Parmesan cheese

In a large sauté pan over medium heat, heat the olive oil. Add the garlic and sauté until it just starts to sizzle. Add the spinach, lemon juice, salt, and pepper to the pan and stir to coat the spinach thoroughly. Sauté until the spinach is soft, about 4 minutes. Add the linguine to the pan, and toss to combine with the spinach. Season with additional lemon juice and salt if needed.

Portion the linguine among 4 plates, and top each with 1 tablespoon of Parmesan.

To store, refrigerate in an airtight container. The pasta will keep for 2 days. Do not freeze.

Tip Turn this side into a main course by increasing the amount of pasta to 12 ounces and adding sliced lemon-pepper chicken breast. Cook the chicken separately, and toss it in with the pasta.

Per serving: Calories 331; Fat 10g; Saturated Fat 2g; Sodium 496mg; Protein 11g; Fiber 8g

Rainbow Quinoa Fusilli
with Artichoke Hearts

VEGANS, ONE POT, 30-MINUTE

SERVES 4 / PREP: 10 MINUTES / COOK: 15 MINUTES

A Mediterranean member of the thistle family, the artichoke plant produces awfully weird-looking buds. You can steam or boil them, then strip off the leaves and scrape off the soft, mildly sweet flesh with your teeth. When you get to the delectable center, you have to remove the bristly, inedible "choke" before eating the heart. But there's an easier way: Buy pre-cleaned frozen or jarred artichoke hearts.

2 tablespoons extra-virgin olive oil, divided

½ cup cooked quinoa

3 garlic cloves, very thinly sliced

1 (9-ounce) package frozen artichoke hearts, thawed, drained, and chopped

¼ cup chopped sun-dried tomatoes

½ teaspoon salt, plus more for seasoning

¼ teaspoon freshly ground black pepper, plus more for seasoning

4 cups cooked rainbow quinoa fusilli, al dente, tossed in olive oil to prevent sticking

¼ cup grated Parmesan cheese

In a medium sauté pan over medium-high heat, heat 1 teaspoon of olive oil. Add the quinoa, and sauté until it's crisp and toasty, 8 to 10 minutes. Set aside.

In a large sauté pan over medium-high heat, heat the remaining 1 tablespoon plus 2 teaspoons of olive oil. Add the garlic, and sauté until it just starts to sizzle. Add the artichoke hearts, and sauté until they are partially browned and crispy, about 5 minutes. Add the sun-dried tomatoes, salt, and pepper and stir to combine thoroughly. Sauté for 2 minutes.

Add the fusilli to the pan, and toss to combine with the vegetables. Add the toasted quinoa, and toss it in evenly. Season with salt and pepper.

Serve each fusilli portion topped with 1 tablespoon of Parmesan.

To store, refrigerate in an airtight container. The pasta will keep for 2 days. Do not freeze.

Per serving: Calories 296; Fat 11g; Saturated Fat 2g; Sodium 492mg; Protein 10g; Fiber 7g

Quinoa Mac 'n' Cheese

SERVES 4 / PREP: 10 MINUTES / COOK: 65 MINUTES

As the story goes, Thomas Jefferson introduced America to pasta, first serving "a pie called macaroni" at an 1802 state dinner. Mac 'n' cheese is arguably still a delicacy, the perfect recipe, a kind of Holy Grail for cooks everywhere. Experiment with this recipe to find your own perfection; you may want to try other cheeses, such as Gruyère or Gouda, or add some cooked ingredients—bacon, ground beef, tomatoes, lobster—to make an even heartier dish.

3 tablespoons butter, plus more for greasing

2 teaspoons extra-virgin olive oil, divided

½ cup cooked quinoa

2 cups dry quinoa macaroni

3 tablespoons Quinoa Flour (page 37) or store bought

1 teaspoon ground dry mustard (optional)

2 cups whole milk, room temperature

8 ounces cream cheese, cubed

8-ounce chunk sharp white cheddar cheese, shredded (not the pre-shredded kind)

Salt

Freshly ground black pepper

Preheat the oven to 350°F.

Grease a 9-by-9-inch baking dish with the butter.

In a medium sauté pan over medium-high heat, heat 1 teaspoon of olive oil. Add the quinoa and sauté until it's crisp and toasty, 8 to 10 minutes. Set aside.

Cook the macaroni until it's very al dente, with a bit of crunch; it's essential to undercook the pasta, because it will finish cooking as it bakes. Toss with the remaining 1 teaspoon of olive oil so it doesn't stick together. Set aside.

In a medium saucepan over medium heat, melt the remaining 3 tablespoons of butter. Whisk in the Quinoa Flour to create a roux (fat and flour paste). Continue whisking the roux until it barely starts to turn light golden, 2 to 3 minutes. Whisk in the mustard powder (if using). Add the milk ¼ cup at a time, whisking constantly to combine with the roux before adding the next portion of milk. Keep whisking until the milk comes to a simmer and thickens, 4 to 6 minutes.

Reduce the heat to low, and add the cream cheese. Stir to combine the cheese with the sauce as it melts, about 2 minutes. Stirring constantly, add the cheddar ½ cup at a time until all the cheese is incorporated and the sauce is smooth. Remove from the heat, and add the macaroni. Stir to coat the macaroni with the sauce. Season with salt and pepper.

Put the mac 'n' cheese in the baking dish, and sprinkle the toasted quinoa over the top. Bake until it is bubbling, about 30 minutes, and serve warm.

Store in an airtight container and refrigerate or freeze. It will keep 5 days in the refrigerator and 2 months in the freezer.

Tip When melted, sharp white cheddar is smoother than extra sharp; it's also smoother than melted orange cheddar.

Per serving: Calories 804; Fat 57g; Saturated Fat 34g; Sodium 675mg; Protein 27g; Fiber 3g

Quinoa Sliders
with Goat Cheese & Roasted Tomatoes

KIDS, LARGE GROUPS, SINGLETONS, VEGETARIANS, MAKE AHEAD

MAKES 8 TO 12 SLIDERS / PREP: 15 MINUTES, PLUS 15 MINUTES TO CHILL / COOK: 15 TO 20 MINUTES

These small bites have game day written all over them. Whether you're hosting a bridal shower or a Super Bowl party, quinoa sliders (or croquettes, if you want to sound fancy) will keep your guests satisfied. If you like, leave off the goat cheese and tomatoes and pile on the ketchup, salsa, jalapeños, or whatever else tickles your taste buds.

¾ cup coarsely grated zucchini

2 eggs, lightly beaten

⅓ cup grated Parmesan cheese

4 teaspoons chopped fresh parsley

2 garlic cloves, minced

¼ teaspoon freshly ground black pepper

Pinch saffron, soaked in ¼ cup hot water for 10 minutes

2 cups cooked quinoa, cooled

1 cup gluten-free pretzels, ground into crumbs (about ½ cup)

Salt

⅓ cup extra-virgin olive oil, divided

6-inch log fresh goat cheese, cut into 8 to 12 rounds

8 oven-roasted plum tomatoes (see the Crispy-Skin Barramundi on Saffron Quinoa recipe, page 211)

8 whole parsley leaves

Put the grated zucchini on a paper towel or clean kitchen towel, roll it up, and squeeze out the liquid. In a large mixing bowl, mix together the zucchini and eggs. Stir in the Parmesan, parsley, garlic, pepper, and saffron water. Mix in the quinoa and pretzel crumbs until just combined. Season with salt. Chill for 15 minutes.

Gently pack a ¼-cup measuring cup full of the quinoa mixture. Turn the mixture out into your hands, and lightly roll and press the portion to form a ½-inch-thick patty. Place the patty on a sheet of parchment or waxed paper. Repeat for the rest of the quinoa, making 8 to 12 patties.

In a medium sauté pan over medium heat, heat 1 tablespoon of olive oil. When the oil is hot, add 4 patties to the pan. Fry until the patties are crisp and golden on the bottom, about 3 minutes. Add 1 more tablespoon of oil to the pan and flip the patties, frying until crisp and golden on the underside, about 3 minutes. Remove the sliders to paper towels to drain. Repeat this step until you have fried all the patties.

Place the sliders on a warm serving platter, and top each with a round of goat cheese and a slice of roasted tomato. Garnish with a parsley leaf and serve.

To store, layer the sliders separated by waxed paper or plastic wrap and place in an airtight container. They will last 5 days in the refrigerator and 2 months in the freezer.

Tip Use this recipe as a base for making larger, sandwich-size burgers. Simply mix in 1 cup of cooked black beans plus another egg and 2 tablespoons more of pretzel crumbs. These additions will yield 4 big quinoa burgers.

Per serving: Calories 185; Fat 11g; Saturated Fat 4g; Sodium 131mg; Protein 9g; Fiber 4g

Cucumber Boats Stuffed
with Red Quinoa & Parmesan

LARGE GROUPS, ONE POT, SINGLETONS, VEGETARIANS, 30-MINUTE

MAKES 14 PIECES / PREP: 25 MINUTES

These cool and refreshing treats juxtapose the crispness of cucumber with the toothsome bite of quinoa. They're excellent low-calorie, low-fat snacks as well as hors d'oeuvres your guests will crave. For easy prep, dress the quinoa ahead of time and assemble the boats just before serving.

2 tablespoons extra-virgin olive oil
1 tablespoon white wine vinegar or
    champagne vinegar
2 loosely packed teaspoons julienned fresh
    basil leaves
1½ cups cooked red quinoa, cooled
Salt
Freshly ground black pepper
1 (14-inch) English cucumber, peeled
2 ounces Parmesan cheese, shaved into
    ½-inch-wide strips

In a medium mixing bowl, whisk together the olive oil and vinegar. Stir in the basil. Add the quinoa and toss to coat evenly. Season with salt and pepper. Set aside.

Cut the cucumber in half lengthwise and scoop out the seeds. Cut each half-cucumber crosswise into 2-inch segments.

Spoon 2 tablespoons of quinoa into each cucumber "boat." Add one or two Parmesan shavings on top and serve.

This dish doesn't lend itself well to leftovers, but if you don't finish them all in one sitting, put them in an airtight container and refrigerate. The boats will keep for 1 day.

Tip **Julienned basil is cut into very, very thin strips. To julienne, stack the leaves on a cutting board in a 2-by-2-inch square. Roll the square up like a cigar. With a sharp knife, slice across the cigar in very small increments to produce thin strips.**

Per serving (1 boat): Calories 90; Fat 4g; Saturated Fat 1g; Sodium 39mg; Protein 4g; Fiber 1g

Quinoa-Crusted Tartlets
with Mushrooms & Frizzled Prosciutto

LARGE GROUPS

MAKES 12 TO 16 TARTLETS / PREP: 20 MINUTES / COOK: 40 MINUTES

Who knew that quinoa could transport you to Italy? This recipe melds Mediterranean flavors into little bites of sunshine. Pour yourself a glass of Chianti and enjoy *la dolce vita*.

For the frizzle
2 teaspoons extra-virgin olive oil
4 slices prosciutto, cut lengthwise into very
  thin strips

For the crust
Cooking spray
½ teaspoon ground turmeric
2 cups cooked quinoa
1 egg, lightly beaten
¼ cup Parmesan cheese
2 tablespoons minced basil
½ teaspoon salt
½ teaspoon freshly ground black pepper

For the filling
1 tablespoon extra-virgin olive oil
1 tablespoon minced garlic
1 cup coarsely chopped crimini or
  portobello mushrooms
4 stalks asparagus, steamed and cut into
  ½-inch segments
2 tablespoons chopped oil-cured olives
1 teaspoon minced fresh oregano
Salt
Freshly ground black pepper
⅓ cup diced fontina cheese

To make the frizzle In a medium sauté pan over medium heat, heat the olive oil. Swirl it to coat the bottom of the pan. Add the prosciutto to the pan, separating the strips as much as possible. Sauté until crisp, about 10 minutes. Drain on paper towels.

To make the crust Preheat the oven to 375°F.

Spray a 24-cup mini-muffin tin with the cooking spray.

In a large mixing bowl, add the turmeric to the quinoa and stir to spread the color evenly. Add the egg, Parmesan, basil, salt, and pepper and mix thoroughly.

Measure 2 tablespoons of the quinoa mixture into each muffin cup, and press it evenly into the bottom of the tin and up the sides. Bake the crusts until they're light golden brown, about 10 minutes. Set aside and turn the oven down to 350°F.

To make the filling In a large sauté pan over medium heat, heat the olive oil. Add the garlic and cook until it just starts to sizzle, about 2 minutes. Stir in the mushrooms and sauté until they are fork-tender but not mushy, about 5 minutes. Add the asparagus, olives, and oregano and sauté for 2 minutes. Season with salt and pepper, and remove from the heat.

Transfer the vegetables to a large mixing bowl and allow to cool for 5 minutes. Add the cheese, and toss to distribute the ingredients evenly.

Scoop the filling into the baked crusts in even amounts. Bake the tartlets until the cheese melts, 6 or 7 minutes. Remove the tartlets from the oven, and allow them to cool enough that they're safe to handle.

Run a table knife between the side crust and the tin, and carefully lift each tart out of its cup. Place the tartlets on a warm serving platter, and top each with the frizzled prosciutto.

This dish doesn't lend itself well to leftovers, but if you don't finish them all in one sitting, put them in an airtight container and refrigerate. The tartlets will keep for 1 day.

Per serving (1 tart): Calories 150; Fat 5g; Saturated Fat 2g; Sodium 433mg; Protein 10g; Fiber 2g

Quinoa Canapés
with Cream Cheese, Smoked Salmon & Capers

LARGE GROUPS, MAKE AHEAD

MAKES 12 TO 16 CANAPÉS / PREP: 30 MINUTES / COOK: 10 MINUTES

The classic smoked salmon canapé has made the rounds at cocktail parties since the 1920s. This updated version brings more crunch and better nutrition to the serving platter but falls squarely within the grand tradition of the passed hors d'oeuvre. Broaden your nibbling horizons even further by trying different toppings, such as fresh dill or lemon zest.

For the toasts

¾ cup cooked quinoa, cooled

½ cup gluten-free pretzels, ground into crumbs (about ¼ cup)

1 egg, lightly beaten

2 tablespoons finely minced red onion

¼ teaspoon salt

2 to 2½ tablespoons extra-virgin olive oil, divided

For the canapés

8 ounces cream cheese, at room temperature

2 tablespoons minced chives

2 tablespoons drained capers (optional)

4 ounces thinly sliced smoked salmon, cut into 12 to 16 pieces

12 to 16 sprigs fresh dill

To make the toasts In a large mixing bowl, mix the quinoa, pretzel crumbs, egg, onion, and salt until well combined. Scoop the mixture into your hands, 1 tablespoon at a time, and form patties 1 to 1½ inches in diameter. Place the patties on a sheet of kitchen parchment or waxed paper. You will make 12 to 16 patties.

In a medium sauté pan over medium heat, heat 1 teaspoon of olive oil. When it is hot, lay 4 of the patties in the pan and fry until they are lightly golden on the bottom, 1 to 2 minutes. Add another teaspoon of olive oil to the pan and flip the patties, frying until lightly golden on the underside, 1 to 2 minutes. Remove the toasts to paper towels to drain. Repeat this step until you have made all the patties. Allow the toasts to cool.

To make the canapés In a small bowl, mix together the cream cheese with the chives and capers (if using). Top each quinoa toast with 1 tablespoon of the mixture. Lay a piece of the salmon over each canapé, and garnish each with a sprig of dill. Place the canapés on a serving platter and serve.

To store, refrigerate or freeze the toasts in an airtight container. The toasts will keep for 2 days in the refrigerator and 1 month in the freezer. Do not prepare the canapé toppings until you are ready to serve.

Per serving (1 canapé): Calories 135; Fat 9g; Saturated Fat 4g; Sodium 325mg; Protein 5g; Fiber 41g

sy Ecuadorian Quinoa Balls
ilantro Dip

E GROUPS, VEGETARIANS

OUT 32 BALLS / PREP: 15 MINUTES / COOK: 1 HOUR

Always a crowd pleaser, these Ecuadorian tidbits are perfect for parties. They're a stealth delivery system for quinoa, so they make an especially nutritious snack for kids. Just replace the cilantro dip (also an Ecuadorean original) with ketchup for the pickier eaters.

For the cilantro dip

1 egg, lightly beaten
¼ cup minced cilantro
2 jalapeño peppers, deribbed, deseeded, and minced
2 garlic cloves, crushed
¾ cup sunflower or canola oil, divided
Juice of 1 lime
6 ounces queso fresco, crumbled
Salt

For the quinoa balls

2½ cups water, plus more if needed
1 cup dry quinoa, rinsed
½ teaspoon salt, plus more for seasoning
½ cup Quinoa Flour (page 37) or store bought
1 egg, lightly beaten
4 ounces Monterey Jack cheese, grated
1 teaspoon baking powder
⅔ cup canola oil, plus more if needed

To make the dip In a blender or food processor, blend the egg, cilantro, jalapeño, garlic, and ¼ cup of sunflower oil into a smooth purée.

Keeping the blender running, add the remaining ½ cup of sunflower oil in a thin stream. Blend until the sauce starts to thicken. Add the lime juice and queso fresco, and continue blending until the dip is smooth. Stop the blender, season with salt, and pulse to combine. Set aside.

To make the quinoa balls In a medium saucepan over high heat, bring the water to a boil. Add the quinoa and salt, give the mixture a stir, and bring it back to a boil. Turn the heat to low, and cover the pan. Simmer the quinoa for 30 minutes, until it becomes thick. Add a few tablespoons of water if it starts to dry out. Let the quinoa cool.

In a large mixing bowl, mix the cooled quinoa and the Quinoa Flour; then mix in the egg, cheese, and baking powder.

In a large sauté pan over medium heat, heat the canola oil until it shimmers but doesn't smoke. Drop 2 tablespoons of the batter at a time into the oil. Don't put more than 5 or 6 portions into the pan at once, or the oil will cool and the balls will come out greasy.

When the bottom of the balls become golden, about 1 minute, roll them to cook another area of the surface. Keep rolling and cooking the balls until they are golden all over, about 5 minutes total. Remove them from the oil and drain on paper towels. Repeat this step until all the batter is used, being careful to allow the oil to reheat between batches.

Serve the balls warm with the cilantro dip.

The quinoa balls don't keep well. If you do have leftovers, put them in a brown paper bag, the layers separated by paper towels. Put the dip in an airtight container. The balls will keep for 1 day in the refrigerator and the dip for 4 days.

Tip Queso fresco, literally "fresh cheese," is a salty, crumbly cheese most often associated with Mexico. If your supermarket doesn't have it, check any Latin American grocery stores. You can substitute French feta, which is milder than the Bulgarian and Greek varieties.

Per serving (two balls and two tablespoons of dip): Calories 276; Fat 24g; Saturated Fat 5g; Sodium 169mg; Protein 6g; Fiber 1g

Sweet Potato & Cranberry Quinoa Cakes

KIDS, LARGE GROUPS, SINGLETONS, VEGETARIANS, MAKE AHEAD

MAKES 12 CAKES / PREP: 15 MINUTES, PLUS 15 MINUTES TO CHILL / COOK: 25 MINUTES

Second only to blueberries in antioxidant content, cranberries team up with sweet potato—an astounding source of vitamin A and fiber—in this super low-fat nibble. The cakes are a sweet, tangy, crunchy snack that'll get you through the afternoon munchies. They're also tasty for breakfast.

1 cup cooked white quinoa, cooled

1 cup cooked black quinoa, cooled

2 eggs, lightly beaten

1 cup gluten-free pretzels, ground into crumbs (about ½ cup)

½ cup sour cream

1 large sweet potato, peeled, boiled, and mashed

¾ cup dried cranberries, soaked in hot water for 15 minutes and drained

Salt

Preheat the oven to 350°F.

In a large mixing bowl, toss the white and black quinoa with the eggs to coat. Add the pretzel crumbs, and stir until just combined. Mix in the sour cream, sweet potato, and cranberries, making sure the berries are evenly distributed. Season with salt and chill for 15 minutes.

Place ⅓ cup of the quinoa mixture in your hands and form a cake about 2 inches in diameter. Place the cake on a parchment-lined baking sheet. Repeat to make the remaining cakes.

Bake the cakes until they're golden brown and a toothpick inserted in the center comes out clean, 20 to 25 minutes. Serve them warm or at room temperature.

To store, refrigerate or freeze the cakes in an airtight container. They will last 5 days in the refrigerator and 2 months in the freezer.

Per serving (1 cake): Calories 149; Fat 4g; Saturated Fat 2g; Sodium 57mg; Protein 5g; Fiber 3g

Super-Powered Granola Bars

KIDS, SINGLETONS, VEGETARIANS, MAKE AHEAD

MAKES 12 BARS / PREP: 15 MINUTES / COOK: 18 TO 20 MINUTES / TOTAL: 1 HOUR, 50 MINUTES

The granola bar has become ubiquitous in America's food culture, sold everywhere under countless brand names and in countless flavors. With your own homemade granola, you can create fresher, better-for-you bars, tailor-made to your taste. For a sweeter bar, add ¼ cup packed light brown sugar.

4 tablespoons plus 1 teaspoon butter, divided
½ cup honey
⅓ cup almond butter
½ teaspoon vanilla extract
Salt
3½ cups Toasty Quinoa Granola (page 52)

Preheat the oven to 350°F.

Line a 9-by-9-inch baking dish with parchment paper.

In a small saucepan over medium heat, melt 4 tablespoons of butter. Add the honey and almond butter, and cook, stirring occasionally, until the ingredients are melted and fully combined. Stir in the vanilla, and season with salt.

In a large mixing bowl, pour the almond butter mixture over the granola and stir to combine well. Allow the mixture to cool slightly; then transfer it to the baking dish, spreading it as evenly as you can. Grease your hands with the remaining 1 teaspoon of butter, and press down on the granola, smoothing the surface and packing it tightly to create a solid square.

Bake until the edges are slightly browned, 18 to 20 minutes. Refrigerate the baked granola until it's completely chilled, about 1½ hours. Cut the square into 6 even strips 1½ inches wide. Cut the strips in half crosswise to make a total of 12 4½-inch-long bars.

To store, wrap the bars individually in waxed paper or plastic wrap and refrigerate or freeze in an airtight container. The bars will keep 2 weeks in the refrigerator and 2 months in the freezer.

Per serving (1 bar): Calories 316; Fat 18g; Saturated Fat 7g; Sodium 66mg; Protein 5g; Fiber 3g

Movie-Night Rainbow Quinoa "Popcorn"

KIDS, LARGE GROUPS, SINGLETONS, VEGANS, ONE POT, 30-MINUTE

MAKES 2 CUPS / COOK: 25 MINUTES

In South America, popping is a common way of preparing quinoa. Hardly bigger than unpopped quinoa, this favorite snack is also eaten as breakfast cereal and in snack bars prepared by street vendors. It's incredibly easy to pop up a batch of golden, toasty, light quinoa.

6 teaspoons canola oil (optional), divided
1½ cups dry rainbow quinoa, rinsed and thoroughly dried, divided
Salt (optional)

In a deep, heavy sauté pan or saucepan over medium-high heat, heat 1 teaspoon of canola oil until it shimmers but doesn't smoke. You can also pop the quinoa in a dry pan if you prefer a slightly lighter result.

Add ¼ cup of quinoa, just enough to cover the bottom of the pan in a single layer. As soon as the quinoa starts to pop (within a few seconds), lift the pan off the burner. Shake the pan to keep the quinoa from burning while it pops. The popping grains will jump a little, but not explosively, like popcorn. Return the pan to the burner for a few seconds if the popping slows down or stops before most of the grains have popped.

Remove the pan from the heat as soon as the popped grains are golden brown. Quickly transfer the popped quinoa and the yummy unpopped grains to a large serving bowl.

Repeat the popping process for the rest of the quinoa. If you wish, season with salt before serving.

Per serving (1 cup): Calories 566; Fat 21g; Saturated Fat 2g; Sodium 6mg; Protein 17g; Fiber 8g

Quinoa Chips with Hot Pepper Dip

KIDS, LARGE GROUPS, VEGANS, MAKE AHEAD

SERVES 4 / PREP: 20 MINUTES / COOK: 11 TO 18 MINUTES

Known as *aji criollo*, the dip for these chips is a traditional Ecuadorian condiment found on every home and restaurant table there. You can make it with a variety of hot peppers, such as jalapeño (mild), serrano (medium), Thai (hot), or habanero (killer), depending on your taste for heat. The quinoa chips go great with just about any other dip, as well, from salsa or guacamole to hummus or mild Cilantro Dip (page 120).

For the dip
4 hot peppers
1½ cups loosely packed chopped fresh cilantro (stems and leaves)
3 garlic cloves
1 tablespoon freshly squeezed lime juice
½ teaspoon ground cumin
½ cup water
3 tablespoons minced white onion
Salt

For the chips
2 teaspoons extra-virgin olive oil or cooking spray
1 cup Toasted Quinoa (page 36)
¼ teaspoon salt, plus more for seasoning
¾ cup water, divided

To make the dip In a blender or food processor, blend the peppers, cilantro, garlic, lime juice, cumin, and water until smooth. Stir in the onion, and season with salt.

If you do have leftovers, refrigerate the dip in an airtight container. It will keep for 2 or 3 days.

To make the chips Preheat the oven to 450°F.

Grease a baking sheet with the olive oil.

In a blender, blend the Toasted Quinoa, salt, and ¼ cup of water, gradually adding more water, until a very thick batter forms. You'll need about ¾ cup of water in all.

Scrape the batter onto the baking sheet. Spread it out evenly, to a ¼-inch thickness. If you like, sprinkle more salt over the top.

Bake until the edges are browned, about 6 to 8 minutes.

Remove the pan from the oven, and let it cool until it's safe to handle. Using a knife or pizza cutter, cut the dough into the chip shape you prefer—square, rectangle, or triangle—about 1½ inches on its longest side. Return the chips to the oven until they're browned, 5 to 10 minutes.

Serve the chips warm or cooled, along with the dip.

Store the cooled chips in an airtight container at room temperature. They will keep for 4 or 5 days.

Per serving: Calories 195; Fat 5g; Saturated Fat 1g; Sodium 198mg; Protein 7g; Fiber 4g

6

Salads

Quinoa with Asparagus & Shaved Parmesan

SINGLETONS, VEGETARIANS, 30-MINUTE, ONE POT

SERVES 4 / PREP: 5 MINUTES

A play on Italian flavors, this recipe is as simple as the cooking of Italy. It's great as a side dish or, if you double the serving size, as a light meal for two. For a more formal presentation, toss only half the asparagus into the salad and arrange the remaining tips on top of each serving, along with the cheese.

4 cups cooked quinoa
2 cups steamed fresh asparagus tips
2 teaspoons minced fresh oregano
Salt
Freshly ground black pepper
2 ounces Parmesan cheese, shaved into thin strips
1 cup Balsamic Vinaigrette (page 43)

In a large mixing bowl, toss together the quinoa, asparagus, and oregano. Season with salt and pepper.

Portion the salad onto 4 plates, and top each with the Parmesan shavings. Serve warm or at room temperature with the Balsamic Vinaigrette on the side.

To store, refrigerate in an airtight container. The salad will keep for 2 days. Do not freeze.

Tip To shave the Parmesan, use a handheld triangular cheese slicer. If you don't have one, a vegetable peeler works, too.

Per serving: Calories 566; Fat 40g; Saturated Fat 8g; Sodium 181mg; Protein 15g; Fiber 6g

Quinoa with Baby Spinach & Blue Cheese

KIDS, SINGLETONS, VEGETARIANS, ONE POT, 30-MINUTE

SERVES 4 / PREP: 5 MINUTES

Spinach and blue cheese, a classic combination, gets a makeover here from the crisp red pepper and chewy quinoa. Make it when corn is in season for the sweetest, freshest results. You can modify the salad for meat lovers by topping it with sliced grilled sirloin or crumbled bacon.

4½ cups cooked quinoa

1 large red bell pepper, seeded and diced

1 cup fresh steamed corn, cut off the cob, or cooked frozen corn

¾ cup crumbled blue cheese

¾ cup Lemon-Thyme Vinaigrette (page 44), plus more if desired

Salt

Freshly ground black pepper

1 pound baby spinach

4 lemon wedges

In a large mixing bowl, toss together the quinoa, red pepper, corn, blue cheese, and Lemon-Thyme Vinaigrette. Season with salt and pepper, and gently toss in the spinach. Serve at room temperature, garnished with a lemon wedge.

To store, refrigerate the quinoa mixture and spinach in separate airtight containers. Each will keep for 2 days.

Per serving: Calories 699; Fat 38g; Saturated Fat 8g; Sodium 520mg; Protein 23g; Fiber 9g

Garden Quinoa
with Summer Squash & Tomatoes

LARGE GROUPS, VEGANS, ONE POT, 30-MINUTE

SERVES 4 / PREP: 5 MINUTES

Sometime midsummer, the zucchini and yellow squash in your garden get out of control. You've got much, much more than you know what to do with, and you start trying to give them away to your friends, coworkers, and your dentist's receptionist. But tomatoes are coming into season, and in this quinoa salad, they help make summer squash exciting again.

4 cups cooked quinoa

1 medium zucchini, cut into ½-inch cubes

1 medium yellow summer squash, cut into ½-inch cubes

2 large tomatoes, seeded and diced

2 tablespoons julienned fresh basil

¾ cup Tarragon-Dijon Vinaigrette (page 45), plus more if desired

Salt

Freshly ground black pepper

In a large bowl, toss together the quinoa, zucchini, squash, tomatoes, basil, and Tarragon-Dijon Vinaigrette, and season with salt and pepper. Serve at room temperature.

To store, refrigerate in an airtight container. The salad will keep for 2 days, but the tomatoes may turn mealy. Do not freeze.

Per serving: Calories 506; Fat 33g; Saturated Fat 5g; Sodium 261mg; Protein 10g; Fiber 6g

Rainbow Quinoa Tricolore Salad

SINGLETONS, VEGANS, ONE POT, 30-MINUTE

SERVES 4 / PREP: 5 MINUTES

In Italian, *tricolore* means "three colors," and *tricolore* salad is a traditional combination of green arugula, white endive, and red radicchio. This salad is truly a riot of colors, with the rainbow quinoa adding a fourth: contrasting black. In keeping with the Italian theme, add some shaved Parm if you want.

4 cups cooked rainbow quinoa
1 (5-ounce) bag arugula
1 cup chopped Belgian endive
1 cup shredded radicchio
2 tablespoons chopped fresh basil
Salt
Freshly ground black pepper
1 cup Balsamic Vinaigrette (page 43)

In a large bowl, toss together the quinoa, arugula, endive, radicchio, and basil. Season with salt and pepper. Serve at room temperature with the Balsamic Vinaigrette on the side.

To store, refrigerate the salad and dressing in separate airtight containers. The salad will keep for 1 day.

Per serving: Calories 570; Fat 40g; Saturated Fat 4g; Sodium 357mg; Protein 10g; Fiber 5g

Quinoa—Cabbage Slaw

LARGE GROUPS, SINGLETONS, VEGANS, MAKE AHEAD, ONE POT, 30-MINUTE

SERVES 4 / PREP: 5 MINUTES

Used extensively in the cuisines of China, Japan, and Korea, napa cabbage isn't named for the California wine country region. It's known also as Chinese cabbage, and you might recognize its oblong shape and pale, crinkly leaves. Its flavor is milder than that of the cabbage typically used in American cooking, allowing quinoa's nutty charm to shine through in this unusual slaw.

3 cups cooked quinoa

3 cups shredded napa cabbage

2 carrots, cut into matchsticks

1 large red bell pepper, seeded and cut into thin strips

½ cup chopped scallions

¾ cup Cilantro-Lime Dressing (page 47), plus more if desired

Salt

Freshly ground black pepper

In a large bowl, toss together the quinoa, cabbage, carrots, bell pepper, scallions, and Cilantro-Lime Dressing. Season with salt and pepper, and serve chilled or at room temperature.

To store, refrigerate in an airtight container. The salad will keep for 4 days. Do not freeze.

Per serving: Calories 432; Fat 28g; Saturated Fat 1g; Sodium 938mg; Protein 9g; Fiber 6g

Super-Quinoa
with Sweet Potatoes

KIDS, SINGLETONS, VEGETARIANS, MAKE AHEAD, 30-MINUTE

SERVES 4 / PREP: 5 MINUTES / COOK: 15 TO 20 MINUTES

This dish gives quite the bang for your superfood buck, combining quinoa with sweet potato. A medium baked sweet potato contains four times as much vitamin A as you need in a day, a third of your vitamin C, and 4 grams of dietary fiber. If you like, add sliced almonds or diced apples—two more members of the superfood club.

2 large sweet potatoes, peeled and diced
1 tablespoon extra-virgin olive oil
1 teaspoon salt, plus more for seasoning
4 cups cooked quinoa
1 tablespoon chopped fresh chives
1 teaspoon ground cumin
Freshly ground black pepper
¾ cup Harissa-Cinnamon Dressing
   (page 48), plus more if desired

Preheat the oven to 450°F.

Line a baking sheet with parchment.

In a large bowl, toss the sweet potatoes with the olive oil and salt. Spread them out on the baking sheet in a single layer. Roast, stirring occasionally, until the potatoes start to brown, 15 to 20 minutes. The potatoes should be tender but not soft. Remove them from the oven, and allow them to cool until they're safe to handle.

In a large bowl, toss together the roasted sweet potatoes, quinoa, chives, and cumin. Season with salt and pepper. Serve hot, warm, or at room temperature with the Harissa-Cinnamon Dressing.

To store, refrigerate or freeze in an airtight container. The salad will keep 3 days in the refrigerator or 2 months in the freezer.

Per serving: Calories 667; Fat 38g; Saturated Fat 6g; Sodium 827mg; Protein 10g; Fiber 9g

Black Quinoa
with Corn Salsa & Pepitas

SERVES 4 / PREP: 5 MINUTES

This stunning yet cheery salad has "potluck" written all over it. It's full of Mexican flavors, including pepitas, or toasted pumpkin seeds, which appear in street snacks and thick sauces called *mole,* including *mole poblano.* To appeal to meat lovers, you can add *carne asada* (page 242).

1 cup fresh corn, cut off the cob and steamed, or steamed frozen corn
¾ cup chopped tomatoes
1 small onion, chopped
¼ cup finely chopped red bell pepper
¼ cup extra-virgin olive oil
2 tablespoons minced fresh cilantro
2 tablespoons freshly squeezed lime juice
1 jalapeño pepper, seeded and minced
¼ teaspoon ground ancho or chipotle chile
4 cups cooked black quinoa
½ cup toasted, unsalted pepitas
Salt
Freshly ground black pepper

In a large bowl, toss together the corn, tomatoes, onion, bell pepper, olive oil, cilantro, lime juice, jalapeño, ancho, quinoa, and pepitas. Season with salt and pepper, and serve at room temperature.

To store, refrigerate in an airtight container. The salad will keep for 3 days, though the tomatoes might get mealy. Do not freeze.

Tip To remove the kernels from a fresh ear of corn, hold the ear vertically on a cutting board, wide-end down. Grasping it firmly at the top, position a sharp knife just under your fingers. Cutting at about ⅔ the depth of the kernels, gently saw down the length of the ear to remove a strip of kernels. Turn the cob a little, and repeat the cutting to remove the next strip. Repeat until you have cut all the kernels off the cob. One ear of corn yields about ½ cup of kernels.

Per serving: Calories 479; Fat 25g; Saturated Fat 4g; Sodium 24mg; Protein 15g; Fiber 7g

Holiday Quinoa
with Oranges & Kale

KIDS, LARGE GROUPS, VEGANS, MAKE AHEAD, ONE POT, 30-MINUTE

SERVES 4 / PREP: 5 MINUTES

The fruity brightness of this salad appeals to kids—and makes it perfect for a party. A gorgeous addition to your Thanksgiving table, it cheers up any meal from fall through winter. The pomegranate seeds add a nice crunch, but make sure to use navel oranges, which are seedless.

1 cup tightly packed deribbed, chopped kale
¾ cup Citrus Dressing (page 46), plus more if desired
4½ cups cooked quinoa
2 navel oranges, segmented and halved
Seeds of 2 pomegranates
1 cup frozen cranberries, thawed
Salt
Freshly ground black pepper

In a large mixing bowl, massage the kale with the Citrus Dressing until it softens. Toss the softened kale with the quinoa, oranges, pomegranate seeds, and cranberries. Season with salt and pepper, and serve chilled or at room temperature.

To store, refrigerate in an airtight container. The salad will keep for 3 days. Do not freeze.

Per serving: Calories 590; Fat 23g; Saturated Fat 1g; Sodium 477mg; Protein 12g; Fiber 9g

Rainbow Quinoa
with Red, Black & Green Beans

LARGE GROUPS, VEGANS, MAKE AHEAD, 30-MINUTE

SERVES 4 / PREP: 10 MINUTES

Tricolor quinoa plus tricolor beans equals a celebration in your mouth, complete with confetti. In this twist on the standard three-bean salad, a spicy chipotle vinaigrette keeps the party going. Be sure not to cook the fresh color out of the green beans; you don't want any soggy, drab creeps killing the mood.

For the chipotle vinaigrette

⅓ cup canola oil

3 tablespoons freshly squeezed lime juice

1 can chipotle pepper in adobo, minced

4 teaspoons adobo

3 garlic cloves, crushed

1 tablespoon agave nectar

¼ teaspoon ground cumin

Salt

For the salad

4½ cups cooked rainbow quinoa

1 (15-ounce) can low-sodium red beans, such as kidney beans or small red beans, drained and rinsed

1 (15-ounce) can low-sodium black beans, drained and rinsed

½ pound fresh green beans, lightly steamed and cut into 1-inch pieces

Salt

Freshly ground black pepper

To make the chipotle vinaigrette In a small bowl, whisk together the canola oil, lime juice, chipotle, adobo, garlic, agave nectar, and cumin. Season with salt and set aside.

To make the salad In a large bowl, toss together the quinoa and red, black, and green beans. Add the vinaigrette, and toss to coat. Season with salt and pepper. Serve at room temperature.

To store, refrigerate or freeze in an airtight container. The salad will keep for 5 days in the refrigerator or 1 month in the freezer.

Tip Found in the Latin foods section of most supermarkets, canned chipotles in adobo are smoked jalapeño peppers in a thick, smoky sauce of tomatoes, garlic, vinegar, and spices. The chipotle itself is usually quite hot, while the adobo is tangy and sometimes a little sweet.

Per serving: Calories 638; Fat 24g; Saturated Fat 2g; Sodium 837mg; Protein 23g; Fiber 20g

Moroccan-Style Quinoa
with Chickpeas & Roasted Carrots

SINGLETONS, VEGETARIANS, MAKE AHEAD

SERVES 4 / PREP: 15 MINUTES / COOK: 25 MINUTES

In this North African-inspired dish, quinoa stands in for couscous, a staple that's considered the region's signature dish. When steamed as it should be, couscous—tiny beads of semolina (durum wheat)—is light and fluffy. Its similarity to quinoa ends there: Unlike couscous, quinoa is gluten-free.

3 medium carrots, peeled and cut into ¼-inch-thick rounds

1 tablespoon extra-virgin olive oil

1 teaspoon salt, plus more for seasoning

4½ cups cooked quinoa

1 (15-ounce) can low-sodium chickpeas, drained and rinsed

½ cup raisins, steeped in hot water for 10 minutes and drained

½ cup chopped fresh flat-leaf parsley

¾ cup Harissa-Cinnamon Dressing (page 48), plus more if desired

Freshly ground black pepper

Preheat the oven to 450°F.

Line a baking sheet with parchment.

In a large bowl, toss the carrot slices with the olive oil and salt. Spread them out on the baking sheet in a single layer. Roast, stirring and flipping occasionally, until the carrots start to brown, 20 to 25 minutes. The carrots should be tender but not soft. Remove them from the oven, and allow them to cool until they're safe to handle.

In a large bowl, toss together the roasted carrots, quinoa, chickpeas, raisins, parsley, and Harissa-Cinnamon Dressing. Season with salt and pepper. Serve hot, warm, or at room temperature.

To store, refrigerate or freeze in an airtight container. The salad will keep for 3 days in the refrigerator or 2 months in the freezer.

Per serving: Calories 753; Fat 39g; Saturated Fat 6g; Sodium 932mg; Protein 18g; Fiber 11g

Red Quinoa
with Radishes & Apple

SINGLETONS, VEGANS, MAKE AHEAD, ONE POT, 30-MINUTE

SERVES 4 / PREP: 5 MINUTES

Light as can be, this salad shines alongside a cheese platter. You can turn it into a Waldorf-like salad by adding some walnuts. If you're still hungry, bring in some cubed boneless, skinless chicken breast.

4 cups cooked red quinoa

3 Granny Smith apples, chopped

½ cup thinly sliced radishes

½ cup dried cherries, steeped in hot water for 10 minutes and drained

¼ cup finely chopped yellow bell pepper

¾ cup Tarragon-Dijon Vinaigrette (page 45), plus more if desired

Salt

Freshly ground black pepper

¼ cup mixed bean sprouts

4 lime wedges

In a large bowl, toss together the quinoa, apples, radishes, cherries, yellow pepper, and Tarragon-Dijon Vinaigrette. Season with salt and pepper.

Portion the salad among 4 plates, top each with the sprouts, and garnish each dish with a slice of lime. Serve at room temperature.

To store, leave the sprouts off and refrigerate in an airtight container. The salad will keep for 2 days. Do not freeze.

Per serving: Calories 497; Fat 18g; Saturated fat 2g; Sodium 136mg; Protein 10g; Fiber 12g

Quinoa with Avocado & Orange Peppers

SINGLETONS, VEGANS, ONE POT, 30-MINUTE

SERVES 4 / PREP: 5 MINUTES

This appealing salad splendidly melds the textures of creamy avocado, snappy bell pepper, and fluffy quinoa. It's delightful at brunch or for a lunch with friends, or just on its own as an afternoon snack. Add a little something extra by making the vinaigrette with extra-virgin avocado oil, an emerald-green elixir with an avocado-grass-butter flavor.

4 cups cooked quinoa
1 cup chopped orange bell pepper
¼ cup chopped fresh flat-leaf parsley
¾ cup Tarragon-Dijon Vinaigrette
   (page 45), plus more if desired
Salt
Freshly ground black pepper
2 ripe avocados, chopped
2 cups microgreens

In a large bowl, toss together the quinoa, bell pepper, parsley, and Tarragon-Dijon Vinaigrette. Season with salt and pepper. Gently toss in the avocados.

Portion the salad among 4 plates, and top each with ½ cup of microgreens. Serve at room temperature.

This recipe does not refrigerate or freeze well.

Tip **Microgreens are tiny vegetable seedlings less than 14 days old. Used mostly as a garnish, microgreens include shoots of vegetables such as spinach, peas, beets, and red cabbage.**

Per serving: Calories 479; Fat 25g; Saturated Fat 4g; Sodium 24mg; Protein 15g; Fiber 7g

Mediterranean Quinoa
with Olives & Feta

LARGE GROUPS, SINGLETONS, VEGETARIANS, MAKE AHEAD, ONE POT, 30-MINUTE

SERVES 4 / PREP: 5 MINUTES

With one foot in Greece, this salad incorporates many of the ingredients for which Greek cuisine is famous. Briny feta, pungent oregano, and piquant Kalamata olives are signatures of that country's everyday cooking. If you can, use Greek olive oil.

4 cups cooked quinoa
½ cup pitted, quartered Kalamata olives
½ cup chopped fresh parsley
⅓ cup crumbled feta
¼ cup freshly squeezed lemon juice
¼ cup extra-virgin olive oil
1 teaspoon minced fresh oregano
Salt
Freshly ground black pepper

In a large bowl, toss together the quinoa, olives, parsley, feta, lemon juice, olive oil, and oregano. Season with salt and pepper, and serve at room temperature.

To store, refrigerate or freeze in an airtight container. The salad will keep for 3 days in the refrigerator or 1 month in the freezer.

Tip In 2005, the European Union's highest court ruled that feta may only be produced in certain regions of Greece, and that no other EU nations can use the name. Nonetheless, French and Bulgarian "feta" is widely sold in American supermarkets.

Quinoa with Apricots & Pistachios

KIDS, LARGE GROUPS, SINGLETONS, VEGETARIANS, MAKE AHEAD, 30-MINUTE

SERVES 4 / PREP: 5 MINUTES / COOK: 6 TO 8 MINUTES

Pistachios and dried apricots are typical in Turkish cooking, which has its origins in the Ottoman Empire. This salad takes its cues from that melting-pot region, the cuisine of which fuses Balkan, Central Asian, Middle Eastern, and other influences. Serve this salad alongside lamb.

1 tablespoon unsalted butter
1 medium white onion, chopped
¼ teaspoon ground cumin
⅛ teaspoon ground allspice
4 cups cooked quinoa
½ cup chopped dried apricots
½ cup chopped pistachios
¾ cup Harissa-Cinnamon Dressing
    (page 48), plus more if desired
Salt
Freshly ground black pepper

In a large sauté pan over medium-high heat, melt the butter. Add the onion, cumin, and allspice and sauté until the onion browns at the edges, 6 to 8 minutes. Remove from the heat and allow to cool.

In a large bowl, toss together the onion, quinoa, apricots, pistachios, and Harissa-Cinnamon Dressing. Season with salt and pepper, and serve at room temperature.

To store, refrigerate or freeze the salad in an airtight container. The salad will keep for 4 days in the refrigerator and 2 months in the freezer.

Tip **If you want to make a more savory salad, add some grilled *merguez*, a North African sausage spiced with cumin and chile pepper; ½ or ¾ cup of sliced *merguez* will impart distinctive flavor and aroma.**

Per serving: Calories 637; Fat 44g; Saturated Fat 8g; Sodium 323mg; Protein 13g; Fiber 7g

Quinoa Macaroni Picnic Salad

KIDS, LARGE GROUPS, MAKE AHEAD, 30-MINUTE

SERVES 8 / PREP: 5 MINUTES

A picnic is not complete without macaroni salad. This version is fully gluten-free and will satisfy everyone—even the ants.

For the dressing
2 cups gluten-free mayonnaise
4 tablespoons vinegar
2 tablespoons prepared yellow mustard
2 teaspoons sugar
Salt
Freshly ground black pepper

For the salad
2 celery stalks, thinly sliced
1 medium green bell pepper, diced
1 medium red bell pepper, diced
½ medium red onion, finely chopped
6 cups cooked quinoa elbow macaroni
Salt
Freshly ground black pepper

To make the dressing In a medium bowl, whisk together the mayonnaise, vinegar, mustard, and sugar until thoroughly combined. Season with salt and pepper.

To make the salad In a large bowl, toss together the celery, green and red bell peppers, onion, and macaroni along with half of the dressing until the dressing completely coats the salad and the vegetables are distributed evenly. If desired, toss in more dressing. Season with salt and pepper, and serve cool or at room temperature.

To store, refrigerate in an airtight container. The salad will keep for 3 days. Do not freeze.

Tip Contrary to popular belief, mayonnaise is not prone to spoil in the heat and make you sick. Store-bought mayo is highly acidic and actually slows the growth of bacteria in food. When your mayo-dosed food goes bad, it's usually the fault of other ingredients in the dish. To be on the safe side, keep your macaroni salad in a cooler if you're headed somewhere hot and sunny.

Per serving: Calories 416; Fat 21g; Saturated Fat 3g; Sodium 446mg; Protein 6g; Fiber 2g

Bistro Quinoa
with Beets & Goat Cheese

VEGETARIANS

SERVES 4 / PREP: 40 MINUTES / COOK: 25 TO 50 MINUTES

Replacing greens with quinoa turns a culinary classic into a heartier dish with a completely different personality. For the deepest, sweetest flavor, the beets are roasted rather than boiled or steamed. If you like, you can swap the almonds for walnuts.

For the dressing
1 cup mayonnaise
2 tablespoons white wine vinegar or champagne vinegar
1 tablespoon half-and-half
1 tablespoon agave nectar
¾ teaspoon dry mustard
¼ teaspoon ground sage
Salt

For the salad
3 medium beets, tops and roots removed
1 tablespoon extra-virgin olive oil
4 cups cooked quinoa
½ cup chopped toasted almonds
¼ cup currants
Salt
Freshly ground black pepper
8-ounce log fresh goat cheese
1 bunch fresh basil (about 64 leaves)

To make the dressing In a large bowl, whisk together the mayonnaise, vinegar, half-and-half, agave, mustard, and sage. Season with salt and set aside.

⇒⟶

To make the salad Preheat the oven to 400°F.

On a baking sheet, lay out a sheet of foil large enough to wrap the beets.

Place the beets on the foil, and rub them with the olive oil until completely coated. Fold the foil into a packet around the beets, and crimp it closed. Roast the beets until they are tender. Depending on their size, beets can take up to an hour to roast.

When they're done, remove the beets from the oven and carefully open the hot foil packet. Allow the beets to cool until they're safe to handle. Rub each beet with your fingers to slip off its jacket. Set aside.

In a large bowl, toss together the quinoa, almonds, and currants. Season with salt and pepper.

Slice the beets in half from top to bottom, and cut each half into ¼-inch-thick crescents.

Cut the goat cheese log into ¼-inch-thick rounds, and cut each round in half.

Portion the quinoa mixture between 4 plates. Arrange the beets on top, then the goat cheese. Scatter the basil evenly across the plates. Serve with the dressing on the side.

This recipe does not stand up well to refrigeration or freezing.

Tip If you find it easier, you can remove the beets' jackets with a vegetable peeler before roasting.

Per serving: Calories 871; Fat 54g; Saturated Fat 19g; Sodium 743mg; Protein 31g; Fiber 8g

Black Quinoa
with Red Lentils & Almonds

SINGLETONS, VEGANS, MAKE AHEAD, 30-MINUTE

SERVES 4 / PREP: 5 MINUTES / COOK: 11 TO 23 MINUTES

Split red lentils, actually more orange in color, make for a dramatic contrast to the black quinoa in this dish. Easily found in the dried bean or bulk section of your supermarket, lentils of all colors are excellent in soups and stews, but in this recipe, a short cooking time gives them the perfect texture for a quinoa salad. Before cooking the lentils, carefully sort through them for tiny pieces of stone or other bits of debris.

1 cup dry red lentils, picked over and rinsed
1 teaspoon extra-virgin olive oil
3 celery stalks, cut into ¼-inch crescents
½ cup chopped onion
4 cups cooked black quinoa
1 cup sliced almonds
¾ cup Lemon-Thyme Vinaigrette (page 44), plus more if desired
Salt
Freshly ground black pepper
8 leaves Boston or butter lettuce

In a medium saucepan over high heat, bring the lentils and enough water to cover them by 1 inch to a boil. Do not salt the water. Reduce the heat to low and simmer the lentils, stirring occasionally, until they're tender but not mushy, 5 to 15 minutes.

Drain the lentils into a fine-mesh sieve, and rinse them under cold water. Shake to remove any excess water. Pour the lentils into a large bowl and set aside.

In a large sauté pan over medium-high heat, heat the olive oil. Add the celery and onion, and sauté until the onion browns at the edges, 6 to 8 minutes. Remove from the heat and allow to cool.

In the large bowl, gently toss the lentils with the onion, celery, quinoa, almonds, and Lemon-Thyme Vinaigrette. Season with salt and pepper. Serve at room temperature on a bed of lettuce.

To store, leave out the lettuce and refrigerate or freeze in an airtight container. The salad will keep for 5 days in the refrigerator or 3 months in the freezer.

Per serving: Calories 799; Fat 44g; Saturated Fat 5g; Sodium 240mg; Protein 26g; Fiber 22g

Red Quinoa
with Spicy Grilled Calamari

KIDS, SINGLETONS, 30-MINUTE

SERVES 4 / PREP: 15 MINUTES / COOK: 8 TO 11 MINUTES

You might happily munch on fried calamari, but do you realize you're eating squid? So you *do* like squid after all! Here, grilled (you can broil if preferred) squid marinated in lemon and garlic may surprise you with its tender sweetness. If you don't have a grill, use a grill pan on your stove instead.

¾ pound fresh, cleaned squid (tubes and tentacles)

2 tablespoons minced flat-leaf parsley

2 teaspoons freshly squeezed lemon juice

3 garlic cloves, minced

¼ teaspoon crushed red chili flakes (optional)

¼ teaspoon salt, plus more for seasoning

¼ teaspoon freshly ground black pepper, plus more for seasoning

1 tablespoon plus 1 teaspoon extra-virgin olive oil, divided

1 small white onion, chopped

Cooking spray

4 cups cooked red quinoa

¾ cup Lemon-Thyme Vinaigrette (page 44), plus more if desired

Preheat the grill to its highest heat setting.

Lay a sheet of foil on your grill grate; perforate the foil with small holes every 4 inches.

Rinse the squid and pat it dry. Cut the tubes into ⅓-inch rings, and cut any large tentacles in half.

In a large bowl, toss the calamari with the parsley, lemon juice, garlic, chili flakes (if using), salt, pepper, and 1 tablespoon of olive oil. Coat the calamari thoroughly. Set aside to marinate.

Heat the remaining 1 teaspoon of olive oil in a large sauté pan over medium-high heat. Add the onion and sauté until it browns at the edges, 6 to 8 minutes. Remove from the heat and allow to cool.

Spray the foil on your grill with non-stick spray. Spread out the squid in a single layer on the foil, and discard any excess marinade. Grill, turning every 30 seconds or so, until the calamari just turns opaque, 2 to 3 minutes in total. If you want a char on your calamari, cook for a few minutes more, but if it starts to turn rubbery, immediately remove it from the heat.

In a large bowl, toss together the onion, quinoa, and Lemon-Thyme Vinaigrette. Season with salt and pepper. Portion the mixture among 4 plates and top with the calamari. Serve warm or at room temperature.

To store, refrigerate the quinoa and calamari separately in airtight containers. The calamari will keep for 1 day, and the quinoa will keep for 4 days. Do not freeze the calamari; the quinoa will keep for 2 months in the freezer.

Per serving: Calories 607; Fat 36g; Saturated Fat 4g; Sodium 413mg; Protein 22g; Fiber 5g

Coconut Quinoa
with Shrimp & Snow Peas

KIDS, SINGLETONS, 30-MINUTE

SERVES 4 / PREP: 15 MINUTES / COOK: 3 MINUTES

Shrimp, snow peas, and rice are frequent ingredients in Asian cooking. With the addition of peanuts, this salad narrows its flavor profile to that of Thailand. If you or a fellow diner have a peanut allergy, you can replace them with crushed cashews; if seafood's your nemesis, switch the shrimp out for cubed boneless, skinless chicken breast.

¾ pound fresh medium shrimp, shelled and deveined

1 tablespoon extra-virgin olive oil

2 garlic cloves, sliced very thin

½ teaspoon salt, plus more for seasoning

¼ teaspoon freshly ground black pepper, plus more for seasoning

4 cups cooked quinoa

12 ounces fresh snow peas, steamed

1 cup toasted coconut flakes or shreds

¾ cup Cilantro-Lime Dressing (page 47), plus more if desired

8 leaves Boston or butter lettuce

2 tablespoons crushed peanuts

Tip The key to good results with shrimp is to cook it quickly. When the shrimp curls into a C shape, it's done; if it curls into an O shape, it's overdone and rubbery.

Rinse the shrimp and pat them dry.

In a large sauté pan over medium heat, heat the olive oil. Add the shrimp, garlic, salt, and pepper and sauté until the shrimp just turns pink and opaque, about 1½ minutes. Using tongs, flip the shrimp halfway through the cooking time. Do not overcook, or the shrimp will be tough. When done, immediately remove the shrimp from the heat and transfer to a bowl to cool.

In a large bowl, toss together the quinoa, snow peas, coconut, and Cilantro-Lime Dressing. Season with salt and pepper.

Portion the quinoa among four lettuce-lined plates. Top each plate with the shrimp. Garnish each plate with a sprinkle of peanuts, and serve warm or at room temperature.

To store, refrigerate the quinoa and shrimp separately in airtight containers. The shrimp will keep for 1 day, and the quinoa will keep for 4 days. Do not freeze the shrimp; the quinoa will keep for 2 months in the freezer.

Per serving: Calories 759; Fat 43g; Saturated Fat 11g; Sodium 1,052mg; Protein 35g; Fiber 11g

Asian-Flavor Quinoa
with Chicken, Cashews & Edamame

KIDS, MEAT LOVERS, SINGLETONS, MAKE AHEAD, 30-MINUTE

SERVES 4 / PREP: 5 MINUTES / COOK: 7 TO 9 MINUTES

Combining the cashew stir-fries of Southeast Asia and the edamame snacks of Japan, this salad adds quinoa's nutty chewiness to the mix. A light lager—especially one from Asia—matches well with the dish. You'll welcome that lager if you include the Thai chile!

¾ pound boneless, skinless chicken breasts

½ teaspoon salt, plus more for seasoning

¼ teaspoon freshly ground black pepper, plus more for seasoning

1 tablespoon canola oil

2 garlic cloves, sliced very thin

1 teaspoon crushed Thai chili flakes (optional)

4 cups cooked quinoa

1 cup steamed, shelled edamame beans

1 cup roasted cashews

½ cup plus 1 tablespoon chopped scallion, divided

¾ cup Sesame-Ginger Dressing (page 49), plus more if desired

Tip The slices of chicken breast will cook very fast. After sautéing them for about 5 minutes, test for doneness by removing a strip from the pan, cutting it in two, and seeing if it's pink inside. If so, return it to the pan and sauté another minute or two before testing another strip.

Wash the chicken breasts, and pat them dry. Cut them on the bias into ½-inch-thick strips. Sprinkle with the salt and pepper.

In a large sauté pan over medium-high heat, heat the canola oil. Add the garlic and chili flakes (if using), and sauté until the garlic just starts to sizzle, about 30 seconds. Add the chicken strips to the pan and cook, flipping once, until they are cooked through, 6 to 8 minutes.

In a large bowl, toss together the quinoa, edamame, cashews, and ½ cup of scallions. Season with salt and pepper. Portion the quinoa among 4 plates, and top each with the chicken. Sprinkle the remaining 1 tablespoon of scallions over the 4 plates, and serve warm or at room temperature with the Sesame-Ginger Dressing.

To store, refrigerate the quinoa and chicken separately in airtight containers. The chicken will keep for 2 days, and the quinoa will keep for 3 days. Do not freeze the chicken; the quinoa will keep for 2 months in the freezer.

Per serving: Calories 925; Fat 62g; Saturated Fat 9g; Sodium 828mg; Protein 40g; Fiber 8g

Traditional Quinoa Tabbouleh

LARGE GROUPS, SINGLETONS, VEGANS, MAKE AHEAD, ONE POT, 30-MINUTE

SERVES 4 / PREP: 5 MINUTES

This classic Middle Eastern salad is usually dominated by bulgur and parsley, but in this recipe, quinoa takes center stage. It's also the gluten-free stand-in for tabbouleh's traditional bulgur wheat base. Chicken-thigh, lamb, or beef kebabs partner well.

4 cups cooked quinoa
2 cups chopped fresh parsley
2 large tomatoes, seeded and diced
2 medium cucumbers, peeled, seeded, and diced
1 medium red onion, finely diced
½ cup chopped fresh mint
½ cup extra-virgin olive oil
½ cup freshly squeezed lemon juice
Salt
4 lemon wedges

In a large bowl, toss together the quinoa, parsley, tomato, cucumber, onion, mint, olive oil, and lemon juice. Season with salt, and serve at room temperature with the lemon wedges for garnish.

To store, refrigerate in an airtight container. The salad will keep for 2 days. Do not freeze.

Per serving: Calories 513; Fat 29g; Saturated Fat 4g; Sodium 38mg; Protein 12g; Fiber 7g

Autumn Quinoa
with Chicken, Kale & Pumpkin

MEAT LOVERS, SINGLETONS, MAKE AHEAD

SERVES 4 / PREP: 20 MINUTES / COOK: 32 TO 46 MINUTES

Fall's confetti of falling leaves is hinted at in this recipe, in which rainbow quinoa is studded with orange pumpkin, dark green kale, and browned chicken. The salad makes a cozy side or main in the cold, dark months of fall and winter. For an even heartier dish, use lamb instead of chicken.

2 tablespoons plus 1 teaspoon extra-virgin olive oil, divided

1 (2-pound) cheese pumpkin or butternut squash

2 teaspoons minced fresh sage

1 teaspoon salt, divided, plus more for seasoning

¾ teaspoon freshly ground black pepper, divided, plus more for seasoning

¾ pound boneless, skinless chicken thighs

1 small white onion, chopped

1 teaspoon balsamic vinegar

1 teaspoon honey

4 cups cooked rainbow quinoa

2 cups deribbed, torn, steamed kale

2 tablespoons chopped hazelnuts

¾ cup Balsamic Vinaigrette (page 43), plus more if desired

4 teaspoons chopped chives

Preheat the oven to 400°F.

Grease a rimmed baking sheet with 1 teaspoon of olive oil.

Quarter, peel, and seed the pumpkin, making sure to remove all the fibers from the interior. Cut the pumpkin into ½-inch cubes.

In a large bowl, toss the pumpkin with 1 tablespoon of olive oil, the sage, ½ teaspoon of salt, and ½ teaspoon of pepper until the pumpkin is thoroughly coated. Spread out the pumpkin in a single layer on the baking sheet. Bake until it is tender and slightly browned, 20 to 30 minutes. Set aside.

Wash the chicken thighs, pat them dry, and remove any visible fat. Cut the chicken into ½-inch cubes. Sprinkle with the remaining ½ teaspoon of salt and ¼ teaspoon of pepper.

In a large sauté pan over medium-high heat, heat the remaining 1 tablespoon of olive oil. Add the onion and sauté until it browns at the edges, 6 to 8 minutes. Add the chicken, vinegar, and honey to the pan, and stir well to combine. Sauté until the chicken is cooked through, 6 to 8 minutes.

In a large bowl, toss together the pumpkin, chicken mixture, quinoa, kale, hazelnuts, and Balsamic Vinaigrette. Season with salt and pepper. Serve warm or at room temperature, garnished with the chives.

To store, refrigerate in an airtight container. The salad will keep for 3 days. Do not freeze.

Per serving: Calories 856; Fat 47g; Saturated Fat 6g; Sodium 905mg; Protein 37g; Fiber 10g

Tropical Quinoa
with Chicken & Mango

KIDS, LARGE GROUPS, MEAT LOVERS, MAKE AHEAD

SERVES 4 / PREP: 20 MINUTES / COOK: 12 TO 16 MINUTES

Whether it's the dead of winter or the height of summer, everyone can do with a taste of the tropics. Think warm breezes, blue water, white-sand beaches, and piña coladas. Put your feet up and let your mind wander as you enjoy this sweet-and-spicy salad.

¾ pound boneless, skinless chicken breasts
1 teaspoon Caribbean jerk seasoning
1 tablespoon extra-virgin olive oil
1 small white onion, chopped
4½ cups cooked quinoa
1 (15-ounce) can low-sodium adzuki beans, drained and rinsed
2 mangoes, chopped
2 kiwifruit, chopped
¾ cup Citrus Dressing (page 46), plus more if desired
Salt
Freshly ground black pepper
8 leaves Boston or butter lettuce

Tip **Most often associated with Jamaica, jerk seasoning is a Caribbean spice blend that varies from island to island and cook to cook. Typical ingredients include ground allspice, chile peppers, cinnamon, and nutmeg; powdered thyme, garlic, and onion; and cracked black peppercorns, salt, and sugar. You can find it in the spices or international section of your supermarket.**

Wash the chicken breasts, pat them dry, and cut them into 1-inch cubes. In a large bowl, toss together the chicken and jerk seasoning.

In a large sauté pan over medium-high heat, heat the olive oil. Add the onion and sauté until it browns at the edges, 6 to 8 minutes. Add the chicken and sauté until it's cooked through, 6 to 8 minutes. Set aside to cool.

In a large bowl, toss together the chicken and onions with the quinoa, beans, mangoes, kiwi, and Citrus Dressing. Season with salt and pepper. Lay two lettuce leaves on each of 4 plates. Scoop equal amounts of the salad in mounds onto the lettuce. Serve cool or at room temperature.

To store, refrigerate in an airtight container. The salad will keep for 2 days.

Per serving: Calories 1,052; Fat 33g; Saturated Fat 7g; Sodium 356mg; Protein 55g; Fiber 21g

Herby Quinoa Linguine
with Chicken & Broccoli

MEAT LOVERS, SINGLETONS, 30-MINUTE

SERVES 4 / PREP: 10 MINUTES / COOK: 3 TO 6 MINUTES

A light yet satisfying dish, this salad is best in summer, when basil and oregano are taking over your garden. When preparing the broccoli, make sure the florets are small, so they don't overpower the delicate quality of the dish.

¾ pound boneless, skinless chicken breasts

1 teaspoon salt, divided, plus more for seasoning

½ teaspoon freshly ground black pepper, divided, plus more for seasoning

1 tablespoon extra-virgin olive oil

3 garlic cloves, thinly sliced

4 cups cooked quinoa linguine, al dente, tossed in olive oil to prevent sticking

½ cup freshly grated Parmesan cheese, plus more for garnish

1 lemon, zested

2 teaspoons chopped fresh basil

1 teaspoon chopped fresh oregano

1½ cups steamed broccoli florets

4 teaspoons chopped fresh parsley

Tip **This salad lends itself well to pre-preparation. Cook the chicken and broccoli the day before you serve the salad. On the day of, cook the linguine, prep the herbs and Parmesan, and put it all together.**

Wash the chicken breasts, pat them dry, and cut them on the bias into ¼-inch-thick strips. Sprinkle with ½ teaspoon of salt and ¼ teaspoon of pepper.

In a large sauté pan over medium-high heat, heat the olive oil. Add the garlic and sauté until it just starts to sizzle, about 30 seconds. Stir in the chicken and sauté until it's cooked through, 3 to 6 minutes. Set aside.

In a large bowl, toss together the linguine, Parmesan, lemon zest, basil, oregano, and the remaining ½ teaspoon of salt and ¼ teaspoon of pepper. Season if needed with more salt and pepper. Add the chicken and broccoli to the bowl, and toss to combine.

Serve warm or at room temperature, each plate garnished with parsley and accompanied by grated Parmesan on the side.

To store, refrigerate in an airtight container. The salad will keep for 2 days. Do not freeze.

Per serving: Calories 478; Fat 17g; Saturated Fat 5g; Sodium 802mg; Protein 39g; Fiber 5g

Quinoa Penne
with Chicken & Pesto

MEAT LOVERS, SINGLETONS

SERVES 4 / PREP: 25 MINUTES / COOK: 6 TO 8 MINUTES

The pesto used in this recipe is as true as possible to the original version from Liguria in north-west Italy. A simple combination of garlic, pine nuts, basil, salt, and Parmesan, it does stray from tradition in that it's made in a blender rather than a mortar and pestle. Of course, you can buy pesto in the supermarket, but fresh-made tastes better by leaps and bounds.

For the pesto

2 cups chopped fresh basil leaves

1⅓ cups freshly grated Parmesan cheese

⅔ cup extra-virgin olive oil, divided

½ cup pine nuts

4 garlic cloves

½ teaspoon salt, plus more for seasoning

For the salad

¾ pound boneless, skinless chicken breast

½ teaspoon salt, plus more for seasoning

¼ teaspoon freshly ground black pepper, plus more for seasoning

1 tablespoon extra-virgin olive oil

2 garlic cloves, minced

4 cups cooked quinoa penne, al dente, tossed in olive oil to prevent sticking

2 cups halved cherry tomatoes

1 cup diced fresh mozzarella

¼ cup pine nuts

To make the pesto In a blender, combine the basil, Parmesan, ¼ cup of olive oil, the pine nuts, garlic, and salt. Put the lid on the blender with the hole at the top open. Start the blender, and once the ingredients have combined, start drizzling in the remaining ⅓ cup of olive oil through the lid until the pesto is smooth and creamy. Scrape down the sides of the blender as necessary. Season the pesto with more salt if needed. You should have about 1 to 1½ cups of pesto.

To make the salad Wash the chicken breasts, pat them dry, and cut them into ¾-inch cubes. Sprinkle with the salt and pepper.

In a large sauté pan over medium-high heat, heat the olive oil. Add the garlic and sauté until it starts to sizzle, 15 to 30 seconds. Add the chicken and sauté until it's cooked through, 6 to 8 minutes. Set aside to cool.

In a large bowl, toss the penne with half of the pesto. Add the chicken, tomatoes, and mozzarella and toss to combine. If desired, toss in more pesto. Season with salt and pepper.

Portion the pasta among 4 plates and garnish with the pine nuts. Serve warm or at room temperature.

To store, refrigerate in an airtight container. The salad will keep for 2 days, though the tomatoes might get mealy. Do not freeze.

Tip You can save pesto in the fridge in an airtight container, with a scant layer of olive oil over the surface; it will keep up to a week this way. Alternatively, you can freeze it in an airtight container, or in ice cube trays for smaller portions. When the cubes freeze, transfer them to a plastic zip-top bag. In the freezer, pesto will keep about three months.

Per serving: Calories 837; Fat 70g; Saturated Fat 16g; Sodium 875mg; Protein 29g; Fiber 4g

7

Soups, Stews & Chilis

Delicate Quinoa– Mushroom Soup

SINGLETONS, VEGANS, MAKE AHEAD, ONE POT

SERVES 4 / PREP: 10 MINUTES / COOK: 21 MINUTES

Clean and refined, this soup brings quinoa to the fore. Its slightly crunchy texture and nutty flavor are accentuated by the clear yet deeply flavored broth. If you can't find chanterelles, you can substitute cremini or shiitake mushrooms.

1 tablespoon extra-virgin olive oil
2 garlic cloves, minced
1½ cups chanterelle mushroom caps
½ teaspoon salt, plus more for seasoning
1 cup dry quinoa, rinsed
1 quart Vegetable Stock (Chicken Stock substitution tip, page 41)
3 cups water
2 tablespoons minced fresh parsley
Freshly ground black pepper
2 cups baby arugula
1 small white onion, sliced thin
1 lemon, zested

In a large saucepan over medium-high heat, heat the olive oil. Add the garlic and sauté until it just starts to sizzle, about 30 seconds. Add the mushrooms and salt and sauté for 3 minutes.

Stir in the quinoa; then add the Vegetable Stock and water. Partially cover and bring the soup to a boil; then reduce the heat to medium and cook until the quinoa starts to soften, about 12 minutes. Add the parsley and cook, uncovered, 5 minutes more. Season with salt and pepper.

Ladle the hot soup into 4 bowls. Garnish with the arugula, onion, and lemon zest, and serve.

To store, leave off the garnishes and refrigerate or freeze in an airtight container or zip-top bag. The soup will keep for 5 days in the refrigerator and 3 months in the freezer.

Per serving: Calories 238; Fat 8g; Saturated Fat 1g; Sodium 1,068mg; Protein 12g; Fiber 4g

Tomato & "Rice" Soup

KIDS, SINGLETONS, MAKE AHEAD

SERVES 4 / PREP: 15 MINUTES / COOK: 1 HOUR, 10 MINUTES

About as comforting as comforting can be, tomato soup and grilled cheese is one of the culinary world's great pairings. In this take on tomato-rice soup, quinoa takes the place of rice, arguably with yummier results. Go get some gluten-free white bread, and griddle up a gooey partner in crime.

1 tablespoon extra-virgin olive oil
1 celery stalk, chopped
½ small onion, chopped
1 garlic clove, chopped
1 cup Chicken Stock (page 40) or store bought
2 (28-ounce) cans low-sodium tomato sauce
2 cups cooked quinoa
2 cups whole milk
¼ teaspoon dried basil
¼ teaspoon dried thyme
Salt
Freshly ground black pepper
Sugar, for sweetening (optional)

In a large saucepan over medium heat, heat the olive oil. Add the celery, onion, and garlic and sauté until tender, about 10 minutes. Do not brown.

Transfer the sautéed vegetables to a blender, and add the Chicken Stock. Purée until smooth. Return the mixture to the saucepan, and stir in the tomato sauce, quinoa, milk, basil, and thyme.

Turn the heat up to high, and bring the soup to a boil, stirring occasionally. When it boils, turn the heat down to low and simmer the soup, uncovered, for 1 hour, stirring every 15 minutes. If the soup is too thick, add some water; if it's too thin, turn the heat up to medium and continue cooking, stirring often, until it reaches the consistency you desire.

Season the soup with salt and pepper. If you want to replicate the tomato soup of your childhood, add sugar. Ladle the hot soup into 4 bowls and serve.

To store, refrigerate or freeze in an airtight container or zip-top bag. The soup will keep for 5 days in the refrigerator and 3 months in the freezer.

Per serving: Calories 320; Fat 10g; Saturated Fat 3g; Sodium 2,364mg; Protein 14g; Fiber 9g

Thai Chicken Soup
with Coconut Milk

LARGER GROUPS, MEAT LOVERS, ONE POT

SERVES 4 / PREP: 15 MINUTES / COOK: 30 MINUTES

You've probably tasted *tom kha gai*, Thailand's famous coconut milk-chicken soup, at your local Thai restaurant, but you've probably never made it. All those strange ingredients—galangal, kaffir lime leaves, lemongrass, fish sauce—are intimidating, not to mention the hot chiles. In fact, one of the most important elements of the recipe is plain old rice, here replaced with quinoa. As for the other components, you can make a fair imitation of *tom kha gai* with mostly familiar ingredients.

1 pound boneless skinless chicken breasts
Salt
Freshly ground black pepper
2 tablespoons vegetable oil, divided
2 tablespoons thinly sliced scallion
2 tablespoons minced fresh ginger
½ pound whole oyster mushrooms or stemmed shiitake mushrooms
2 Thai bird or serrano chiles, whole
3 cups unsweetened coconut milk
3 cups water
2 medium tomatoes, each cut into 8 wedges
¼ cup fish sauce (see ingredient tip)
¼ cup freshly squeezed lime juice
4 teaspoons fresh cilantro leaves
4 cups cooked quinoa, hot

Wash the chicken breasts, and pat them dry. Cut them into ¾-inch cubes, and season with salt and pepper.

In a large saucepan over medium heat, heat 1 tablespoon of vegetable oil. Add the chicken and sauté until it's no longer pink, about 5 minutes. Transfer it to a bowl and set aside.

Turn up the heat to medium-high, and heat the remaining 1 tablespoon of vegetable oil. Add the scallions and ginger and sauté until they are soft, about 4 minutes. Add the mushrooms and chiles and sauté until the mushrooms are fork tender, about 3 minutes.

Stir in the coconut milk, water, and tomatoes. Bring the soup almost to a boil; then turn the heat to low. Stir in the fish sauce and lime juice. Simmer the soup for 10 minutes, stirring occasionally. Return the chicken to the pot to warm through, about 5 minutes. Stir in the cilantro.

Put 1 cup of hot quinoa into each of 4 bowls, ladle the hot soup over the quinoa, and serve.

To store, refrigerate the soup and quinoa in separate airtight containers or zip-top bags. You may want to remove the chiles from the soup, as they will continue to impart spiciness as the soup sits. The soup will keep 1 day in the refrigerator. Do not freeze.

Tip The only potentially unfamiliar necessity in this recipe is fish sauce, which might sound awfully unappetizing. Without it, though, your soup just won't taste right. A Thai staple, fish sauce imparts umami—that wonderful savory flavor—to all kinds of dishes, and surprisingly, virtually no fishy flavor. You can find fish sauce in the Asian section of your supermarket, or at Asian specialty stores. If a Thai version isn't available, other Asian fish sauces are fine.

Per serving: Calories 948; Fat 62g; Saturated Fat 42g; Sodium 1,806mg; Protein 47g; Fiber 9g

Two-Season Soup
with Spinach & Butternut Squash

SINGLETONS, VEGETARIANS, MAKE AHEAD, ONE POT

SERVES 4 / PREP: 15 MINUTES / COOK: 26 TO 28 MINUTES

This soup straddles the seasons, bringing together summer's last spinach with autumn's characteristic butternut squash. It's light enough for warm nights, but substantial enough for cooler weather. Using chicken stock and adding sautéed strips of chicken breast would be a tasty addition, although the dish would no longer be vegetarian.

1 tablespoon extra-virgin olive oil
½ cup chopped white onion
1½ cups diced butternut squash
½ teaspoon salt, plus more for seasoning
1 cup dry quinoa, rinsed
1 quart Vegetable Stock (Chicken Stock substitution tip, page 41)
1 cup chopped baby spinach
1 tablespoon chopped fresh oregano
1 tablespoon chopped fresh basil
3 cups water
Freshly ground black pepper
2 ounces pecorino romano cheese

In a large saucepan over medium-high heat, heat the olive oil. Add the onion and sauté until it softens, about 5 minutes. Add the squash and salt, and sauté until the squash starts to soften, about 5 minutes.

Stir in the quinoa; then add the Vegetable Stock, spinach, oregano, basil, and water. Partially cover and bring the soup to a boil; then reduce the heat to medium and cook until the quinoa becomes tender but still firm, about 15 minutes. Season with salt and pepper.

Ladle the hot soup into 4 bowls, shave a few strips of pecorino on top, and serve.

To store, refrigerate or freeze the soup in an airtight container or zip-top bag. The soup will keep for 3 days in the refrigerator and 2 months in the freezer.

Per serving: Calories 305; Fat 11g; Saturated Fat 4g; Sodium 1,240mg; Protein 16g; Fiber 5g

Old-World Minestrone

LARGE GROUPS, VEGETARIANS, MAKE AHEAD, ONE POT

SERVES 4 / PREP: 20 MINUTES / COOK: 45 TO 52 MINUTES

It's all vegetables all the time with minestrone. This satisfying, substantial Italian soup gains richness from vegetables that are cooked to a very soft state and a heartiness from the quinoa, which stands in for pasta. There's no set recipe for minestrone, which has traditionally been made from whatever produce is on hand, so leave out or add in ingredients according to your taste.

4 tablespoons extra-virgin olive oil, divided

2 medium white onions, diced

2 medium potatoes, peeled and diced

1 large carrot, diced

2 garlic cloves, crushed

1 medium zucchini, diced

2 celery stalks, cut into ¼-inch crescents

5 ounces string beans, cut into 1-inch pieces

1 (16-ounce) can low-sodium cannellini beans, drained and rinsed

1 bay leaf

½ teaspoon chopped fresh thyme

½ teaspoon salt, plus more for seasoning

¼ teaspoon freshly ground black pepper, plus more for seasoning

4 cups Vegetable Stock (Chicken Stock substitution tip, page 41)

1 (15-ounce) can low-sodium crushed tomatoes, undrained

2 cups cooked quinoa

½ cup grated fresh Parmesan cheese, divided

½ cup chopped fresh parsley

In a large saucepan over medium-high heat, heat 2 tablespoons of olive oil. Add the onions, potatoes, carrot, and garlic and sauté until the vegetables are fork tender, 5 to 10 minutes. Add the zucchini, celery, string beans, cannellini beans, bay leaf, thyme, salt, and pepper and sauté for an additional 5 to 7 minutes.

Stir in the Vegetable Stock and tomatoes with their juice, and bring to a boil. Lower the heat, and simmer for about 15 minutes. Add the quinoa, and cook for another 20 minutes.

Ladle the hot soup into 4 bowls, drizzle each with the remaining 2 tablespoons of olive oil, and sprinkle 1 tablespoon of Parmesan on top of each serving. Garnish with the parsley, and serve the remaining Parmesan on the side.

To store, refrigerate or freeze in an airtight container or zip-top bag. The minestrone will keep for 4 days in the refrigerator and 3 months in the freezer.

Tip **For additional depth to the minestrone, toss in a Parmesan rind with the tomatoes, or stir in some Pesto (Quinoa Penne with Chicken and Pesto recipe, page 162) before serving.**

Per serving: Calories 863; Fat 22g; Saturated Fat 5g; Sodium 1,456mg; Protein 57g; Fiber 40g

Brazilian Fish Stew

SERVES 4 / PREP: 30 MINUTES / COOK: 20 MINUTES / TOTAL: 2 HOURS, 20 MINUTES

This stick-to-your-ribs stew, called *moqueca* in Portuguese, springs from Brazil's vibrant Afro-Brazilian culture. Traditionally made with red-colored palm oil (*dende*), an African ingredient with a very strong flavor that can be an acquired taste, the stew is here made with bacon fat or extra-virgin olive oil. You can make *moqueca* with any firm-fleshed white fish, such as halibut, striped bass, or monkfish.

4 cups cooked quinoa

½ teaspoon ground turmeric

1½ pounds boneless, skinless catfish or tilapia filets

½ teaspoon salt, plus more for seasoning

¼ teaspoon freshly ground black pepper, plus more for seasoning

4 tablespoons extra-virgin olive oil, divided

2 tablespoons freshly squeezed lime juice

4 garlic cloves, minced, divided

½ teaspoon chopped fresh thyme

1 small yellow onion, chopped

1 red bell pepper, chopped

1 yellow bell pepper, chopped

2 tomatoes, cored, seeded, and finely chopped, divided

1½ cups Chicken Stock (page 40) or store bought

1 cup unsweetened coconut milk

1 tablespoon bacon fat or extra-virgin olive oil

½ cup chopped cilantro, divided

In a medium bowl, toss the quinoa with the turmeric. Set aside.

Wash the fish, pat it dry, and cut it into 2-inch chunks. Season it with salt and pepper.

In a large bowl, toss together the fish, 2 tablespoons of olive oil, the lime juice, half of the garlic, thyme, and the salt and pepper. Transfer the mixture to a zip-top bag and refrigerate for 2 hours. Take the bag out of the fridge about 30 minutes before you need it to bring it to room temperature.

In a large saucepan over medium-high heat, heat the remaining 2 tablespoons of olive oil. Add the onion, red and yellow bell peppers, and remaining garlic and sauté until the vegetables soften, about 5 minutes. Add the tomatoes and sauté until they melt, about 5 minutes.

Add the Chicken Stock, coconut milk, and bacon fat, and bring the stew to a boil. Turn the heat down to medium-low. Drain and discard the marinade from the fish, and add the fish to the pot. Allow the soup to simmer for 10 to 12 minutes. Season with salt and pepper, and stir in ¼ cup of cilantro.

Portion the quinoa among 4 bowls, and ladle the stew on top. Garnish with the remaining ¼ cup of cilantro and serve.

To store, refrigerate the quinoa and stew in separate airtight containers or zip-top bags. The soup will keep for 2 days. Do not freeze.

Per serving: Calories 965; Fat 59g; Saturated Fat 21g; Sodium 138; Protein 44g; Fiber 10g

Gazpacho

LARGE GROUPS, SINGLETONS, VEGANS, MAKE AHEAD, ONE POT

SERVES 4 / PREP: 20 MINUTES, PLUS 2 HOURS TO CHILL

This classic no-cook Spanish soup is a superb meal or snack on a hot day, both for the people eating it and the person preparing it. Traditionally thickened with bread or almonds, this recipe puts gluten-free, nut-free quinoa in that role instead. Given the size of most blenders, you'll probably have to work in batches and mix them all together in a bowl at the end.

2½ pounds tomatoes, seeded and roughly chopped, divided

2 red bell peppers, roughly chopped

1 medium cucumber, peeled, seeded, and roughly chopped

1 medium red onion, roughly chopped

1 cup cooked quinoa

3 garlic cloves

⅓ cup extra-virgin olive oil

3 tablespoons sherry vinegar

1 medium fresh jalapeño, roughly chopped (optional)

Salt

Freshly ground black pepper

¾ cup chopped green bell pepper

½ cup chopped white onion

In a blender, blend 2 cups of tomatoes, the red bell peppers, cucumber, onion, quinoa, garlic, olive oil, vinegar, and jalapeño (if using) until smooth, adding cold water as needed to bring the soup to the consistency of a smoothie. Season with salt and pepper. Chill the soup in an airtight container in the refrigerator for 2 hours.

Ladle the soup into 4 bowls, garnish with the remaining tomatoes, green bell pepper, and white onion, and serve.

To store, refrigerate or freeze the soup in an airtight container or zip-top bag. The soup will keep for 5 days in the refrigerator and 2 months in the freezer.

 Tip For a chunkier gazpacho, use a food processor instead of a blender.

Per serving: Calories 309; Fat 18g; Saturated Fat 3g; Sodium 24mg; Protein 7g; Fiber 7g

Curried Red Quinoa & Chicken Stew

LARGE GROUPS, MEAT LOVERS, MAKE AHEAD, ONE POT

SERVES 4 / PREP: 15 MINUTES / COOK: 25 MINUTES

This colorful stew is chock full of vegetables that are integral to Indian cuisine. The sweetness of the onion and carrot and the creaminess of the coconut milk balance the mild spice of the curry, making this an adventure in aroma rather than heat. For a heartier experience, add some diced potato.

1 tablespoon unsalted butter

1 large yellow onion, thinly sliced

1 large carrot, diced

3 cloves minced garlic

4 teaspoons Indian curry powder

1 teaspoon salt, plus more for seasoning

4 cups Chicken Stock (see page 40) or store bought

1 cup dry red quinoa

1½ pounds cooked boneless, skinless chicken breast, cut into ½-inch cubes

2 medium tomatoes, chopped

2 cups cauliflower florets

1 (14-ounce) can unsweetened coconut milk

1½ cups frozen peas

1 tablespoon chopped fresh cilantro

1 lemon, cut into wedges

In a large saucepan over medium-high heat, melt the butter. Add the onion, carrot, garlic, curry powder, and salt and sauté until the carrot softens, 5 to 7 minutes.

Add the Chicken Stock and quinoa to the pot and stir well. When the liquid comes to a simmer, reduce the heat to medium and continue simmering for 10 minutes. Add the chicken, tomatoes, cauliflower, and coconut milk and simmer until the cauliflower is fork-tender, 5 to 7 minutes.

Add the peas and cook them just enough to turn bright green. Season with salt.

Ladle the hot stew into 4 bowls, garnish each with the cilantro, and serve with lemon wedges on the side.

To store, refrigerate in an airtight container or zip-top bag. The stew will keep for 3 days. Do not freeze.

Per serving: Calories 785; Fat 36g; Saturated Fat 23g; Sodium 1,613mg; Protein 69g; Fiber 11g

Spicy Spanish Chicken Stew

LARGE GROUPS, SINGLETONS, MEAT LOVERS, MAKE AHEAD, ONE POT

SERVES 4 / PREP: 20 MINUTES / COOK: 20 TO 25 MINUTES

Quinoa takes on the vivid color of paprika in this robust Spanish-style stew, which is zestier the fresher your paprika is. The stew is quick to make and easy on the wallet, and you can save even more money by using chicken thighs in place of the chicken breast. Another variation is to turn this into a mixed seafood rather than poultry stew; good options are firm, white fish, such as cod or monkfish, clams, shrimp, and squid.

1 tablespoon extra-virgin olive oil

½ cup finely chopped white onion

4 teaspoons finely chopped garlic

½ cup finely chopped carrots

½ cup finely chopped celery

1 tablespoon ground paprika

½ teaspoon salt, plus more for seasoning

¼ teaspoon freshly ground black pepper, plus more for seasoning

3 cups cooked quinoa

1 (15-ounce) can low-sodium diced tomatoes, undrained

1½ quarts Chicken Stock (page 40) or store bought, plus more if needed

1 hot chile, finely chopped

2 cups diced cooked chicken breast

2 tablespoons chopped fresh parsley

In a large saucepan over medium heat, heat the olive oil. Add the onion and garlic and sauté until the onion browns at the edges, about 5 minutes. Stir in the carrots, celery, paprika, salt, and pepper, and sauté until the carrots soften, 5 to 10 minutes.

Thoroughly mix the quinoa into the pot. Add the diced tomatoes with their liquid, Chicken Stock, and chile and stir well. Bring the stew up to a vigorous simmer (do not boil) and cook for 10 minutes, adding more stock if the stew gets too thick.

Turn the heat down to low, and add the chicken. Cook until the chicken is warmed through. Season with salt and pepper.

Ladle the hot stew into 4 bowls, garnish each with the parsley, and serve.

To store, refrigerate or freeze in an airtight container or zip-top bag. The stew will keep for 4 days in the refrigerator and 2 months in the freezer.

Per serving: Calories 381; Fat 10g; Saturated Fat 1g; Sodium 1,553mg; Protein 34g; Fiber 6g

New England Clam Chowder

LARGE GROUPS, MEAT LOVERS, SINGLETONS, ONE POT, 30-MINUTE

SERVES 4 / PREP: 10 MINUTES / COOK: 20 MINUTES

In this easy version of a classic recipe, quinoa stands in for potatoes, canned clams for fresh, and bacon for salt pork. If you make the chowder the day before you serve it, it will thicken a little more in the fridge.

4 slices slab or thick-cut bacon, diced
1 medium onion, finely chopped
1 celery stalk, finely chopped
4 tablespoons unsalted butter
3 tablespoons Quinoa Flour (page 37) or store bought
3 (6.5-ounce) cans whole clams, drained, with liquid reserved
1½ cups milk
4 cups cooked quinoa
1½ cups half-and-half
1 (8-ounce) bottle clam juice
Salt
Freshly ground black pepper
4 teaspoons chopped fresh parsley
Gluten-free crackers or bread (optional)

Tip If you want to use fresh clams, you can buy 4 quarts of hard-shell clams such as cherrystones, littlenecks, or quahogs (the traditional choice). Steam them and reserve the resulting liquor. Alternatively, you can buy 1 pint of pre-shucked clams with their broth and a bottle of clam juice. You don't have to steam them; just chop them into a ¼-inch dice.

In a large saucepan over medium heat, cook the bacon until it's almost crisp. Add the onion and celery and cook, stirring, until they are tender, about 5 minutes. Add the butter and let it melt; then sprinkle the Quinoa Flour over the pan and stir the contents to blend thoroughly.

Add the reserved clam liquid and milk to the pan. Bring the liquid to a simmer, stirring often while the temperature comes up. Add the quinoa, and simmer for 8 to 10 minutes.

Add the clams and half-and-half to the pan. Check the thickness of the chowder, and add as much of the bottled clam juice as needed to create the thickness you want. Simmer until the clams are heated through, 2 to 3 minutes. Don't cook the clams too long, or they will be tough. Season the chowder with salt and pepper.

Ladle the hot chowder into 4 bowls and garnish with the parsley. Serve with crackers or bread if desired.

To store, refrigerate in an airtight container or zip-top bag. The chowder will keep for 3 days in the refrigerator. Do not freeze.

Per serving: Calories 768; Fat 40g; Saturated Fat 19g; Sodium 1,493; Protein 27g; Fiber 6g

Creamy Beef & Mushroom Soup

KIDS, LARGE GROUPS, MEAT LOVERS, ONE POT

SERVES 4 / PREP: 10 MINUTES / COOK: 1 HOUR, 20 MINUTES

A little bit cream of mushroom soup, a little bit beef stroganoff, this is about as indulgent as soup gets. If you want to go deeper, add a splash of dry white wine to the pot after the mushrooms brown and before you add the stock. If you want to be bit more virtuous, switch out the sour cream for plain nonfat Greek yogurt—or leave out the dairy altogether.

1 pound beef chuck, cut into 1-inch cubes
½ teaspoon salt, plus more for seasoning
½ teaspoon freshly ground black pepper, plus more for seasoning
¼ cup extra-virgin olive oil, divided
1 medium white onion, chopped
3 cups sliced button mushrooms
1 teaspoon chopped fresh thyme
⅛ teaspoon ground nutmeg
6 cups Chicken Stock (page 40) or store bought
1 cup dry quinoa, rinsed
1 cup sour cream
2 tablespoons chopped flat-leaf parsley

In a large bowl, sprinkle the meat with the salt and pepper. Toss the cubes to coat.

In a large saucepan over high heat, heat 2 tablespoons of olive oil. Add the meat and sear, turning often, until the cubes are browned on all sides, about 4 minutes. Transfer the meat to a bowl and set aside.

Reduce the heat to medium-high, and heat the remaining 2 tablespoons of olive oil. Add the onion and sauté until it softens, about 5 minutes. Stir in the mushrooms, thyme, and nutmeg and sauté until the mushrooms start to brown, about 5 minutes.

Add the Chicken Stock to the pot, and bring it to a boil. Turn the heat down to medium, and add the quinoa. Return the meat and its juices to the pot and stir thoroughly. Simmer until the meat is very tender, about 1 hour. Remove the pot from the heat, and stir in the sour cream. Season with salt and pepper.

Ladle the hot soup into 4 bowls, garnish each with the parsley, and serve.

To store, refrigerate in an airtight container or zip-top bag. The soup will keep for 4 days. Do not freeze.

Per serving: Calories 627; Fat 35g; Saturated Fat 13g; Sodium 1,549mg; Protein 45g; Fiber 4g

Chilled Zucchini-Quinoa Soup with Chive Oil

SINGLETONS, VEGANS, MAKE AHEAD

SERVES 4 / PREP: 40 MINUTES, PLUS 1 HOUR TO CHILL / COOK: 20 MINUTES / TOTAL: 6 HOURS, 20 MINUTES

This soup is summertime at its finest and freshest. Purée the abundance of garden-fresh zucchini with quinoa for a creamy yet light soup. Likewise, it's simple to make the chive oil yourself; do it at least a day before you make the soup, so the flavors have time to meld.

For the chive oil
2 large bunches chives (about 2½ ounces), cut in half crosswise
1 cup extra-virgin olive oil

For the soup
1 tablespoon extra-virgin olive oil
1 small white onion, chopped
2 medium zucchini, chopped
2 tablespoons chopped fresh dill (optional)
2 teaspoons lemon zest
½ teaspoon salt, plus more for seasoning
1 cup dry quinoa, rinsed
1 quart Vegetable Stock (Chicken Stock substitution tip, page 41)
3 cups water
1 teaspoon cracked black peppercorns (see ingredient tip)
¼ cup pepitas
¼ cup pine nuts

To make the chive oil In a small saucepan of water, bring the chives to a boil and blanch until they're bright green, about 10 seconds. Drain the chives, and run them under cold water. Pat them dry on paper towels.

Roughly chop the chives, and put them in a blender. Place the lid on the blender with the hole open. Turn on the blender, and drizzle in the olive oil to purée. Let the purée stand at least 1 hour, or as long as overnight.

Line a fine-mesh sieve with damp cheese-cloth, and pour the oil through to filter out the solids. Press the solids gently to drain out as much oil as possible. Don't press too hard, or the oil will become cloudy.

Pour the oil into an airtight container until you're ready to use it. Store it at room temperature, or for 1 month in the refrigerator.

To make the soup In a large saucepan over medium-high heat, heat the olive oil. Add the onion and sauté until it softens, about 5 minutes. Add the zucchini, dill (if using), lemon zest, and salt, and sauté for 3 minutes.

Stir in the quinoa; then add the Vegetable Stock and water. Partially cover the pan, and bring the soup to a boil. Reduce the heat to medium, and cook until the quinoa starts to soften, about 12 minutes. Season with salt and the cracked pepper. Allow the soup to cool until it's safe to handle.

Pour the soup into a blender; you may have to work in batches. Purée it until it's smooth. As you complete the batches, pour them together into a large bowl, stirring the batches together for uniform flavor. Refrigerate the soup for 5 or 6 hours to chill.

Ladle the soup into 4 bowls, garnish each with the pepitas and pine nuts, and drizzle with the chive oil.

To store, refrigerate or freeze the soup in an airtight container or zip-top bag. The soup will keep for 4 days in the refrigerator and 3 months in the freezer.

Tip You can buy cracked pepper at any supermarket, but if you take a few minutes to crack whole peppercorns at home, you'll get a much more aromatic result. To crack peppercorns, put about 1 tablespoon of whole peppercorns in a sturdy zip-top bag and seal it, pressing out the air. Lay the bag on a flat work surface. Using the flat side of a meat tenderizing mallet, a rolling pin, or the bottom of a heavy sauté pan, pound, roll over, or press down on the peppercorns to crack them. Crack them to whatever coarseness you desire; for this recipe, it's best to go fairly fine.

Per serving: Calories 737; Fat 64g; Saturated Fat 9g; Sodium 1,070mg; Protein 14g; Fiber 5g

Chicken & "Stars" Soup

KIDS, SINGLETONS, MAKE AHEAD, ONE POT

SERVES 4 / PREP: 15 MINUTES / COOK: 28 TO 32 MINUTES

You'll feel good about serving your kids this homemade soup with healthy, gluten-free quinoa, rather than the who-knows-what's-in-it canned variety. Just as tasty and just as fun, it also qualifies as a folk remedy for the common cold. You can also make the soup with chicken legs or turkey.

1 pound boneless, skinless chicken breast
Salt
Freshly ground black pepper
2 tablespoons extra-virgin olive oil, divided
1 cup diced celery
1 cup diced carrots
2½ quarts Chicken Stock (page 40) or
    store bought
3 cups cooked quinoa
½ teaspoon minced fresh marjoram
½ teaspoon minced fresh thyme
1 bay leaf

Wash the chicken breasts, pat them dry, and season both sides with salt and pepper.

In a large saucepan over medium-high heat, heat 1 tablespoon of olive oil. Reduce the heat to medium, and add the chicken. Cook, turning occasionally, until the juices run clear, 8 to 12 minutes. Transfer the chicken to a large plate and allow it to cool. Tear the chicken into bite-size pieces (not too small).

Add the remaining 1 tablespoon of olive oil to the pan. Turn the heat to medium-high. When the oil is hot, add the celery and carrots and sauté until tender.

Return the chicken to the pan, add the Chicken Stock, quinoa, marjoram, thyme, and bay leaf, and bring the soup to a simmer. Turn the heat to medium-low, and allow the soup to simmer for 20 minutes. Season with salt and pepper.

Ladle the hot soup into 4 bowls and serve.

To store, refrigerate or freeze in an airtight container or zip-top bag. The soup will keep for 5 days in the refrigerator and 3 months in the freezer.

Per serving: Calories 526; Fat 17g; Saturated Fat 17g; Sodium 2,080mg; Protein 55g; Fiber 4g

Cheesy Quinoa—Ham Soup

KIDS, MEAT LOVERS, ONE POT, 30-MINUTE

SERVES 4 / PREP: 10 MINUTES / COOK: 20 MINUTES

Okay, it's true: Quinoa is super-healthy, but this soup is not. Sometimes, though, you just need something cheesy, and the little grains of quinoa floating around in this soup make it all the more fun to eat. If you're not a big cheddar fan, try using another cheese that melts well, such as Monterey Jack (pepper Jack!), Gouda, or asiago.

2 tablespoons extra-virgin olive oil

½ medium white onion, diced

¼ teaspoon salt, plus more for seasoning

¼ teaspoon freshly ground black pepper, plus more for seasoning

¼ teaspoon mustard powder

¼ teaspoon ground paprika

3 cups cooked quinoa

3 cups Chicken Stock (page 40) or store bought

2 cups milk

8 ounces mild orange cheddar cheese, shredded, or American cheese, chopped

8 ounces cured, ready-to-serve ham or Canadian bacon, diced

In a large saucepan over medium-high heat, heat the olive oil. Add the onion, salt, pepper, mustard powder, and paprika and sauté until the onion softens, about 5 minutes. Add the quinoa and stir well to coat it with the spices. Sauté for 5 minutes.

Pour in the Chicken Stock, and bring it to a boil. Reduce the heat to simmer and cook for 5 minutes.

Turn the heat down as low as it will go and add the milk, cheese, and ham. Stir the soup until the cheese melts and blends in. Season with salt and pepper. Leave the pot on the heat for 5 minutes, stirring occasionally.

Ladle the hot soup into 4 bowls and serve.

To store, refrigerate in an airtight container or zip-top bag. The soup will keep for 3 days. Do not freeze.

Tip **When shopping for ham, pay attention to the labels "fully cooked" or "cook before eating." Ham steaks need cooking, but canned hams are fully cooked. Virginia hams and other "country hams" are dry-cured, then smoked and aged. Fresh hams must be cooked before eaten.**

Per serving: Calories 624; Fat 36g; Saturated Fat 17g; Sodium 1,872mg; Protein 35g; Fiber 4g

Ecuadorian Quinoa–Pork Chowder

MEAT LOVERS, SINGLETONS, MAKE AHEAD, ONE POT

SERVES 4 / PREP: 15 MINUTES / COOK: 1 HOUR, 15 MINUTES

The climate in the high Andes is cold, and this simple Ecuadorean soup is great when it's raw and rainy outside. No wonder all kinds of soup are so popular in Ecuador—and it doesn't hurt that they're inexpensive to make. If you prefer, you can also make this recipe with stew beef.

2 tablespoons extra-virgin olive oil
1 pound pork shoulder, cut into 1-inch cubes
1 large yellow onion, finely chopped
2 garlic cloves, minced
6 cups Chicken Stock (page 40) or store bought
1 medium carrot, cut into ¼- to ½-inch slices
2 medium potatoes, peeled and cut into 1-inch cubes
2 cups cooked quinoa
1 cup frozen peas
Salt
1 tablespoon chopped cilantro

In a large saucepan over medium-high heat, heat the olive oil. Add the pork, onion, and garlic and sauté until the meat is browned, about 7 minutes.

Add the Chicken Stock, and bring it to a boil. Turn the heat down to medium-low, and simmer the soup for 30 minutes. Add the carrot and simmer for 15 minutes. Add the potatoes, and bring the chowder to a boil over medium-high heat. Turn down the heat to medium-low and cook at a rapid simmer until the potatoes are fork tender, about 15 minutes.

Turn the heat down to low, and stir in the quinoa and peas. Simmer for 5 minutes. Season with salt.

Ladle the hot chowder into 4 bowls, garnish each with the chopped cilantro, and serve.

To store, refrigerate or freeze in an airtight container or zip-top bag. The chowder will keep for 4 days in the refrigerator and 3 months in the freezer.

Per serving: Calories 642; Fat 34g; Saturated Fat 10g; Sodium 1,310mg; Protein 36g; Fiber 8g

Rustic Lentil Soup

KIDS, SINGLETONS, VEGANS, MAKE AHEAD, ONE POT

SERVES 4 / PREP: 20 MINUTES / COOK: 35 MINUTES

Super-easy and super-fast to make, this lentil soup keeps hunger pangs at bay. It's packed with nutrition, too, not only from the quinoa but from the lentils, which deliver an impressive amount of fiber and protein. If you're focused on indulgence and you aren't set on a vegan dish, add some diced ham when you put in the lentils and quinoa.

2 tablespoons extra-virgin olive oil

1½ cups chopped onions

2 large carrots, cut into ¼-inch rounds

1 cup chopped celery

½ teaspoon minced fresh savory (see ingredient tip)

½ teaspoon salt, plus more for seasoning

¼ teaspoon freshly ground black pepper, plus more for seasoning

6 cups Vegetable Stock (Chicken Stock substitution tip, page 41)

1 (14.5-ounce) can low-sodium diced tomatoes

1¼ cups dry brown lentils, picked over and rinsed

2 to 3 cups cooked quinoa

1 cup seeded, chopped fresh tomatoes

¼ cup chopped fresh parsley

In a large saucepan over medium-high heat, heat the olive oil. Add the onions, carrots, celery, savory, salt, and pepper and sauté until the vegetables begin to soften, about 5 minutes.

Add the Vegetable Stock, tomatoes, lentils, and quinoa, and bring to a boil. Turn the heat down to low, cover, and simmer, stirring occasionally, until the lentils are tender, about 30 minutes.

As the lentils cook, some will break down and thicken the soup. But if the finished soup is too thin for your taste, use an immersion blender or vegetable masher to break down the lentils until the soup reaches the desired consistency. If the soup is too thick, add water or stock. Season with salt and pepper.

Ladle the hot soup into 4 bowls, garnish each bowl with the chopped tomatoes and parsley, and serve.

To store, refrigerate or freeze in an airtight container or zip-top bag. The soup will keep for 2 days in the refrigerator and 3 months in the freezer.

Per serving: Calories 506; Fat 12g; Saturated Fat 2g; Sodium 1,498mg; Protein 39g; Fiber 25g

New Orleans Red Beans & Quinoa

LARGE GROUPS, MEAT LOVERS, MAKE AHEAD, ONE POT

SERVES 4 / PREP: 20 MINUTES / COOK: 45 TO 60 MINUTES

Alongside jambalaya, gumbo, and étouffé, red beans and rice ranks as one of Louisiana's signature contributions to America's culinary lexicon. In New Orleans, Monday night is traditionally red beans and rice night. Cook red beans and quinoa any night of the week to *laissez les bon temps rouler*!

2 tablespoons extra-virgin olive oil

1 medium yellow onion, chopped

3 garlic cloves, chopped

1 celery stalk, chopped

1 medium green bell pepper, chopped

1 teaspoon chopped fresh thyme

½ teaspoon salt, plus more for seasoning

½ teaspoon freshly ground black pepper, plus more for seasoning

½ pound andouille sausage or other smoked sausage, cut into ½-inch slices

1 ham hock or 1 smoked turkey leg

5 cups Chicken Stock (page 40) or store bought

2 (15-ounce) cans low-sodium kidney beans, drained and rinsed

2 bay leaves

4 cups cooked quinoa, hot

¼ cup chopped scallions

Hot sauce (see ingredient tip), for serving

In a large saucepan over medium-high heat, heat the olive oil. Add the onion, garlic, celery, bell pepper, thyme, salt, and pepper. Sauté until the vegetables soften, about 5 minutes. Add the sausage and ham hock and cook, stirring occasionally, until they brown, about 5 minutes.

Add the Chicken Stock, beans, and bay leaves to the pan, stir well, and bring the liquid to a boil. Turn the heat down to medium-low and simmer, uncovered, stirring occasionally, until the beans start to thicken the liquid, about 30 minutes. If the stew becomes too thick and dry, add ¼ cup of water at a time.

Take 2 cups of beans out of the pot, and put them in a blender. Purée them and return them to the pot.

Continue cooking the stew until the remaining whole beans are tender and the stew is creamy, 5 to 20 minutes. Discard the ham hock and bay leaves. Season with salt and pepper.

Put 1 cup hot quinoa into each of 4 bowls, and ladle the hot beans on top. Garnish each bowl with the scallions, and serve with the hot sauce on the side.

To store, refrigerate or freeze the quinoa and beans in separate airtight containers or zip-top bags. The beans will keep for 5 days in the refrigerator and 3 months in the freezer.

Tip · You've probably got a bottle of Tabasco—that famous hot sauce made from tabasco peppers—in your kitchen, but the Pelican State produces many other sauces of note. Two of those are Louisiana Hot Sauce, a much milder sauce made with cayenne pepper, and Crystal Hot Sauce, another cayenne-based sauce that lies somewhere in between.

Per serving: Calories 983; Fat 50g; Saturated Fat 15g; Sodium 2,643mg; Protein 51g; Fiber 15g

All-American Beef & Vegetable Soup

KIDS, LARGE GROUPS, MEAT LOVERS, MAKE AHEAD, ONE POT

SERVES 4 / PREP: 10 MINUTES / COOK: 1 HOUR, 15 MINUTES

Quintessentially American food like this keeps your feet on the ground and your eye on the ball. A gluten-free takeoff on beef-barley soup, this recipe delivers a serious wallop of flavor and nutrition. It's a great make-ahead lunch for the gang on a blustery fall day.

1 pound beef chuck, cut into 1-inch cubes

¾ teaspoon salt, divided, plus more for seasoning

½ teaspoon freshly ground black pepper, divided, plus more for seasoning

2 tablespoons extra-virgin olive oil, divided

1 medium yellow onion, chopped

2 medium carrots, chopped

3 celery stalks, chopped

2 tablespoons tomato paste

1 cup dry quinoa, rinsed

2 quarts Chicken Stock (page 40) or store bought

1 (14.5-ounce) can diced tomatoes

2 teaspoons chopped fresh thyme

1 bay leaf

2 cups coarsely chopped steamed green beans

In a large bowl, sprinkle the meat with ½ teaspoon of salt and ¼ teaspoon of pepper. Toss the cubes to coat them.

In a large saucepan over medium-high heat, heat 1 tablespoon of olive oil. Add the meat and sear, turning often, until the cubes are browned on all sides, about 4 minutes. Transfer the meat to a bowl and set aside.

Heat the remaining 1 tablespoon of olive oil in the pan. Add the onion, carrots, and celery and cook, stirring often, until the vegetables begin to brown, about 6 minutes. Mix in the tomato paste to coat the vegetables evenly.

Add the quinoa, Chicken Stock, tomatoes, thyme, bay leaf, the remaining ¼ teaspoon of salt and ¼ teaspoon of pepper, and the meat with its juices. Bring the soup to a boil; then turn the heat down to medium-low. Cover the pot and simmer until the beef is very tender, about 1 hour. If the soup becomes too thick, stir in a little water.

Add the green beans and cook until heated through, about 1 minute. Season with salt and pepper.

Ladle the hot soup into 4 bowls and serve.

To store, refrigerate or freeze in an airtight container or zip-top bag. The soup will keep for 5 days in the refrigerator and 2 months in the freezer.

Per serving: Calories 507; Fat 18g; Saturated Fat 4g; Sodium 2,091mg; Protein 44g; Fiber 8g

Kickin' Slow Cooker Chili con Carne

KIDS, LARGE GROUPS, MEAT LOVERS, SINGLETONS, MAKE AHEAD, ONE POT

SERVES 4 / PREP: 15 MINUTES / COOK: 7½ HOURS

Is this authentic chili? Well, there's no such thing. Here, quinoa substitutes for beans (which many would argue don't belong in chili anyway). Regardless, a slow cooker is a great chili-maker, and Quinoa-Jalapeño Cornbread (page 107) is a great side.

2 pounds beef chuck, cut into 1-inch cubes

1 tablespoon packed light brown sugar

2 teaspoons salt, plus more for seasoning

3 tablespoons vegetable oil

1 medium onion, chopped

1 (28-ounce) can diced tomatoes

1 cup dry quinoa, rinsed

1 large poblano or Anaheim chile, chopped

3 tablespoons chili powder

1 tablespoon ground cumin

½ teaspoon chipotle powder

½ teaspoon dried oregano

2 cups water

2 teaspoons white sugar (optional)

Juice of 1 lime (optional)

1 cup shredded cheddar or Monterey Jack cheese

¼ cup sour cream

¼ cup chopped scallions

Mexican hot sauce

In a large bowl, toss the beef with the brown sugar and salt.

In a large sauté pan over medium-high heat, heat the vegetable oil. Add half the meat and sear, turning often, until the cubes are browned on all sides, about 4 minutes. Transfer the meat to a 4- to 6-quart slow cooker, brown the remaining meat, and transfer it to the slow cooker as well.

Add the onion to the pan and cook until it's soft, about 5 minutes. Transfer the onion to the slow cooker. Add the tomatoes, quinoa, chile, chili powder, cumin, chipotle powder, oregano, and water to the cooker and stir well.

Close the cooker, and cook on low for 7 hours. When the cycle is done, open the cooker and adjust the chili for seasoning. If it seems too spicy, dissolve the white sugar in the lime juice and stir the mixture into the chili. Season with salt;

then set the cooker's heat to high and cook, uncovered, until the chili thickens slightly, about 15 minutes.

Ladle the hot chili into 4 bowls. Top each with the cheese, sour cream, and scallions, and serve with Mexican hot sauce on the side.

To store, refrigerate or freeze in an airtight container or zip-top bag. The chili will keep for 5 days in the refrigerator and 3 months in the freezer.

Tip The chili powders sold on your supermarket spice shelves often contain other ingredients, such as cumin or salt. Look for labels that list only one ingredient—chile peppers. You may have the best luck in the international foods aisle; Mexican groceries are sure to have pure chili powders as well.

Per serving: Calories 898; Fat 41g; Saturated Fat 16g; Sodium 1,575mg; Protein 85g; Fiber 8g

Irish Lamb Stew

SERVES 8 / PREP: 25 MINUTES / COOK: 2 HOURS

Hardcore Irish stew contains only mutton (grown-up lamb), potatoes, onions, and water, but this modern version adds carrots, and in place of some of the potatoes, quinoa. The original stew was a product of necessity: Sheep raised for their wool eventually became tough mutton that needed long cooking times, and potatoes were the foundation of the Irish diet. This humble stew yields incredible results.

2 tablespoons butter

1½ pounds lamb stew meat, cut into 1-inch cubes

2 small onions, thinly sliced

3 medium carrots, cut into 1-inch chunks

1 teaspoon salt, divided, plus more for seasoning

½ teaspoon freshly ground black pepper, divided, plus more for seasoning

1 cup dry quinoa, rinsed

4 medium potatoes, peeled and halved

3 tablespoons chopped fresh parsley

In a large pot over medium-high heat, melt the butter. Add the lamb and sear, turning often, until the cubes are browned on all sides, about 4 minutes. Turn off the heat, transfer the meat to a bowl, and set aside.

Arrange half the onions across the bottom of the pot. Scatter half the carrots over the onions. Return the lamb and its juices to the pot, and distribute the meat evenly over the layer of carrots. Sprinkle the lamb with ½ teaspoon of salt and ¼ teaspoon of pepper.

Pour the quinoa evenly over the lamb. Layer on the remaining onion, then the remaining carrots. Sprinkle the top with the remaining ½ teaspoon of salt and ¼ teaspoon of pepper.

Add enough water to the pot to come halfway up the top layer of carrots. Arrange the halved potatoes, cut-side down, on top of the carrots, making sure they don't touch the water.

Turn on the heat to medium-high, and bring the water to a boil. Cover the pot, and turn the heat down to low. Simmer until the meat is fully cooked and very tender, and the potatoes are soft inside, about 1½ hours. Season with salt and pepper.

Spoon the hot stew into bowls, garnish each with the parsley, and serve.

To store, refrigerate or freeze in an airtight container or zip-top bag. The stew will keep for 5 days in the refrigerator and 3 months in the freezer.

Per serving: Calories 352; Fat 10g; Saturated Fat 4g; Sodium 401mg; Protein 29g; Fiber 5g

8

Main Dishes

Quinoa & Roasted Vegetable Bowl

SINGLETONS, VEGANS, MAKE AHEAD

SERVES 4 / PREP: 50 MINUTES / COOK: 1 HOUR, 10 MINUTES TO 1 HOUR, 30 MINUTES

Roasting brings such depth and sweetness to vegetables that it's a wonder anyone cooks them any other way. This recipe is time consuming but absolutely worth it. When you taste the combination of sweet vegetables and nutty quinoa, you'll add this to your permanent recipe collection.

Cooking spray

4 cups cooked quinoa

½ cup plus 1 teaspoon extra-virgin olive oil, divided

1 tablespoon plus 1¼ teaspoons salt, divided, plus more for seasoning

¼ teaspoon freshly ground black pepper, plus more for seasoning

2 bulbs garlic, skins on

12 baby carrots, tops removed

2 medium red bell peppers

3 medium beets, tops and roots removed

1 tablespoon chopped fresh thyme

½ cup water

½ cup whole flat-leaf parsley leaves

Preheat the oven to 450°F.

Line a rimmed baking sheet with parchment or foil, and lightly grease it with cooking spray or a drizzle of oil.

In a large bowl, toss the quinoa with 2 tablespoons of olive oil, 1 teaspoon of salt, and the pepper. Transfer it to a large casserole dish, put the lid on, and set aside.

Strip the papery white skin from the outside of the garlic bulbs, leaving each bulb intact and the skins on the cloves. Cut off the pointy end of each bulb so the flesh of the cloves is visible.

In a large bowl, toss the garlic bulbs, carrots, bell peppers, and beets with ¼ cup of olive oil and 1 tablespoon of salt until they're coated thoroughly. Wrap each garlic bulb in foil, and place it upright on the baking sheet. Spread out the rest of the vegetables on the baking sheet in a single layer.

Roast the vegetables, turning occasionally. When the vegetables begin to brown, start testing for tenderness every 5 minutes by piecing with a fork. The carrots will be ready first, tender but not soft, at about 20 minutes; transfer them to the casserole dish. The garlic and peppers should be ready next, at about 30 minutes. The garlic should be very soft, like a paste, inside its skin. Transfer it to a dish to cool. The bell peppers are ready when their skins are wrinkled and a bit charred. Remove them to a brown paper bag, and fold the top to seal it tightly. Set aside for 30 minutes. The beets will take longest, 40 minutes to 1 hour. When they're done, remove them from the oven on the baking sheet, and allow them to cool until they're safe to handle. Turn down the oven to 350°F.

Separate the garlic cloves from the bulbs. Squeeze their flesh into a medium bowl. Using a fork, mash them together into a paste. Whisk in the remaining 2 tablespoons of olive oil and ¼ teaspoon of salt, and the thyme and water, combining thoroughly.

Pour half of the garlic mixture over the quinoa and carrots, and toss to coat. Season with salt and pepper. Set aside the rest of the garlic mixture.

Rub each beet with your fingers to slip off its jacket; it should come off easily. If necessary, use a knife. Cut the beets crosswise into ½-inch slices, and put them in a large bowl.

Take the bell peppers out of the paper bag. Cut each in half, top to bottom. Remove the stem and seeds, and peel off the skin. Cut the peppers top to bottom into ¼-inch slices. Add them to the bowl with the beets.

Pour the remaining garlic mixture over the beets and peppers, and stir gently to coat the vegetables. Season with salt and pepper. Transfer the vegetables to the casserole dish, and gently toss all the ingredients together. Put the lid back on the dish, and bake the casserole until it's warmed through and steaming, about 30 minutes.

Spoon the quinoa and vegetables into bowls, garnish with parsley, and serve hot.

To store, refrigerate or freeze in an airtight container or zip-top bag. The dish will keep for 3 days in the refrigerator and 1 month in the freezer.

Per serving: Calories 536; Fat 33g; Saturated Fat 4g; Sodium 2,417mg; Protein 11g; Fiber 9g

Black-and-White Portobello Mushrooms

SERVES 4 / PREP: 10 TO 15 MINUTES / COOK: 20 TO 25 MINUTES

Oh so elegant, this is a great dish for an intimate dinner party. It's easy, too, to whip up at the last minute, while chatting with friends and enjoying a glass of wine. Just make the quinoa stuffing earlier in the day, or even the day before, and reheat it while the mushrooms are baking.

Cooking spray

4 large portobello mushrooms, cleaned and stemmed

¼ cup extra-virgin olive oil, divided

Salt

Freshly ground black pepper

2 garlic cloves, minced

1 teaspoon chopped fresh thyme

1 tablespoon balsamic vinegar

3 cups cooked black quinoa

2 tablespoons chopped fresh basil

4-ounce log fresh goat cheese, cut into 8 slices

4 sprigs fresh basil

Preheat the oven to 350°F.

Cover a baking sheet with foil, and lightly grease it with cooking spray or a drizzle of oil.

Place the mushrooms on the baking sheet, underside up. Drizzle them with 1 tablespoon of olive oil and season with salt and pepper. Cover the baking sheet with foil, and cook until the mushrooms are tender, 15 to 20 minutes. Remove from the oven and leave the foil cover on.

In a large saucepan over medium-high heat, heat the remaining 3 tablespoons of olive oil. Add the garlic and sauté until it just starts to sizzle, about 30 seconds. Stir in the thyme and vinegar. Cook for 1 minute. Add the quinoa, and toss to coat. Season with salt and pepper. Remove the pan from the heat, and toss in the chopped basil.

Place one mushroom, underside up, on each of 4 plates. Spoon about ¾ cup of quinoa onto each mushroom. Arrange 2 slices of goat cheese on top of each mushroom, garnish with a sprig of basil, and serve.

To store, gently pat down the cheese- and basil-free quinoa a little and tightly wrap each serving in plastic wrap. Refrigerate or freeze in airtight containers or zip-top bags. The stuffed mushrooms will keep for 2 days in the refrigerator and 1 month in the freezer.

 Tip **To make this a vegan dish, simply leave off the goat cheese.**

Per serving: Calories 381; Fat 22g; Saturated Fat 6g; Sodium 320mg; Protein 14g; Fiber 5g

Stuffed Acorn Squash
with Maple-Hazelnut Quinoa

KIDS, VEGETARIANS, MAKE AHEAD, 30-MINUTE

SERVES 4 / PREP: 10 MINUTES / COOK: 10 TO 15 MINUTES

Since time immemorial, cooks have been stuffing acorn squash with anything they can dream up. This time it's quinoa, and not just any quinoa: A little sweet and a little spicy, it's 100 percent wonderful.

Cooking spray
2 acorn squash, halved, baked, seeds and fibers removed
1 tablespoon extra-virgin olive oil
¾ teaspoon salt, divided, plus more for seasoning
4 tablespoons butter
3 tablespoons maple syrup
1 teaspoon grated fresh ginger
¼ cup chopped hazelnuts
4 cups cooked quinoa
¼ cup chopped fresh parsley
Freshly ground black pepper

Preheat the oven to 300°F. Cover a baking sheet with foil, and lightly grease it with cooking spray or a drizzle of oil.

Rub each baked squash half with the olive oil, and sprinkle them with ½ teaspoon of salt. Place the halves, cut-side down, on the baking sheet. Keep them warm in the oven until you're ready to use them.

In a large saucepan over medium heat, melt the butter. When it foams, stir in the maple syrup, ginger, and the remaining ¼ teaspoon of salt. Cook for 1 minute. Add the hazelnuts, and stir to coat. Cook for 1 minute.

Add the quinoa to the pot, and toss to combine. Turn the heat to medium-low, cover the pot, and heat the quinoa, stirring occasionally, until it's steaming, 5 to 10 minutes. If the quinoa seems to be drying out, add water a tablespoon at a time. Stir in the parsley, and season with salt and pepper.

Place a squash half, cut-side up, on each of 4 plates. Scoop about 1 cup of quinoa on top of each squash half in a mound. Serve immediately.

To store, gently pat down the quinoa and tightly wrap each serving in plastic wrap. Refrigerate or freeze in airtight containers or zip-top bags. The stuffed squash will keep for 4 days in the refrigerator and 2 months in the freezer.

Per serving: Calories 513; Fat 22g; Saturated Fat 9g; Sodium 533mg; Protein 11g; Fiber 8g

Quinoa California Rolls

SERVES 4 / PREP: 1 HOUR / COOK: 30 TO 45 SECONDS

Making sushi isn't difficult once you've had a little practice. Depending on where you live, the real challenge might be finding a few of the ingredients: wasabi paste; pickled ginger; the seaweed sheets, called nori; and the artificial crab sticks used here. If your supermarket doesn't carry them and there's no Asian market nearby, you can order them online.

2 tablespoons rice vinegar

2 tablespoons sugar

1 teaspoon salt

2 cups cooked quinoa, warm

2 sheets nori, cut crosswise

⅓ cup toasted sesame seeds

1 medium avocado, cut into ¼-inch-thick slices and sprinkled with the juice of ½ lemon

1 small cucumber, peeled, seeded, and cut into matchsticks

4 artificial crab sticks (see ingredient tip), pulled lengthwise into strips

4 teaspoons wasabi paste

16 slices pickled ginger

Tamari, for dipping

In a small, microwave-safe bowl, stir together the rice vinegar, sugar, and salt. Microwave the mixture on high for 30 to 45 seconds. Stir to dissolve the sugar and salt. Allow to cool until it's safe to handle.

In a large bowl, toss together the quinoa and the vinegar mixture. Toss and fold for several minutes to make sure all the quinoa is coated with the vinegar.

Lay a sushi mat (or, alternatively, a clean kitchen towel) on a flat work surface with the flat sides of the slats facing up. Cover the mat (or towel) with a piece of plastic wrap. With dry hands, place a half sheet of nori on the mat, shiny-side up.

Moistening your hands in a small bowl of water, place ½ cup of quinoa on the nori. Using the tips of your fingers, spread the quinoa in an even layer, about ¼-inch deep. Sprinkle a bit more than 1 table-spoon of sesame seeds across the quinoa, and very lightly press in the seeds. Flip over the nori so it is quinoa-side down.

Along the long edge of the nori, place ¼ of the avocado slices in a line about 1½ inches wide. Top with ¼ of the cucumber, then ¼ of the crab sticks. If there seems to be too much filling, remove a little of each ingredient.

With your thumbs under the mat at the filled edge, gently roll the nori over the filling. Roll tightly enough that the filling is tucked in snugly when the quinoa on the outside edge of the roll first touches the inner nori. Continue rolling the quinoa-covered nori away from you, gently pushing down so everything stays together, until it's all rolled up. Form the roll into an even cylindrical shape. Cover with a damp cloth and set aside.

Repeat this process with the remaining nori, quinoa, sesame seeds, avocado, cucumber, and crab, changing the plastic wrap between rolls.

When all the rolls are complete, use a very sharp knife to slice each in half. Cut each half in half, then cut each quarter in half. Each roll becomes 8 pieces.

Arrange 8 pieces of sushi on each of 4 plates. Add 1 teaspoon of wasabi to each plate, and garnish with 4 slices of pickled ginger. Serve with a small dipping bowl at each place setting. Place a cruet of tamari on the table to fill the bowls. Provide chopsticks for each diner.

Storing sushi is not recommended. If it's not eaten right away, the nori will become soggy and tough. But if necessary, refrigerate the sushi in a tightly sealed container. Do not freeze.

Tip The crab sticks, also known as "krab," in California rolls contain not a morsel of crab. They're a processed combination of white fish such as pollock and sea bream, which is mixed into a paste and cooked. *Surimi,* as these products are called in Japan, are widely used in Japanese cuisine. It takes many different forms, including *kanikawa,* the stringy imitation crabmeat used in California rolls. It's sold in the refrigerated section.

Per serving: Calories 362; Fat 19g; Saturated Fat 3g; Sodium 849mg; Protein 11g; Fiber 7g

Shrimp Scampi
on Quinoa "Polenta"

KIDS, 30-MINUTE

SERVES 4 / PREP: 10 MINUTES / COOK: 10 MINUTES

There's not a tomato to be found in this recipe, but shrimp scampi is a staple in the kind of Italian-American red-sauce restaurants that have red-and-white checkered tablecloths. Polenta-style creamy quinoa takes the place of the typical pasta, and toasted quinoa is the topping instead of breadcrumbs. Rest assured that the alcohol in the wine cooks off long before the shrimp's done.

5 tablespoons unsalted butter, divided

3 cups cooked quinoa

¼ cup milk

3 tablespoons grated Parmesan cheese

Salt

Freshly ground black pepper

1 pound jumbo shrimp (about 24 pieces), peeled and deveined

¼ cup extra-virgin olive oil

4 garlic cloves, minced

1 teaspoon chopped fresh oregano

1 cup dry white wine or vermouth (not cooking wine)

8 teaspoons Toasted Quinoa (page 36)

2 tablespoons chopped parsley

4 lemon wedges

In a medium saucepan over medium heat, melt 1 tablespoon of butter. Add the quinoa, milk, and Parmesan, and stir to combine. Season with salt and pepper. Warm the mixture until it's steaming, about 2 minutes. Cover the pot and set aside.

Wash the shrimp, pat them dry, and season with salt and pepper.

In a large sauté pan over medium-high heat, melt the remaining 4 tablespoons of butter in the olive oil. Add the garlic and sauté until it just starts to sizzle, about 30 seconds. Stir in the oregano and wine, and simmer for 2 minutes. Add the shrimp and sauté, flipping them occasionally, until they just turn pink and opaque, about 2 minutes.

Portion the Toasted Quinoa among 4 plates. Using tongs, transfer the shrimp onto the quinoa; then drizzle the sauce from the pan over the top. Garnish each plate with the toasted quinoa and parsley. Serve immediately with a lemon wedge.

To store, refrigerate the quinoa and shrimp separately in airtight containers or zip-top bags. The shrimp will keep for 1 day and the quinoa for 3 days in the refrigerator. You can freeze the quinoa; it will keep for 3 months.

Tip   **Shrimp scampi is traditionally served over spaghetti, and you can indeed serve it with any pasta shape. It's also good on its own, with some gluten-free bread on the side to swipe up the sauce.**

Per serving: Calories 670; Fat 36g; Saturated Fat 14g; Sodium 525mg; Protein 39g; Fiber 4g

Crispy-Skin Barramundi
on Saffron Quinoa

SINGLETONS

SERVES 4 / PREP: 20 TO 25 MINUTES / COOK: 40 MINUTES

This Mediterranean-flavored recipe using South American quinoa features a fish from Southeast Asia. Similar to snapper, grouper, and striped bass (all of which you can use here), barramundi has firm, flaky white flesh with a mild flavor. But unlike other white-fleshed fish, barramundi packs as much omega-3s as salmon.

2 plum tomatoes, halved lengthwise

5 tablespoons extra-virgin olive oil, divided

⅓ teaspoon salt, plus more for seasoning

4 cups cooked quinoa, warm

2 pinches saffron, soaked in hot water for 5 minutes

3 garlic cloves, sliced thin

½ cup slivered Kalamata olives, divided

¼ cup toasted pine nuts

Freshly ground black pepper

4 thick fillets barramundi, about 1½ pounds total

2 plum tomatoes, seeded and slivered lengthwise

4 teaspoons chopped chives

¼ cup pea shoots

Preheat the oven to 450°F.

Cover a rimmed baking sheet with foil. Place the halved plum tomatoes on the pan, drizzle them with 2 teaspoons of olive oil, and sprinkle with the salt. Toss to coat the tomatoes; then arrange the tomatoes cut-side up. Roast them until they are soft (not mushy) and somewhat caramelized, about 30 minutes. Remove from the oven and allow them to cool until they're safe to handle.

Cut each tomato half in half lengthwise and then crosswise. Return them to the baking sheet and set aside.

In a large bowl, mix the quinoa with the saffron water and threads, tossing well to combine evenly. Set aside.

■——→

In a large saucepan over medium-high heat, heat 2 tablespoons of olive oil. Add the garlic and sauté until it just starts to turn a bit golden, about 30 seconds. Turn down the heat to low, and add the roasted tomatoes with their oil and juices, the quinoa, ¼ cup of olives, and the pine nuts. Stir and toss to heat through and combine. Season with salt and pepper. Cover the pot and set it aside.

Wash the barramundi fillets, and pat them dry. Using a very sharp knife, score the skin with 3 or 4 small parallel cuts that go through the skin, but not into the flesh. Season all over with salt and pepper.

In a large sauté pan over medium-high heat, heat 1 tablespoon of olive oil. When the oil's very hot but not smoking, place 2 fillets in the pan skin-side down. Sear until the skin is crispy and brown, 2 to 3 minutes. Flip the fillets, and cook them until barely cooked through, 1 to 2 minutes. Transfer the fillets to a plate, cover, and set aside. Repeat this step for the remaining 2 fillets.

Put 1 cup of quinoa on each of 4 plates. Rest a fillet on each quinoa bed. Garnish the plate with the remaining ¼ cup of olives and the slivered tomatoes, chives, and pea shoots. Serve immediately.

To store, refrigerate the quinoa and fish in separate airtight containers. The fish will keep for 1 day and the quinoa for 2. Do not freeze.

Per serving: Calories 586; Fat 30g; Saturated Fat 4g; Sodium 548mg; Protein 35g; Fiber 7g

Quinoa Penne Puttanesca with Tuna

SERVES 4 / PREP: 15 MINUTES / COOK: 15 MINUTES

Quick and easy to prepare with stuff you probably already have in your pantry, this aromatic Southern Italian dish shows off some of the region's signature ingredients. The tuna is a recent twist (and you can omit it if you prefer), but puttanesca has always relied on pungent anchovies. You don't have to use them, but give them a try: They melt and disappear into the sauce, adding a depth of flavor and a kick of umami.

4 tablespoons extra-virgin olive oil, divided
4 garlic cloves, minced
4 or more anchovy fillets (optional)
¾ cup roughly chopped pitted Kalamata, Gaeta, or other black olives
3½ cups Marinara Sauce (page 42)
2 teaspoons chopped fresh oregano
½ teaspoon crushed red pepper flakes
Salt
Freshly ground black pepper
½ pound fresh tuna fillet
3 tablespoons capers, rinsed and drained
1 pound quinoa penne, cooked to al dente
½ cup freshly grated Parmesan cheese, plus more for serving
¼ cup chopped fresh flat-leaf parsley
1 teaspoon freshly grated lemon zest

In a large saucepan over medium-high heat, heat 3 tablespoons of olive oil. Add the garlic and sauté until it sizzles, about 30 seconds. Add the anchovies (if using), and mash them with the back of a spoon. Add the olives and sauté until they sizzle, about 30 seconds. Pour in the Marinara Sauce, and stir in the oregano and red pepper. Season with salt and pepper. Bring the sauce to a boil; then turn down the heat to medium and simmer for 10 minutes, stirring occasionally.

Wash the tuna, and pat it dry. Remove the stripe of dark-red flesh. Cutting across the grain, slice the fish into ½-inch strips, then cut each strip in half crosswise. Season the fish with salt and pepper.

In a large sauté pan over high heat, heat the remaining 1 tablespoon of olive oil to just short of smoking. Add the tuna and sauté it quickly, stirring and tossing the fish, until the pieces are seared outside and pink inside, about 2 minutes. The fish will finish cooking in the sauce.

Transfer the tuna to the pot with the sauce, add the capers, and stir. Turn the heat to low. Add the pasta to the sauce; stir and toss to combine. (If your saucepan isn't large enough for everything, you can plate the pasta and spoon the sauce on top.) Just before serving, stir in the Parmesan, parsley, and lemon zest.

Spoon the puttanesca into shallow bowls, and serve with additional Parmesan on the side.

Store the pasta and sauce separately. Toss the pasta with a scant amount of olive oil to prevent it sticking together. Refrigerate the pasta and sauce in separate airtight containers or zip-top bags. They will keep for 2 days. Do not freeze.

Per serving: Calories 941; Fat 34g; Saturated Fat 7g; Sodium 2,218mg; Protein 37g; Fiber 15g

Cheesy Quinoa-Zucchini Bake

KIDS, LARGE GROUPS, VEGETARIANS, MAKE AHEAD

SERVES 4 / PREP: 15 MINUTES / COOK: 40 MINUTES

Ah, the miracle that is cheese. This casserole is one sneaky way to get kids to eat their vegetables, and to slip in nutritious quinoa under the radar. Don't pretend you're not susceptible to the charms of cheese, either: You'll be heating up this bake for lunch every chance you get.

Cooking spray
1½ cups shredded Gruyère, divided
1½ cups orange cheddar, divided
2 tablespoons Quinoa Flour (page 37) or store bought
2 tablespoons extra-virgin olive oil
3 garlic cloves, thinly sliced
1 cup diced zucchini
1 cup halved cherry tomatoes
1 cup steamed broccoli florets
4 cups cooked quinoa, cooled
Salt
Freshly ground black pepper
1 medium zucchini, thinly sliced

Preheat the oven to 350°F.

Grease a large casserole dish with cooking spray.

In a medium bowl, toss together the Gruyère, cheddar, and Quinoa Flour. Set aside.

In a large sauté pan over medium-high heat, heat the olive oil. Add the garlic, and sauté until it just starts to sizzle, about 30 seconds. Add the diced zucchini and the tomatoes, and sauté until both are tender and the tomatoes have started to melt, about 5 minutes. Add the broccoli, and stir to coat with the oil. Allow the vegetables to cool until they're safe to handle.

In a large bowl, toss together the quinoa and half of the cheese mixture. Add the sautéed vegetables, and toss to combine. Season with salt and pepper.

→

Transfer the quinoa-vegetable combination to the casserole dish, and spread it out evenly. Layer the zucchini slices over the top, overlapping their edges so they completely cover the quinoa. Evenly spread the remaining cheese over the top. Put on the casserole lid or cover snugly with foil.

Bake the casserole for 20 minutes; then remove the cover. Continue baking until the cheese inside is melted and the cheese on top is bubbling, about 15 minutes.

Portion the hot casserole onto plates and serve.

To store, tightly cover the casserole dish and refrigerate; it will keep for 3 days. To freeze, transfer it to an airtight container; it will keep for 2 months in the freezer.

Tip **If you like your melted cheese brown, slip the finished casserole under the broiler for a minute or two.**

Per serving: Calories 659; Fat 37g; Saturated Fat 18g; Sodium 405mg; Protein 33g; Fiber 7g

Peruvian Green Chicken

LARGE GROUPS, MEAT LOVERS, MAKE AHEAD, ONE POT

SERVES 4 / PREP: 12 MINUTES / COOK: 55 MINUTES

Most countries have their own version of chicken-and-rice. In Spanish-speaking countries, it's called *arroz con pollo,* and Peru has its own special *verde* (green) twist. In this recipe, rice bows out for one of Peru's most important crops: quinoa.

1 bunch (2½ to 3 ounces) cilantro, leaves and stems coarsely chopped

3 tablespoons water

1 pound boneless, skinless chicken thighs, fat trimmed away

1 teaspoon ground cumin

½ teaspoon salt, plus more for seasoning

Freshly ground black pepper

2 tablespoons extra-virgin olive oil

4 garlic cloves, minced

1 cup diced onion

1 red bell pepper, chopped

1 cup beer or Chicken Stock

2 cups Chicken Stock (page 40) or store bought

2 cups dry quinoa, rinsed

2 carrots, diced

½ cup frozen peas

Aji criollo (Quinoa Chips with Hot Pepper Dip recipe, page 126)

In a blender, purée the cilantro with the water. Set aside.

Wash the chicken, and pat it dry. Cut the thighs into quarters. Sprinkle all over with the cumin and season with salt and pepper.

In a large saucepan over medium-high heat, heat the olive oil. Add the chicken and cook, turning occasionally, to brown it on all sides, about 5 minutes. Remove it from the pan and set aside.

Turn down the heat to medium. Add the garlic, onion, and bell pepper to the pan and sauté until softened, 4 to 5 minutes.

Turn up the heat to medium-high. Add the beer, Chicken Stock, cilantro purée, and the ½ teaspoon of salt to the pan and stir well. Bring the liquid to a boil, add the quinoa, and stir to combine. Turn the heat down to medium-low.

Add the carrots, and return the browned chicken to the pan. Cover and cook for 15 minutes; then stir and adjust the seasoning with salt and pepper. If the quinoa seems too dry, add a few tablespoons of water. Replace the cover, and cook for 10 more minutes. Stir, and add the peas, adding a little water if needed. Cook for another 10 minutes.

Spoon the quinoa and chicken into bowls, and serve with *aji criollo*.

To store, refrigerate or freeze in an airtight container or zip-top bag. It will keep for 4 days in the refrigerator and 3 months in the freezer.

Per serving: Calories 661; Fat 21g; Saturated Fat 4g; Sodium 826mg; Protein 47g; Fiber 9g

Mixed Quinoa Paella

LARGE GROUPS, MEAT LOVERS, ONE POT

SERVES 4 / PREP: 15 MINUTES / COOK: 1 HOUR, 15 MINUTES

Purists wouldn't think of making paella in anything but a paella pan—a circular, flat-bottomed steel pan with angled walls and handles on opposite sides. They also wouldn't use anything but Spanish bomba variety rice. But quinoa works just as well, and a big, heavy sauté pan does the job.

1 pound boneless chicken thighs

Salt

Freshly ground black pepper

3 tablespoons extra-virgin olive oil

8 ounces fresh (uncooked) chorizo or other smoked sausage, cut crosswise into ½-inch slices

1 medium onion, finely chopped

2 tablespoons chopped pimentos

1 tablespoon minced garlic

¼ teaspoon ground paprika

1 cup dry quinoa, rinsed

1¾ cups Chicken Stock (page 40) or store bought

1 cup canned diced tomatoes

½ cup dry white wine

1 bay leaf, crumbled

Pinch saffron, dissolved in ¼ cup hot water

1¼ pounds (about 12) littleneck or other hard-shell clams, well-scrubbed

1 cup fresh or thawed frozen peas

½ cup chopped fresh flat-leaf parsley

1 lemon, cut into wedges

Preheat the oven to 325°F.

Wash the chicken, pat it dry, and season with salt and pepper.

In a large, ovenproof sauté pan over high heat, heat the olive oil. Add the chicken and fry until it's golden on all sides and cooked through, 12 to 15 minutes. Remove it to a plate and set aside.

Put the chorizo in the pan, and cook until it's browned all over, 5 or 6 minutes. Add the onion, pimentos, and garlic and sauté until the onion is soft, about 5 minutes. Stir in the paprika.

Add the quinoa to the pan, and stir to coat it well with the oil. Pour in the Chicken Stock, tomatoes, wine, bay leaf, and saffron water. Season with salt and pepper. Bring the liquid to a boil; then reduce the heat to low. Cover the pan and cook until the quinoa is tender and the liquid is absorbed, about 15 minutes.

Remove the pan from the heat. Push the chicken pieces down into the quinoa so they are surrounded. Distribute the clams throughout the pan, pushing them into the quinoa with their hinges down and opening edges up.

Put the pan in the oven and bake, uncovered, for 20 minutes. Remove the pan from the oven, and stir in the peas. Cover the pan, and let the paella rest for 10 minutes.

Spoon the paella into shallow bowls. Garnish each with the parsley, and serve with lemon wedges on the side.

To store, refrigerate it in an airtight container. The paella will keep for 1 day.

 Tip **Saffron is costly, so if you wish, substitute ¼ teaspoon turmeric.**

Per serving: Calories 908; Fat 53g; Saturated Fat 15g; Sodium 1,676mg; Protein 44g; Fiber 8g

Oven–"Fried" Chicken Fingers
with Honey–Mustard Dip

KIDS, LARGE GROUPS, MEAT LOVERS, MAKE AHEAD

SERVES 4 / PREP: 40 MINUTES / COOK: 30 MINUTES

Quinoa brings new life to an old favorite, giving the crust on these chicken fingers a pleasing nubbly texture. Done in the oven, they're doubly healthy for you and just as crave-busting as their unhealthy fried cousins. For dipping, don't stop at honey-mustard: barbecue sauce, Buffalo sauce, chipotle mayo—whatever sounds good to you *is* good.

For the dip
¼ cup honey
¼ cup yellow mustard
2 tablespoons mayonnaise

For the fingers
Extra-virgin olive oil, for greasing and drizzling
1½ to 2 pounds boneless, skinless chicken breasts
2 cups Quinoa Flour (page 37) or store bought
1 teaspoon ground paprika
4 eggs, lightly beaten
3 cups cooked quinoa
1 teaspoon salt, plus more for seasoning
1 teaspoon freshly ground black pepper, plus more for seasoning

To make the dip In a small bowl, mix together the honey, mustard, and mayonnaise. Set aside.

To make the fingers Preheat the oven to 375°F.

Line a baking sheet with parchment paper, and lightly grease it with olive oil.

Wash the chicken, and pat it dry. Slice the breasts lengthwise into ¾-inch-thick fingers. Set them aside.

In a small bowl, mix the Quinoa Flour with the paprika. Transfer it to a shallow, wide bowl.

Put the eggs in a second shallow, wide bowl.

In a large bowl, toss the quinoa with the salt and pepper. Transfer half of the quinoa into a third shallow, wide bowl, and set the rest aside.

Dredge a chicken finger in the flour, lightly coating it all over. Shake off the excess flour; then dip the finger into the egg to coat it all over. Transfer it to the bowl of quinoa, and press the grains onto the chicken so they stick on every side. Lay the finger on the baking sheet. Repeat this process for all the fingers,

replenishing the quinoa as needed. Leave space between the fingers on the baking sheet. Just before putting them in the oven, drizzle them with a little bit of oil on both sides.

Bake until the chicken is cooked through, about 30 minutes.

Serve on a platter with the honey-mustard dip on the side.

To store, refrigerate the dip in an airtight container. Refrigerate or freeze the fingers in an airtight container or zip-top bag. The fingers and dip will keep for 3 days in the refrigerator; the fingers will keep for 2 months in the freezer.

Tip **The quinoa crust on these tenders lends itself to endless variations. Try tossing the quinoa with 1 cup of grated Parmesan; 1 or 2 teaspoons of chopped herbs, such as chives or parsley; 1 teaspoon of garlic powder, onion powder, or cayenne; or just about anything else.**

Per serving: Calories 1,029; Fat 31g; Saturated Fat 7g; Sodium 1,077mg; Protein 86g; Fiber 9g

Irresistible Turkey Meatloaf

This meatloaf is addictive. In this straightforward recipe, the quinoa's hidden, but it's got a big presence, adding body to what can sometimes be a mushy dish. If you're in the mood, swap out turkey for 85 percent lean beef, or pull out your own meatloaf tricks and have at it.

For the sauce
¼ cup ketchup
1 tablespoon cider vinegar
½ teaspoon brown sugar
½ teaspoon dry mustard
Dash hot sauce

For the meatloaf
1 tablespoon extra-virgin olive oil
1 cup chopped onion
2 cups cooked quinoa
1 pound ground turkey
2 eggs
⅓ cup ketchup
⅓ cup minced flat-leaf parsley
4 teaspoons Worcestershire sauce
1¼ teaspoons salt
¾ teaspoon ground mustard
½ teaspoon freshly ground black pepper

To make the sauce In a small bowl, mix together the ketchup, vinegar, sugar, mustard, and hot sauce. Set aside.

To make the meatloaf Preheat the oven to 350°F.

In a large saucepan over medium-high heat, heat the olive oil. Add the onion and sauté until it softens, about 5 minutes. Allow it to cool until it's safe to handle.

In a large bowl, using your hands, mix together the quinoa, turkey, eggs, ketchup, parsley, Worcestershire sauce, salt, mustard, and pepper until well combined.

Spread the meat mixture in an ungreased loaf pan, or shape it into a loaf on a rimmed, parchment-lined baking sheet. Spread half of the sauce over the top of the meatloaf.

Bake the meatloaf for 45 minutes; then spread the remaining half of the sauce over the meatloaf. Bake until the meat is no longer pink in the center and the internal temperature reaches 160°F, about 15 minutes.

Let the meatloaf rest for 10 minutes before cutting it into 1-inch-thick slices and serving.

To store, refrigerate or freeze in an airtight container. The meatloaf will keep for 3 days in the refrigerator and 3 months in the freezer.

Per serving: Calories 454; Fat 21g; Saturated Fat 4g; Sodium 1,329mg; Protein 39g; Fiber 3g

Mango–Chicken Quinoa with Cashews

SINGLETONS, MAKE AHEAD, MEAT LOVERS

SERVES 4 / PREP: 15 MINUTES / COOK: 25 MINUTES

A combination of sweet and savory flavors and soft and crunchy textures make this chicken dish anything but ho-hum. With the aromas of coconuts and herbs, it's a warm-weather dish that you can serve either warm or cool. It's also delicious made with shrimp.

1 cup unsweetened coconut milk
1 cup water
1 cup dry quinoa, rinsed
½ teaspoon salt, plus more for seasoning
¼ teaspoon sugar
1 pound boneless, skinless chicken breast
2 teaspoons curry powder
2 tablespoons extra-virgin olive oil
2 garlic cloves, minced
½ cup diced red onion
1½ teaspoons chopped fresh mint
1½ teaspoons chopped fresh basil
1 mango, cubed
1 cup unsalted, roasted cashew halves

In a medium saucepan over high heat, bring the coconut milk and water to a boil. Add the quinoa, salt, and sugar. Give the mixture a stir, and bring it back to a boil. Turn the heat to low, and cover the pan. Simmer the quinoa 15 minutes. Remove from the heat and set aside, covered, for 10 minutes.

Wash the chicken, and pat it dry. Cut each breast into several large chunks of roughly the same size. Sprinkle them with the curry powder and season with salt.

In a large sauté pan over medium-high heat, heat the olive oil. Add the garlic and sauté until it just starts to sizzle, about 30 seconds. Add the chicken and sauté, turning occasionally, until it's browned and cooked through, about 5 minutes depending on the size of the chunks. Set aside.

Transfer the quinoa to a large bowl, and toss it with the onion, mint, and basil. Gently toss in the mango.

Scoop the quinoa into 4 bowls. Arrange the chicken on top, scatter the cashews over each bowl, and serve.

To store, refrigerate or freeze the quinoa and chicken in separate airtight containers or zip-top bags. They will keep for 2 days in the refrigerator and 1 month in the freezer.

Per serving: Calories 820; Fat 47g; Saturated Fat 18g; Sodium 442mg; Protein 51g; Fiber 7g

Pork Fried "Rice"

SERVES 4 / PREP: 2 MINUTES / COOK: 12 MINUTES

About as fast and easy as it gets, this recipe is a perfect way to use up leftover pork. With just a few other ingredients, you can prepare a home-cooked meal in just a few minutes at the end of a hectic day. This is a kitchen sink dish: Leave out or add in any ingredients you please.

For the sauce
1 tablespoon hot water
1 teaspoon honey
1 teaspoon sesame or peanut oil
1 teaspoon Chinese Shaoxing wine or dry sherry (optional)
4 teaspoons tamari
¼ teaspoon freshly ground black pepper

For the fried rice
2 tablespoons canola oil
½ cup chopped onion
2 cups cooked pork (any kind), diced
3 cups cold cooked quinoa
1 cup mung bean sprouts
2 eggs, scrambled
2 scallions, chopped
Salt

To make the sauce In a small bowl, mix together the water, honey, sesame oil, wine, tamari, and pepper. Set aside.

To make the fried rice In a large sauté pan over medium-high heat, heat the canola oil. Add the onion and sauté until it softens, about 5 minutes. Add the pork and stir for 1 minute. Mix in the quinoa; then add half of the sauce. Toss and stir to coat all the ingredients with the sauce. Sauté, stirring often, for 5 to 6 minutes.

Add the bean sprouts, eggs, and scallions. Toss everything together and cook for 2 minutes, stirring often. Season with salt.

Scoop the quinoa into bowls, and serve with the remaining sauce on the side.

To store, refrigerate or freeze in an airtight container or zip-top bag. The quinoa will keep for 3 days in the refrigerator and 3 months in the freezer.

Per serving: Calories 797; Fat 33g; Saturated Fat 8g; Sodium 464mg; Protein 39g; Fiber 9g

Pork Tenderloin
with Sweet-and-Sour Apples

MEAT LOVERS, ONE POT

SERVES 4 / PREP: 20 MINUTES / COOK: 50 MINUTES

Ideal for the depths of winter, this soul-warming meal takes its cues from Central Europe. The subtle nuttiness of the quinoa noodles is a delightful complement to the tangy apples and mellow pork. Note: Pork tenderloin is extremely lean and can easily overcook and become dry. Monitor the roasting process closely.

1½ pounds pork tenderloin, silver skin trimmed off

3 tablespoons extra-virgin olive oil, divided

1 teaspoon salt, plus more for seasoning

½ teaspoon freshly ground black pepper, plus more for seasoning

1 large onion, cut into ½-inch wedges

2 Rome or Braeburn apples, cored and cut into ½-inch wedges

½ cup unsweetened apple juice

¼ cup apple cider vinegar

1 tablespoon minced fresh rosemary

1 cup Chicken Stock (page 40) or store bought

1 tablespoon cold unsalted butter

1 pound quinoa fettuccine, cooked to al dente and tossed with butter to prevent sticking

Preheat the oven to 425°F.

Wash the tenderloin, and pat it dry. Brush the tenderloin with 1 tablespoon of olive oil, and sprinkle it all over with the salt and pepper.

In a large, ovenproof sauté pan over medium-high heat, heat 1 tablespoon of olive oil until it shimmers. Place the tenderloin in the pan and cook, turning occasionally, until it's browned on all sides, about 10 minutes. Transfer the tenderloin to a plate and set aside.

Add the remaining 1 tablespoon of olive oil to the pan, and heat until it shimmers. Add the onion wedges and sauté until they start to brown at the edges, about 8 minutes. Add the apples and sauté until they are golden on each side, about 8 minutes. Stir in the apple juice and vinegar. Season with salt and pepper.

Sprinkle the rosemary all over the tenderloin, patting it so it sticks to the meat. Place the tenderloin in the pan on top of the onion and apples.

Bake until the internal temperature is 145°F to 150°F, about 10 to 15 minutes. Turn off the oven and transfer the tenderloin to a baking dish, leaving the onion and apples in the pan. Cover the dish tightly, and put it in the oven to stay warm.

Return the sauté pan to the stove over medium-high heat, and add the Chicken Stock. Bring the liquid to a rapid simmer and cook until it's reduced by half, 3 to 5 minutes. Add the butter and stir while it melts into the sauce.

Remove the tenderloin from the oven, and cut it crosswise into 1-inch slices.

Lay a bed of fettuccine on each of 4 plates. Arrange several slices of pork on the noodles; then top with the apples and onion. Spoon the sauce over the plates.

To store, refrigerate the noodles and pork, onion, and apples in separate airtight containers. They will keep for 3 days in the refrigerator. Do not freeze.

Per serving: Calories 793; Fat 24g; Saturated Fat 6g; Sodium 904mg; Protein 54g; Fiber 8g

Barbecue Stuffed Pork Chops

KIDS, MEAT LOVERS

SERVES 4 / PREP: 25 MINUTES / COOK: 35 TO 60 MINUTES

You can make these chops in the oven or on the grill. They grill up just like regular barbecued chops, taking just a little longer than if done in the oven. Grill them over high heat for 1 minute per side, then 5 minutes per side over low heat. Be gentle when you flip them so the stuffing doesn't make an escape.

Tip **For some extra flavor, prepare the recipe with cold-smoked pork chops.** Hot-smoked chops come already cooked, so they won't work.

3 cups cooked quinoa
1 cup fresh or thawed frozen corn kernels
1 red bell pepper, finely diced
1 jalapeño, minced (optional)
1 tablespoon canola oil
Salt
Freshly ground black pepper
4 (1½-inch-thick) bone-in pork chops
2 cups barbecue sauce

Preheat the oven to 350°F.

Lightly grease a 9-by-13-inch baking dish.

In a large bowl, toss together the quinoa, corn, bell pepper, jalapeño (if using), and canola oil. Season with salt and pepper. Set aside.

If you like, trim the fat from the pork chops. Cut a pocket into each chop all the way back to the bone; make a sizeable pocket, but leave enough meat on either side so the walls are sturdy. Season the chops inside and out with salt and pepper.

Spoon the quinoa mixture into the pockets. The meat will shrink a bit as it cooks, so don't overfill the chops or pack the stuffing tightly. There will be leftover stuffing; set it aside. Close the pockets with toothpicks.

Spread a thin layer of barbecue sauce in the baking dish. Add the chops to the dish, and brush on barbecue sauce to your taste.

Cover the dish with foil, tenting it if necessary so it doesn't touch the chops. Bake the chops for 15 minutes; then remove the foil. Continue baking for another 20 minutes. If the meat is 145°F in its center, it is finished cooking. The stuffing also should be 145°F. Continue cooking until it reaches this temperature. Remove the baking dish from the oven, and allow the chops to rest for 5 minutes.

Warm up the remaining quinoa and barbecue sauce. Spoon a bed of quinoa onto each of 4 plates, and serve with the sauce on the side.

To store, refrigerate or freeze the chops, quinoa, and sauce in separate airtight containers. They will keep for 2 days in the refrigerator and 1 month in the freezer.

Per serving: Calories 787; Fat 35g; Saturated Fat 11g; Sodium 1,521mg; Protein 33g; Fiber 5g

All-American Pork Chop Casserole

KIDS, LARGE GROUPS, MEAT LOVERS, MAKE AHEAD

SERVES 4 / PREP: 10 MINUTES / COOK: 66 TO 78 MINUTES

Here's an update on solid fare from the heartland. Replacing the ubiquitous potatoes, quinoa lightens things up and gives the dish a lot more texture. This casserole is an ideal choice for family gatherings.

4 bone-in pork chops
Salt
Freshly ground black pepper
1 tablespoon canola oil
½ cup chopped onion
¼ cup dry white wine or water
1 (11-ounce) can condensed cream of mushroom soup
1 cup milk
4 teaspoons chopped fresh parsley
4 cups cooked quinoa
1½ cups shredded cheddar cheese

Preheat the oven to 375°F.

Season both sides of the pork chops with salt and pepper. In a large sauté pan over medium-high heat, heat the canola oil. Put the chops in the pan and brown them on both sides, 3 to 5 minutes per side. Transfer the chops to a plate and set aside.

Add the onion to the pan and sauté until it softens, about 5 minutes. Transfer the onion to a large bowl and set aside.

Add the wine to the pan, and bring it to a simmer. Scrape any brown bits off the bottom and sides of the pan, and reduce the wine by half, about 3 minutes. Add the pan juice to the mixing bowl.

Transfer any juices that have escaped from the pork to the mixing bowl. Whisk in the soup, milk, and parsley. Season with salt and pepper and set aside.

Spread the quinoa in an ungreased 9-by-13-inch baking dish. Pour the soup mixture evenly over the quinoa. Place the pork chops on top, and scatter the cheese over the dish. Cover the dish with foil, and bake for 30 minutes. Remove the foil and bake until the casserole edges are bubbly and the pork reaches an internal temperature of 145°F, 20 to 30 minutes.

Place a pork chop on each of four plates. Spoon the quinoa onto the plates beside the chops, and serve immediately.

To store, refrigerate the casserole in an airtight container. It will keep for 3 days in the refrigerator.

Per serving: Calories 904; Fat 44g; Saturated Fat 22g; Sodium 918mg; Protein 48g; Fiber 5g

Shepherd's Pie
with Quinoa "Mashed Potatoes"

LARGE GROUPS, MEAT LOVERS, MAKE AHEAD, ONE POT

SERVES 4 / PREP: 25 MINUTES / COOK: 1 HOUR

It doesn't get any more British than this casserole. Likely originating from eighteenth-century northern England, it would have been a tasty weapon against the perpetually cold, wet weather. If you swap out the lamb for beef, this becomes a "cottage pie."

2 tablespoons extra-virgin olive oil

1½ pounds lamb shoulder, fat trimmed, diced into ½-inch cubes

1 cup diced carrot

½ cup chopped onion

1 teaspoon minced garlic

1 tablespoon water

2 tablespoons Quinoa Flour (page 37) or store bought

2 cups Chicken Stock (page 40) or store bought

1½ cups fresh or thawed frozen peas

1 tablespoon chopped fresh thyme leaves

1 tablespoon minced fresh rosemary leaves

Salt

Freshly ground black pepper

3 cups Quinoa "Mashed Potatoes" (page 98)

1 tablespoon chopped flat-leaf parsley

Preheat the oven to 375°F.

In a large sauté pan over medium-high heat, heat the olive oil. Add the lamb, and brown it on all sides, about 5 minutes. Remove the lamb to a bowl and set aside.

Add the carrot, onion, and garlic to the pan, and sauté about 5 minutes. Add the water and scrape up any brown bits. Stir in the Quinoa Flour, and cook for 2 minutes. Stir in the Chicken Stock, peas, thyme, and rosemary. Season with salt and pepper. Turn down the heat to medium, cover and cook for 15 minutes.

Pour the stew into a 9-by-9-inch baking dish. Cover with the Quinoa "Mashed Potatoes." Run a fork around the surface to create ridges. Bake until crisp and brown and the filling is bubbling, 30 to 35 minutes. Remove the pie from the oven, and let it sit for 15 minutes before serving.

Portion the pie out onto 4 plates, garnish each with the parsley, and serve.

The pie will keep for 4 days in the refrigerator and 2 months in the freezer.

Per serving: Calories 647; Fat 23g; Saturated Fat 6g; Sodium 876mg; Protein 59g; Fiber 9g

Prosciutto-Wrapped Chicken Roulade

LARGE GROUPS, MEAT LOVERS, MAKE AHEAD

SERVES 4 / PREP: 35 MINUTES / COOK: 30 TO 35 MINUTES

This stylish dish is perfect for special occasions, whether a romantic evening *à deux* or a Kentucky Derby party. It's a beautiful meal alongside a simply dressed salad, or an eye-catching hors d'oeuvre accompanied by Parmesan crisps.

For the filling
2 tablespoons extra-virgin olive oil
2 garlic cloves, thinly sliced
3 cups cooked quinoa
⅓ cup chopped sun-dried tomatoes
2 tablespoons chopped oil-cured black olives
4 teaspoons chopped fresh basil
Salt
Freshly ground black pepper

Tip To turn this into a vegan treat, replace the chicken and prosciutto with thin slices of eggplant. Make the sauce with Vegetable Stock (Chicken Stock substitution tip, page 41), and leave out the butter.

For the roulades
2 tablespoons extra-virgin olive oil, plus more for brushing
4 (6- to 8-ounce) boneless, skinless chicken breasts
Salt
Freshly ground black pepper
4 thin slices prosciutto

For the sauce
½ cup dry white wine
½ cup Chicken Stock (page 40) or store bought
2 tablespoons freshly squeezed lemon juice
1 tablespoon cold unsalted butter
Salt
Freshly ground black pepper
4 sprigs fresh basil

To make the filling Heat the oil in a large sauté pan over medium-high heat. Add the garlic and sauté until it just starts to sizzle, about 30 seconds. Add the quinoa, tomatoes, and olives and cook, stirring often, for 3 minutes. Transfer the filling to a bowl, and toss in the basil. Season with salt and pepper. Set aside to cool until it's safe to handle.

▶

To make the roulades Preheat the oven to 450°F.

Line a baking sheet with parchment and brush it with oil.

Wash the chicken, and pat it dry. With the flat end of a tenderizing mallet, a rolling pin, or a large jar, pound the breasts into fillets about ¼-inch thick.

Brush both sides of the fillets with olive oil and season with salt and pepper. Lay them on the baking sheet in a single layer. Spoon a little less than 1 cup of the filling onto each, arranging it in a line along the lengthwise center of the fillet. Flip one long edge of the fillet over the filling, and roll up the chicken like a jelly roll, pressing lightly to make the filling hold together. Secure the edge of each roulade with 2 evenly spaced toothpicks.

In a large sauté pan over medium-high heat, heat 2 tablespoons of olive oil. Place the roulades in the pan and cook, turning, until they are brown on all sides, about 10 minutes.

Transfer the roulades to a clean work surface, and allow them to cool until they're safe to handle. Remove the toothpicks. Wrap each roulade in a slice of prosciutto. Tie kitchen twine around each at 1½-inch intervals. Brush the roulades with olive oil.

Put the roulades in a baking pan with a little space in between each roulade. Bake to an internal temperature of 160°F, 5 to 7 minutes. Remove them from the oven, and allow them to rest for 1 or 2 minutes.

To make the sauce Put the sauté pan used to brown the chicken over medium-high heat. Add the wine, Chicken Stock, and lemon juice, and bring the liquid to a boil. Scrape any brown bits from the bottom and sides of the pan, and stir them into the sauce. Cook until the liquid reduces to about ¾ its original volume, about 5 minutes. Add the butter and stir while it melts, incorporating it into the sauce. Season with salt and pepper.

Cut the strings from the roulades, and cut them crosswise into ¾-inch rounds.

Place 1 sliced roulade on each of 4 plates. Spoon the sauce over the top of each, garnish with a sprig of basil, and serve.

To store, refrigerate the roulades and sauce in separate airtight containers or zip-top bags. The sauce will keep for 2 days and the roulades 3 days. Do not freeze.

Per serving: Calories 750; Fat 37g; Saturated Fat 9g; Sodium 1,024mg; Protein 64g; Fiber 4g

Spicy Ginger Steak
with Sesame–Quinoa Noodles

SERVES 4 / PREP: 30 MINUTES, PLUS 1 TO 24 HOURS TO MARINATE / COOK: 7 TO 12 MINUTES

Chinese flavors infuse this zesty steak-and-noodles meal. With a long marinade, the steak is moist and tender, while the sesame noodles are ever so slightly chewy. You can swap out the steak for chicken, with equally delectable results.

For the marinade and steak

5 tablespoons tamari

3 tablespoons rice vinegar

2 tablespoons sesame oil

1 tablespoon grated fresh ginger

1 tablespoon minced garlic

Salt

Freshly ground black pepper

1½-pound top sirloin steak (1-inch thick)

For the sesame sauce and noodles

¼ cup tamari

¼ cup peanut or canola oil

2 tablespoons rice vinegar

2 tablespoons sesame oil

2 tablespoons Chinese sesame paste, tahini, or unsalted smooth peanut butter

2 tablespoons sugar

1 tablespoon grated fresh ginger

2 teaspoons minced garlic

½ teaspoon chile oil or 2 teaspoons chile paste (optional)

Salt

Freshly ground black pepper

4 cups cooked and cooled quinoa spaghetti

½ medium cucumber, peeled, seeded, and cut into matchsticks

2 tablespoons chopped peanuts (optional)

To make the marinade and steak In a medium bowl, whisk together the tamari, vinegar, sesame oil, ginger, and garlic. Season with salt and pepper.

Pour the marinade into a large zip-top bag, and add the steak. Press the air out of the bag, and zip it shut. Massage the marinade into the steak. Put the bag in the refrigerator for at least 1 hour and as long as 24 hours, periodically massaging the steak with the marinade.

Preheat the grill or broiler to medium-high heat.

Remove the steak from the bag, allowing the excess liquid to drip back into the bag. Do not discard the marinade.

Grill or broil the steak, turning once, to the doneness you like (about 5 minutes per side for medium-rare). Transfer the steak to a cutting board, and let it rest for 5 minutes.

While the steak rests, add the reserved marinade into a small saucepan and bring it to a boil. Turn the heat down and simmer for 2 minutes; then remove from the heat.

To make the sesame sauce and noodles In a medium bowl, whisk together the tamari, canola oil, vinegar, sesame oil, sesame paste, sugar, ginger, garlic, and chile oil (if using). The sauce should be the consistency of maple syrup. If it is too thick, add a little water. Season with salt and pepper.

In a large bowl, pour the sauce over the noodles, and toss to coat them thoroughly.

Portion the noodles onto 4 plates, and garnish them with the cucumber and peanuts (if using). Slice thin strips of the steak on the bias, and place them on each plate. Serve with the marinade on the side.

To store, refrigerate the dressed noodles, unsliced steak, and sauce in separate air-tight containers. The meal will keep for 2 days in the refrigerator. Do not freeze.

Tip The Chinese sesame paste used here is made with roasted sesame seeds, while Middle Eastern tahini is made with unroasted seeds. They taste distinctly different from each other and from peanut butter, but tahini and peanut butter are acceptable substitutes for the Chinese standard.

Per serving: Calories 912; Fat 46g; Saturated Fat 9g; Sodium 2,468mg; Protein 63g; Fiber 6g

Carne Asada Burritos

SERVES 4 / PREP: 30 MINUTES, PLUS 1 TO 48 HOURS TO MARINATE / COOK: 30 TO 35 MINUTES

Carne asada ("grilled meat") is a classic Mexican dish served on its own or in tacos and burritos. The burrito is believed to have made its first appearance in the United States in the 1930s, at the El Cholo Spanish Café in Los Angeles. Since then, Americans have put just about anything in their burritos, with *carne asada* a perennial favorite. Here's a new version that uses quinoa in place of the typical rice.

For the carne asada

½ cup freshly squeezed orange juice
¼ cup freshly squeezed lime juice
2 tablespoons tamari
1 tablespoon minced garlic
¼ teaspoon ancho chili or chipotle powder
Salt
Freshly ground black pepper
1 pound skirt steak or flank steak
Canola oil, for brushing

For the pico de gallo

1 cup chopped tomato
⅔ cup chopped onion
1 jalapeño pepper, minced
⅓ cup finely chopped cilantro
2 tablespoons freshly squeezed lime juice
Salt

For the beans

1 (14½-ounce) can low-sodium black beans, drained and rinsed
1 garlic clove, minced
1 teaspoon hot sauce (optional)
½ teaspoon dried *epazote* (Mexican oregano; don't use regular oregano)
¼ teaspoon ground cumin
⅛ teaspoon ground coriander
¼ cup Chicken Stock (page 40) or store bought
Salt
Freshly ground black pepper

For the burritos

4 large, gluten-free flour (not corn) tortillas of your choice (see tip)
2 cups cooked quinoa, hot
1 cup shredded Monterey Jack or cheddar cheese
¼ cup sour cream
4 sprigs fresh cilantro

To make the carne asada In a medium bowl, whisk together the orange and lime juices, tamari, garlic, and chili powder, and season with salt and pepper. Pour the marinade into a large zip-top bag, and add the steak. Press the air out of the bag, and zip it shut. Massage the marinade into the steak. Refrigerate the steak for at least 1 hour and as long as 2 days, periodically massaging the steak with the marinade.

Preheat the grill or broiler to medium-high heat.

Remove the steak from the bag, allowing the excess liquid to drip off. Discard the marinade. Brush the hot grill or broiler with a little canola oil. Grill or broil the steak, turning several times, to either medium or well done, 6 to 8 minutes per side. Transfer the steak to a cutting board and set aside.

To make the pico de gallo In a medium bowl, gently toss together the tomato, onion, jalapeño, cilantro, and lime juice. Season with salt. Set aside in the refrigerator.

To make the beans In a medium saucepan over medium heat, bring the beans, garlic, hot sauce (if using), *epazote*, cumin, coriander, and Chicken Stock to a rapid simmer. Turn the heat to medium-low, and cover the pot. Cook until the beans thicken slightly, about 15 minutes. Leave the beans as is or mash them partway, leaving at least ⅓ of the beans whole. Season with salt and pepper. Cover the pot and set aside.

To make the burritos Chop the steak into bite-size pieces.

Steam the tortillas by wrapping them together in a double layer of damp paper towels, and heat them on high in the microwave for 1 minute. Keep the tortillas wrapped until you're ready to use them.

Remove 1 tortilla from the paper towels, and put it on a flat work surface. Mound about ½ cup of quinoa onto the tortilla in a line a little closer to one edge than the other. Leave about 1½ inches between the ends of the quinoa and the edges of the tortilla. Spoon about ¼ cup of cheese onto the quinoa, then roughly ¼ cup of beans. Arrange about ¼ cup of meat on top of the beans, and finish with 2 or 3 tablespoons of pico de gallo. Don't overfill your burritos. They'll fall apart and become very messy to eat.

Fold the tortilla away from you and over the filling, squeezing gently to slightly compact the filling within. Fold the side edges of the tortilla inward over the ends of the first fold to create a pocket around the filling. Finish rolling the tortilla away from you, compacting the filling as you go. Place the burrito on a warmed plate, cover it with a slightly damp towel, and repeat the rolling process for the remaining 3 burritos.

Put each burrito on a plate, and top it with 1 tablespoon of sour cream. Garnish with a sprig of cilantro, and serve with the extra pico de gallo on the side.

To store, refrigerate the tortillas and fillings in separate airtight containers or zip-top bags. The pico de gallo will keep for 1 day; the tortillas will keep for 2 days; the meat, beans, and cheese will keep for 3 days; and the quinoa will keep for 4 days. You may freeze the meat and beans for up to 2 months and the quinoa for up to 4 months.

Tip Use store-bought tortillas. Mixed-grain, brown rice, teff, and other varieties are readily available in your supermarket. You can make quinoa tortillas with a very simple recipe of quinoa flour and water, but they won't hold up to burrito rolling and eating.

Per serving: Calories 1,088; Fat 36g; Saturated Fat 18g; Sodium 1,246mg; Protein 73g; Fiber 24g

Spot-On Spaghetti & Meatballs

KIDS, LARGE GROUPS, MAKE AHEAD, MEAT LOVERS

SERVES 4 / PREP: 15 MINUTES / COOK: 20 TO 25 MINUTES

What is there to say about spaghetti and meatballs that hasn't already been said? It's a favorite of kids and grown-ups alike, and this gluten-free version packs a nutritious punch. Red quinoa stays under the radar while lightening up the meatballs.

1½ cups cooked red quinoa

1 pound lean ground beef

2 eggs, lightly beaten

¾ cup freshly grated Parmesan cheese, plus more for garnish

½ cup chopped fresh oregano

½ cup chopped fresh parsley

2 garlic cloves, minced

1 teaspoon salt

½ teaspoon freshly ground black pepper

1 pound quinoa spaghetti, cooked al dente

4 cups Marinara Sauce (page 42)

Preheat the oven to 400°F.

Line a rimmed baking sheet with parchment paper.

In a large bowl, using your hands, mix the quinoa, ground beef, eggs, Parmesan, oregano, parsley, garlic, salt, and pepper.

Divide the meat into 12 equal portions, rolling each portion between your palms into a ball; they should each be about 2½ inches in diameter.

Place the meatballs on the baking sheet, spacing them out evenly. Bake until the meatballs are browned and cooked through, 20 to 25 minutes.

Portion the hot spaghetti out into 4 shallow bowls, and top with 3 meatballs each. Pour 1 cup of Marinara Sauce over the top, and serve with grated Parmesan on the side.

To store, refrigerate the spaghetti, meatballs, and marinara in separate airtight containers or zip-top bags. The spaghetti will keep for 2 days; the meatballs and sauce will keep for 4. You can freeze the meatballs and sauce for up to 4 months.

Per serving: Calories 936; Fat 27g; Saturated Fat 9g; Sodium 1,991mg; Protein 60g; Fiber 16g

Slow Cooker Moroccan Beef Tagine

LARGE GROUPS, MEAT LOVERS, SINGLETONS, MAKE AHEAD

SERVES 8 / PREP: 20 MINUTES / COOK: 6 TO 10 HOURS

Quinoa is a superb gluten-free stand-in for couscous, the tiny pasta that's all-important in Moroccan cooking. Tagines are cooked in a unique ceramic vessel that is itself called a tagine. The tagine is an ancient slow cooker, so tagine recipes like this are perfect for your electric slow cooker.

2 tablespoons extra-virgin olive oil, divided
3 garlic cloves, minced
1 large onion, halved and sliced thick
1½ pounds beef chuck, trimmed and cut into 1½-inch cubes
4 medium carrots, chopped
1 large sweet potato, peeled and cut into ½-inch cubes
1 (14.5-ounce) can chickpeas, drained and rinsed
1 (14.5-ounce) can diced tomatoes
1 cup pitted, quartered prunes
1 tablespoon honey
1 cinnamon stick
2 tablespoons *ras el hanout* (see tip)
Salt
Freshly ground black pepper
8 cups cooked quinoa
¼ cup sliced almonds
¼ cup chopped fresh cilantro

Preheat the slow cooker to low or high. On low, the tagine will take 9 to 10 hours to cook; on high it will take 6 to 7 hours.

In a large sauté pan over medium-high heat, heat 1 tablespoon of olive oil. Add the garlic and sauté until it just starts to sizzle, about 30 seconds. Add the onion and brown it well, about 8 minutes. Transfer the garlic and onion to the slow cooker.

Add the remaining 1 tablespoon of olive oil to the pan, and heat until it shimmers. Add the meat, and brown the cubes all over, about 5 minutes. Transfer the meat and juices to the slow cooker.

Add the carrots, sweet potato, chickpeas, tomatoes, prunes, honey, cinnamon stick, and *ras el hanout* to the slow cooker and stir well. Season with salt and pepper.

Cover and cook, without stirring, on low for 9 to 10 hours or high for 6 to 7 hours. The sweet potato should be tender, and the beef should be starting to fall apart. If the stew seems too thin, open the cover and turn the heat up to high. Simmer until the stew is as thick as you like.

Remove the cinnamon stick from the tagine. Portion the quinoa into 4 shallow bowls, and ladle the tagine over the top. Garnish each bowl with the almonds and cilantro, and serve.

To store, refrigerate or freeze the quinoa and tagine in separate airtight containers or zip-top bags. Both will keep for 3 days in the refrigerator; the tagine will keep 2 months in the freezer and the quinoa 4 months.

Tip **Ras el hanout is a spice mix used throughout Moroccan cuisine. The formula varies widely, but if you can't find any, you can mix up a pretty fair version in your kitchen using 2 parts each ground coriander and cumin, and 1 part each ground ginger and turmeric.**

Per serving: Calories 727; Fat 17g; Saturated Fat 3g; Sodium 124 mg; Protein 47g; Fiber 18g

Wine-Braised Short Ribs
over Creamy Parmesan-Garlic Quinoa

MEAT LOVERS, MAKE AHEAD, ONE POT

SERVES 6 / PREP: 20 MINUTES / COOK: 3 HOURS

At once sophisticated and hearty, this dish is braising at its best. It's strictly a winter dish, unless you crank up the AC in warm weather and take an off-season plunge into these layers of richness. Traditionally served over mashed potatoes, short ribs get a snazzier treatment here with creamy, cheesy quinoa.

5 pounds short ribs

Salt

Freshly ground black pepper

2 tablespoons extra-virgin olive oil

1 large onion, chopped

3 medium carrots, chopped

3 celery stalks, chopped

3 garlic cloves, crushed

1 bottle dry red wine, such as Cabernet Sauvignon or Pinot Noir, divided

3 tablespoons tomato paste

4 sprigs fresh thyme

1 bay leaf

3 cups Chicken Stock (page 40) or store bought

Creamy Parmesan-Garlic Quinoa (page 93)

Preheat the oven to 350°F.

Season the short ribs all over with salt and pepper.

In a large Dutch oven or heavy, oven-proof saucepan over medium-high heat, heat the olive oil. Add the ribs, and brown them on all sides, about 8 minutes. Remove the ribs to a plate and set aside.

Add the onion, carrots, celery, and garlic to the pan, and sauté until the onion is browned, about 8 minutes. Turn the heat up to high, and add half the bottle of wine to the pan. Bring it to a boil, and while it boils, scrape any brown bits off the bottom of the pot. Reduce the heat to medium-high, and add the remaining half bottle of wine and the tomato paste, stirring until it dissolves, about 1 minute. Add the thyme and bay leaf to the pan and stir. Return the ribs and their juices to the pot; then stir in the Chicken Stock. Bring the liquid to a boil, cover the pot, and put it in the oven.

Braise the ribs until tender, about 1½ hours. Uncover the pot and continue to braise until the liquid reduces by half, about 1 hour. Transfer the ribs to a warmed platter, and cover them with foil. The meat will be very tender and may fall off the bones; if so, discard the bones.

Carefully pour the sauce through a fine-mesh strainer into a measuring cup to remove and discard the vegetables and herbs; there should be about 2 cups of sauce. Let it settle for 5 minutes; then skim the fat from its surface.

Scrape any debris out of the braising pot, and return the sauce to the pot. Bring it to a simmer over medium-low heat and cook, stirring frequently, until it darkens and thickens a little, about 5 minutes. Season with salt and pepper. Return the ribs to the pot to heat through.

Scoop a bed of Creamy Parmesan-Garlic Quinoa into each of 4 shallow bowls. Arrange the ribs on top of the quinoa, spoon the sauce over the top, and serve.

To store, refrigerate the quinoa and ribs in the sauce in separate airtight containers or zip-top bags. The ribs and quinoa will keep for 3 days. The ribs will keep for 2 months in the freezer.

Per serving: Calories 902; Fat 37g; Saturated Fat 14g; Sodium 1,968mg; Protein 60g; Fiber 5g

9

Treats

Ecuadorian Quinoa Cookies

KIDS, LARGE GROUPS, SINGLETONS, VEGETARIANS, MAKE AHEAD

MAKES ABOUT 45 COOKIES / PREP: 15 MINUTES, PLUS 1 HOUR TO CHILL
AND 10 MINUTES TO REST / COOK: 8 TO 10 MINUTES

These are Ecuador's version of the sugar cookie. Fast and easy, the recipe ensures you'll be prepared for bake sales, birthday parties, or afternoon tea breaks with a minimum of bother. Gussy up the cookies by sprinkling them with colored sugar before baking, or icing them after they cool.

- ½ cup milk
- 1 medium egg, lightly beaten
- 2 teaspoons vanilla extract
- 1¼ cups Quinoa Flour (page 37) or store bought, plus more for the work surface
- 1¼ cups tapioca flour (see tip)
- 3 tablespoons unsalted butter, cold, cut into 3 chunks
- ½ cup sugar
- 4 teaspoons baking powder
- ½ teaspoon salt

In a medium bowl, whisk together the milk, egg, and vanilla extract. Set aside.

Over a large bowl, sift together the Quinoa Flour and tapioca flour. Cut in the butter until the mixture resembles a coarse meal. Stir in the sugar, baking powder, and salt.

Form the flour mixture into a mound, and make a hollow in the top. Add the milk mixture a little at a time, kneading it in as you go. Try to make a smooth dough with as little kneading as possible.

When the dough is smooth, form it into a disk about 6 inches in diameter. Wrap it in plastic wrap, and refrigerate for 30 minutes.

Line 2 baking sheets with parchment paper. Place the chilled, unwrapped dough on a clean work surface sprinkled with flour. Let it rest for 10 minutes; then roll it out to a thickness of about ¼ inch. Cut the dough into your preferred cookie shape, about 2 inches across the center. Place the shapes on the baking sheets, and refrigerate for 30 minutes.

Preheat the oven to 350°F.

Remove the baking sheets from the refrigerator, and bake the cookies until their edges start to brown, 8 to 10 minutes.

Let the cookies cool on the baking sheets for 2 minutes before transferring them to a wire rack to cool completely. Serve.

To store, refrigerate or freeze the cookies in an airtight container. They will keep for 4 days in the refrigerator and 3 months in the freezer.

Tip Tapioca flour, also known as tapioca starch, is a frequent companion of quinoa and other flours in many gluten-free baked goods. It adds structure usually provided by gluten, giving cookies and cakes a better texture.

Per serving (1 cookie): Calories 34; Fat 1g; Saturated Fat 1g; Sodium 36mg; Protein 1g; Fiber 0g

Cranberry-Pecan Cookies

KIDS, LARGE GROUPS, SINGLETONS, VEGETARIANS, MAKE AHEAD, 30-MINUTE

MAKES 24 TO 36 COOKIES / PREP: 15 TO 20 MINUTES / COOK: 9 TO 11 MINUTES

The combination of quinoa flakes, pecans, and dried cranberries in these cookies may tempt you to sneak them in for breakfast. That's okay: Packed with all of quinoa's protein and fiber, they'll keep you going for hours. You can make this recipe with any mix of nuts and dried berries that you prefer.

1½ cups Quinoa Flour (page 37) or store bought
¾ cup brown rice flour
½ cup quinoa flakes
1 teaspoon baking powder
½ teaspoon salt
½ cup (1 stick) butter, at room temperature
½ cup sugar
½ cup brown sugar, packed
1 teaspoon vanilla extract
2 eggs, lightly beaten
Milk, for mixing (if needed)
1½ cups dried cranberries
1 cup chopped pecans

Preheat the oven to 375°F. Line 2 baking sheets with parchment paper.

In a large bowl, whisk together the Quinoa Flour, brown rice flour, quinoa flakes, baking powder, and salt. Set aside.

In a medium bowl, blend together the butter, sugars, and vanilla extract. Gradually add the eggs, stirring well until the ingredients are thoroughly combined.

A bit at a time, add the dry ingredients to the wet ingredients and stir thoroughly. If the dough seems too thick, add 1 or 2 tablespoons of milk. Fold in the cranberries and pecans.

Drop the batter by rounded tablespoons onto the baking sheets, leaving 2 inches between each. Bake until golden brown, 9 to 11 minutes. Let the cookies cool on the baking sheets for 2 minutes before transferring them to a wire rack to cool completely. Serve.

To store, refrigerate or freeze them in an airtight container. The cookies will keep for 5 days in the refrigerator and 3 months in the freezer.

Per serving (1 cookie): Calories 147; Fat 9g; Saturated Fat 3g; Sodium 59mg; Protein 4g; Fiber 2g

Brown Butter–Salted Caramel Cookies

KIDS, LARGE GROUPS, SINGLETONS, VEGETARIANS, MAKE AHEAD

MAKES 3 DOZEN / PREP: 30 MINUTES, PLUS 15 TO 30 MINUTES TO CHILL / COOK: 13 TO 15 MINUTES

If you've never tasted salted cookies, you're missing out on an eye-rolling pleasure. These cookies can introduce you to a whole new world of baking. They're grown-up cookies that go well with coffee, but kids like them, too (no surprise there).

¾ cup Quinoa Flour (page 37) or store bought

¾ cup tapioca flour

1 teaspoon baking soda

12 tablespoons (1½ sticks) unsalted butter, cut into pieces

½ cup tightly packed light brown sugar

1 teaspoon vanilla extract

1 egg, lightly beaten

Large-flake or medium-grain sea salt (see tip), for sprinkling

Preheat the oven to 325°F.

Line 2 baking sheets with parchment paper.

In a small bowl, whisk together the Quinoa Flour, tapioca flour, and baking soda.

In a medium saucepan over medium-low heat, melt the butter. Turn the heat down to low and cook, occasionally swirling the pot, until the butter is brown and smells nutty, 8 to 10 minutes. There will be brown bits at the bottom of the pot. Be very careful not to burn the butter, or it will become bitter and you'll have to start over.

Pour the brown butter, including any browned bits, into a large bowl. Stir in the sugar and vanilla. Add the flour mixture, and mix until well combined. Add the egg, and mix until well combined. Let the dough cool to room temperature.

Shape the dough into two 6-inch disks. Wrap each in plastic wrap and refrigerate 15 to 30 minutes.

Remove one disk of the dough from the refrigerator. One tablespoon at a time, roll the dough into spheres between your palms. Put them on the baking sheets about 2 inches apart. Flatten the cookies slightly using the flat bottom of a glass, and sprinkle them with salt. Lightly press the salt into the cookies.

Bake the cookies until they're light golden, 13 to 15 minutes. Don't overcook or they will dry out and become crumbly. Let the cookies cool on the baking sheets for 2 minutes before transferring them to a wire rack to cool completely. Serve.

To store, refrigerate or freeze them in an airtight container. The cookies will keep for 4 days in the refrigerator and 3 months in the freezer.

Tip Most supermarkets carry a variety of salts beyond table and kosher salts, each with its own unique flavor and texture. Some of them are excellent complements to sweets such as caramel. For these cookies, choose a sea salt. Maldon, an English flake salt, is relatively common, as is fleur de sel, from various parts of the world.

Per serving (1 cookie): Calories 64; Fat 4g; Saturated Fat 3g; Sodium 65mg; Protein 1g; Fiber 0g

Double-Chocolate Brownies

KIDS, LARGE GROUPS, SINGLETONS, VEGETARIANS, MAKE AHEAD

MAKES 9 BROWNIES / PREP: 15 MINUTES / COOK: 30 TO 35 MINUTES / TOTAL: 55 MINUTES TO 1 HOUR

Cakey or fudgy? Corner, edge, or middle? Nuts or no nuts? Everyone has a strong opinion about brownies, one of America's greatest contributions to chocolate lovers everywhere. And if you love chocolate, you'll love these brownies; you can even raise them to triple-chocolate level by throwing in some whole chocolate chips.

1 teaspoon vegetable oil or cooking spray

⅔ cup Quinoa Flour (page 37) or store bought

⅓ cup almond flour

½ cup unsweetened cocoa powder

¼ teaspoon salt

¼ teaspoon baking powder

½ cup (1 stick) unsalted butter

1 cup semisweet chocolate chips

3 eggs, lightly beaten, at room temperature

½ cup sugar

¼ cup milk

1 teaspoon vanilla extract

1 cup cooked quinoa

Preheat the oven to 350°F.

Lightly grease an 8-by-8-inch baking pan with the vegetable oil.

In a small bowl, whisk together the Quinoa Flour, almond flour, cocoa powder, salt, and baking powder. Set aside.

In a medium saucepan over medium-low heat, melt the butter together with the chocolate chips, stirring often. Pour the chocolate into a medium bowl, and set aside to cool to room temperature.

In a large bowl, whisk together the eggs, sugar, milk, and vanilla extract until smooth. Slowly stir the cooled chocolate into the egg mixture. Add ⅓ of the flour mixture, and stir until it's completely incorporated. Repeat until all of the flour has been blended into the batter. Fold in the cooked quinoa.

Pour the batter into the baking pan. Bake until a toothpick inserted into the middle comes out clean, 30 to 35 minutes. Allow the brownies to cool for at least 10 minutes before cutting them into 2-inch squares and serving.

To store, refrigerate or freeze them, layered with wax paper, in an airtight container. The brownies will keep for 4 days in the refrigerator and 2 months in the freezer.

Tip It's essential to let the chocolate cool to roughly the same temperature as the egg mixture. If the chocolate is much warmer than the eggs, the eggs will scramble when you put the two together. Can't wait for the melted chocolate to cool? Add a tiny bit at a time to the egg mixture while whisking rapidly, to bring up the egg's temperature gradually. Once the temperatures are about equal, you can pour in the rest of the chocolate without risking the eggs.

Per serving (1 brownie): Calories 382; Fat 23g; Saturated Fat 12g; Sodium 165mg; Protein 6g; Fiber 5g

Blueberry Muffins

KIDS, LARGE GROUPS, SINGLETONS, VEGETARIANS, MAKE AHEAD, 30-MINUTE

MAKES 12 MUFFINS / PREP: 10 MINUTES / COOK: 20 TO 25 MINUTES

Yummy as a snack or at breakfast, these muffins give you chewy specks of quinoa alongside juicy pockets of blueberries. Together, each muffin is an antioxidant powerhouse and a sweet treat. Try other berries (cranberries and raspberries work particularly well) or soft fruit such as peeled, diced peach in place of blueberries.

1 cup Quinoa Flour (page 37) or store bought
½ cup brown rice flour
½ cup sugar
2 teaspoons baking powder
½ teaspoon baking soda
¼ teaspoon salt
¼ teaspoon ground cinnamon
1 cup unsweetened almond milk
2 eggs, lightly beaten
¼ cup canola oil
1 teaspoon vanilla extract
1½ cups cooked quinoa
1½ cups fresh or frozen blueberries

Preheat the oven to 375°F.

Put muffin cups in a 12-muffin tin.

In a large bowl, whisk together the Quinoa Flour, brown rice flour, sugar, baking powder, baking soda, salt, and cinnamon. Set aside.

In a medium bowl, whisk together the almond milk, eggs, canola oil, and vanilla extract.

Pour the wet ingredients over the dry ingredients, and stir gently until the ingredients are just combined. The batter will be thick.

Fold in the quinoa and blueberries with as few stirs as possible to distribute them evenly through the batter. Spoon the batter into the muffin cups. The muffins don't rise much, so it's okay if the cups are quite full.

Bake for 20 to 25 minutes, or until the tops are golden brown and a toothpick inserted in the center comes out clean. Let the muffins cool for 10 minutes in the tin; then move the individual muffins to a wire rack to cool.

Serve the muffins warm, with butter or jam.

To store, refrigerate or freeze them, layered with wax paper, in an airtight container. The muffins will keep for 4 days in the refrigerator and 2 months in the freezer.

Per serving (1 muffin): Calories 238; Fat 8g; Saturated Fat 1g; Sodium 131mg; Protein 6g; Fiber 3g

Chocolate Chip Cookies

KIDS, LARGE GROUPS, SINGLETONS, VEGETARIANS, MAKE AHEAD, 30-MINUTE

MAKES 24 COOKIES / PREP: 15 MINUTES / COOK: 11 TO 14 MINUTES

Chocolate chip cookies are the ultimate: Without a doubt, there are more recipes for them than for any other kind of cookie. They also take the prize for most recipes in the gluten-free and quinoa-flour categories. If you like, supplement their deliciousness with chopped walnuts.

2 cups Quinoa Flour (page 37) or store bought
1 cup brown rice flour
1 teaspoon baking soda
1 teaspoon salt
1 cup (2 sticks) butter, at room temperature
1 cup dark brown sugar
2 eggs, lightly beaten
2 teaspoons vanilla extract
1 cup semisweet chocolate chips

Preheat the oven to 350°F.

Line 2 baking sheets with parchment paper.

In a small bowl, whisk together the Quinoa Flour, brown rice flour, baking soda, and salt. Set aside.

In a large bowl, cream the butter with the sugar until smooth. Beat in half the egg until well combined; then add the remaining egg. Beat in the vanilla extract.

Mix the dry ingredients into the creamed butter until just combined. Slowly add the chocolate chips, mixing so they're distributed evenly through the dough.

Drop the dough onto the baking sheets by the tablespoonful. Pat the tops down.

Bake the cookies until they're golden brown on the edges, 11 to 14 minutes. Let the cookies cool on the baking sheets for 2 minutes before transferring them to a wire rack to cool completely. Serve.

To store, refrigerate or freeze them in an airtight container. The cookies will keep for 4 days in the refrigerator and 3 months in the freezer.

Per serving (1 cookie): Calories 212; Fat 12g; Saturated Fat 7g; Sodium 212mg; Protein 2g; Fiber 2g

Almond Cookies

KIDS, LARGE GROUPS, SINGLETONS, VEGETARIANS, MAKE AHEAD

MAKES 24 COOKIES / PREP: 30 MINUTES, PLUS 2½ TO 12 HOURS TO CHILL
AND 10 MINUTES TO REST / COOK: 9 TO 10 MINUTES

Between the quinoa granules, the browned edges, and the almonds on top, these cookies have a satisfying crunch. "Yes, please!" will always be the answer to an offer of this cookie.

1 cup toasted Quinoa Flour (page 37) or store bought, plus more for the work surface

1½ cups toasted almond flour

½ cup (1 stick) unsalted butter, cold

¾ cup Toasted Quinoa (page 36)

1 cup powdered sugar

1 teaspoon baking powder

¼ teaspoon salt

2 eggs

½ teaspoon almond extract

2 egg whites

½ cup sliced almonds, broken up

Sift the Quinoa Flour and almond flour together into a large bowl.

Cut the butter into the flour just until the mixture resembles a coarse meal. Stir in the Toasted Quinoa, sugar, baking powder, and salt.

In a small bowl, lightly beat the 2 whole eggs and almond extract together. Slowly add the egg mixture to the flour mixture, kneading it in as you go. Try to make a smooth dough with as little kneading as possible.

When the dough is smooth, form it into a disk about 6 inches in diameter. Wrap it in plastic wrap, and refrigerate for at least 2 hours, and no more than 12.

Place the chilled, unwrapped dough on a clean, lightly floured work surface. Let it rest at room temperature for 10 minutes.

Line 2 baking sheets with parchment paper. Roll out the dough to a thickness of ¼ inch. Cut the dough into your preferred cookie shape, about 2 inches across the middle. Place the shapes on the baking sheets, and refrigerate for approximately 30 minutes.

Preheat the oven to 350°F.

In a small bowl, lightly beat the egg whites.

Remove the cookies from the refrigerator. Brush each with egg white; then sprinkle with the almonds. Gently press the almonds so they stick to the cookies; it's okay if you have to press them into the dough a bit.

Bake the cookies until they begin to brown around the edges, 9 to 10 minutes. Let the cookies cool on the baking sheets for 2 minutes before transferring them to a wire rack to cool completely. Serve.

To store, refrigerate or freeze the cookies in an airtight container. They will keep for 5 days in the refrigerator and 3 months in the freezer.

Per serving (1 cookie): Calories 147; Fat 9g; Saturated Fat 3g; Sodium 59mg; Protein 4g; Fiber 2g

Chili–Chocolate Cookies

KIDS, LARGE GROUPS, SINGLETONS, VEGETARIANS, MAKE AHEAD, 30-MINUTE

MAKES 36 COOKIES / PREP: 15 MINUTES / COOK: 10 TO 15 MINUTES

Long before the conquistadores arrived in the New World, the Mayans and Aztecs of Mexico and Central America used chocolate. It was a beverage, drunk hot or cold by priests and nobles, and when chili was added, it became the drink of the emperor. Now, North Americans have caught on to the exciting combination. These gluten-free cookies will give you a taste, too.

1¼ cups Quinoa Flour (page 37) or store bought
1¼ cups tapioca flour
¾ cup unsweetened cocoa powder
2 teaspoons chili powder
1 teaspoon ground cinnamon
1 teaspoon baking powder
¾ teaspoon salt
1 cup (2 sticks) butter, at room temperature
1¼ cups sugar
2 eggs, lightly beaten
¼ cup very strong black coffee, cooled
1 teaspoon vanilla extract
Confectioners' sugar, for sprinkling

Preheat the oven to 350°F.

Line 2 baking sheets with parchment paper.

In a medium bowl, whisk together the Quinoa Flour, tapioca flour, cocoa powder, chili powder, cinnamon, baking powder, and salt. Set aside.

In a large bowl, cream the butter with the sugar until smooth. Beat in half the egg until well incorporated; then add the remaining egg. Beat in the coffee and vanilla extract until smooth. Mix in the dry ingredients until just combined.

Drop the dough onto the baking sheets by the tablespoonful, spacing them about 1 inch apart. Bake for 10 to 15 minutes, making sure the bottoms don't burn.

Remove the cookies from the oven, and sprinkle them with confectioners' sugar. Let the cookies cool on the baking sheets for 2 minutes before transferring them to a wire rack to cool completely. Serve.

To store, refrigerate or freeze them in an airtight container. The cookies will keep for 4 days in the refrigerator and 3 months in the freezer.

Per serving (1 cookie): Calories 107; Fat 6g; Saturated Fat 4g; Sodium 93mg; Protein 1g; Fiber 1g

Scottish Shortbread Bars

KIDS, LARGE GROUPS, SINGLETONS, VEGETARIANS, MAKE AHEAD

MAKES 20 BARS / PREP: 20 MINUTES, PLUS 30 MINUTES FOR CHILLING / COOK: 20 TO 25 MINUTES

A very simple recipe, shortbread nonetheless elicits sighs of pleasure. It must be all that butter, which gives them an exceptional richness. Maybe quinoa's heart-healthy qualities balance out all that indulgence . . . .

1⅓ cups Quinoa Flour (page 37) or store bought, plus more for dusting

⅔ cup brown rice flour

¼ teaspoon salt

1 cup (2 sticks) unsalted butter, at room temperature

¾ cup sugar, plus more for sprinkling

1 teaspoon vanilla extract

In a medium bowl, sift together the Quinoa Flour, brown rice flour, and salt. Set aside.

In a large bowl, cream the butter with the sugar until smooth. Mix in the vanilla extract. Then add the dry ingredients to the wet ingredients until just combined.

Form the dough into a 6-inch disk. Wrap it in plastic wrap, and refrigerate for 30 minutes.

Preheat the oven to 350°F. Line 2 baking sheets with parchment.

Place the chilled, unwrapped dough on a clean, lightly floured work surface. Roll the dough out to a thickness of ½ inch. Cut the dough into rectangles about 1 inch wide by 3 inches long. Place them on the baking sheets, and sprinkle with the sugar.

Bake the bars until the edges begin to brown, 20 to 25 minutes. Let them cool for 5 minutes before transferring them to a wire rack to cool completely. Serve.

To store, refrigerate or freeze them in an airtight container. The shortbread will keep for 4 days in the refrigerator and 2 months in the freezer.

Per serving (1 bar): Calories 164; Fat 10g; Saturated Fat 6g; Sodium 98mg; Protein 2g; Fiber 1g

Betty's Lemon Squares

KIDS, LARGE GROUPS, SINGLETONS, VEGETARIANS, MAKE AHEAD

MAKES 24 BARS / PREP: 12 MINUTES / COOK: 50 TO 55 MINUTES

The invention of the kitchen staff at Betty Crocker, lemon squares have graced potluck tables since 1963. Quinoa is the foundation of this particular recipe, which fills a crust of quinoa shortbread with tangy sweetness. The lemony intensity will have your lips puckering while your mouth waters.

1 teaspoon vegetable oil or cooking spray
1 batch Scottish Shortbread dough (page 268)
4 eggs, plus 2 egg yolks
2 cups sugar
1 cup freshly squeezed lemon juice
½ cup Quinoa Flour (page 37) or store bought
½ teaspoon baking powder
2 teaspoons fresh lemon zest
Confectioners' sugar, for sprinkling

Preheat the oven to 350°F.

Lightly grease a 9-by-13-inch baking pan with vegetable oil. Line the pan with crisscrossing sheets of parchment, leaving a 2-inch overhang on all sides.

Flour your hands, and press the shortbread dough evenly across the bottom of the pan, making sure to smooth out any cracks. Press the dough about ½ inch up the sides of the pan.

Bake the crust until it's golden, about 20 minutes. Set the pan aside to cool.

In a large bowl, whisk together the eggs, sugar, lemon juice, flour, baking powder, and lemon zest. Pour the filling into the crust. Bake until the filling is set, 30 to 35 minutes. Put the pan on a wire rack to cool.

Sprinkle confectioners' sugar over the top, cut into squares about 2 by 2 inches, and serve.

To store, refrigerate or freeze them, layered with wax paper, in an airtight container. The squares will keep for 3 days in the refrigerator and 2 months in the freezer.

Per serving (1 square): Calories 225; Fat 10g; Saturated Fat 5g; Sodium 91mg; Protein 3g; Fiber 1g

Red Velvet Cupcakes

YIELDS 24 CUPCAKES / PREP: 25 MINUTES / COOK: 20 TO 22 MINUTES

Why on earth would anyone want to eat red cupcakes? Well, for one thing, they're fun, and for another thing, they taste great. And the vinegar? It reacts with the buttermilk to help make these odd-looking cupcakes moist and fluffy.

For the cream cheese frosting

1 cup (2 sticks) unsalted butter, at room temperature

12 ounces cream cheese, at room temperature

4 cups confectioners' sugar, sifted

1 teaspoon vanilla extract

Milk, for softening (if desired)

For the cupcakes

1 cup Quinoa Flour (page 37) or store bought

1 cup brown rice flour

½ cup tapioca flour

1½ cups sugar

1 tablespoon unsweetened cocoa powder

1½ teaspoons baking soda

1 teaspoon salt

1½ cups vegetable oil

1 cup buttermilk

2 eggs, lightly beaten

2 tablespoons red food coloring

1½ teaspoons distilled white vinegar

1 teaspoon vanilla extract

To make the cream cheese frosting In a large bowl, beat the butter and cream cheese together until fluffy. Add the sugar, 1 cup at a time, and then the vanilla extract; mix the icing until it's smooth. Add more confectioners' sugar if you'd like the frosting stiffer, or a little milk if you want it softer.

To make the cupcakes Preheat the oven to 350°F.

Put muffin cups in two 12-muffin tins.

In a medium bowl, sift together the Quinoa Flour, brown rice flour, tapioca flour, sugar, cocoa powder, baking soda, and salt. Set aside.

In a large bowl, whisk together the vegetable oil, buttermilk, eggs, food coloring, vinegar, and vanilla extract. In three batches, add the dry ingredients to the wet ingredients, and mix until the batter is smooth and thoroughly combined between batches.

Spoon the batter into the cupcake tins, filling each cup about ¾ full. Bake the cupcakes, turning the pans once, until a toothpick inserted into the middle comes out clean, 20 to 22 minutes.

Let the cupcakes cool completely before you remove them from the tins. Spread frosting across the top of each cupcake and serve.

To store, refrigerate or freeze them in an airtight container. The cupcakes will keep for 3 days in the refrigerator and 2 months in the freezer.

Per serving (1 cupcake): Calories 433; Fat 27g; Saturated Fat 11g; Sodium 290mg; Protein 3g; Fiber 1g

Carrot-Spice Cake

MAKES 2 (8-INCH ROUND) CAKES / PREP: 20 TO 25 MINUTES / COOK: 25 TO 30 MINUTES

This cake is a stealth delivery system for nutrition. The carrots are filled with vitamin A and fiber; the quinoa brings protein, fiber, and antioxidants to the mix; and the cinnamon brings a generous dose of manganese and calcium. Yes, carrot cake is health food, but more importantly, it's a treat for everyone to enjoy.

Vegetable oil or cooking spray

1½ cups Quinoa Flour (page 37) or store bought

1 cup almond flour

¼ cup cornstarch

2 teaspoons baking powder

2 teaspoons ground cinnamon

½ teaspoon ground ginger

½ teaspoon salt

1 cup packed dark brown sugar

6 eggs, separated

2 teaspoons vanilla extract

1 cup unsweetened applesauce

3 cups grated carrots

1 cup cooked quinoa

⅔ cup raisins

1 batch Cream Cheese Frosting (page 270), made with ½ teaspoon ground cinnamon

Preheat the oven to 350°F. Grease two 8-inch cake pans with vegetable oil, and line the bottoms with parchment.

Into a large bowl, sift together the Quinoa Flour, almond flour, cornstarch, baking powder, cinnamon, ginger, and salt. Set aside.

In a medium bowl, whisk together the sugar, egg yolks, and vanilla extract. Stir in the applesauce, carrots, quinoa, and raisins. Fold the wet ingredients into the dry ingredients.

In a separate large bowl, beat the egg whites to soft peaks. Gently fold them into the batter until just combined.

Divide the batter between the cake pans. Tap the pans against the counter a few times to get rid of any air bubbles. Bake the cakes until the layers are golden brown, 25 to 30 minutes. A toothpick inserted into the middle of each layer should come out with just a few crumbs, and the centers of the layers should spring back when lightly touched.

Transfer the pans to wire racks, and let the layers cool for about 10 minutes. Run a knife around the edge of the pans, and turn the layers out onto the racks to cool completely.

Place one cooled cake on a serving plate. Spread about ¾ cup of the Cream Cheese Frosting evenly over the entire top of the layer. Carefully place the second cake layer on top of the first, aligning the edges of the layers. Spread the remaining frosting over the top and around the sides of the cake.

To store, refrigerate or freeze in an airtight container. The cake will keep for 4 days in the refrigerator and 2 months in the freezer.

Per serving (1 slice): Calories 670; Fat 31g; Saturated Fat 31g; Sodium 345mg; Protein 10g; Fiber 4g

Meyer Lemon–Olive Oil Cake

LARGE GROUPS, SINGLETONS, VEGETARIANS, MAKE AHEAD

MAKES 1 CAKE / PREP: 10 MINUTES / COOK: 1 HOUR

Here's a very easy cake recipe that yields very sophisticated results. The olive oil makes the cake as moist as can be, its tender insides redolent of lemon and its golden crust lightly crisp. You can even swap out the lemon for orange.

Vegetable oil or cooking spray

1⅓ cups Quinoa Flour (page 37) or store bought

⅔ cup brown rice flour

1½ cups sugar

1½ teaspoons salt

1¼ teaspoons baking powder

1⅓ cups extra-virgin olive oil

1¼ cups milk

3 eggs

¼ cup freshly squeezed Meyer lemon juice (see tip)

1½ tablespoons freshly grated Meyer lemon zest

½ teaspoon lemon extract

Confectioners' sugar, for sprinkling

Preheat the oven to 350°F.

Grease a 9-inch cake pan with the vegetable oil, and line the bottom with parchment paper.

In a medium bowl, whisk together the Quinoa Flour, brown rice flour, sugar, salt, and baking powder. Set aside.

In a large bowl, whisk together the olive oil, milk, eggs, lemon juice, lemon zest, and lemon extract. Then whisk in the dry ingredients until just combined.

Pour the batter into the pan. Tap the pan against the counter a few times to get rid of any air bubbles. Bake until the top is golden brown and a toothpick inserted into the middle comes out clean, about 1 hour. The center of the cake should spring back when you lightly touch the top.

Let the cake cool for 30 minutes. Run a knife around the edge of the pan, and turn the cake out onto the rack to cool completely.

Place the cake on a serving plate, and sprinkle it with the confectioners' sugar.

To store, refrigerate or freeze it in an airtight container. The cake will keep for 3 days in the refrigerator and 1 month in the freezer.

Tip **Possibly a cross between a regular lemon and a mandarin or regular orange, Meyer lemons are quite a different beast. With a rounder shape, thinner rind, and darker flesh, they are sweeter and less acidic than ordinary lemons. If you made this recipe with the familiar supermarket lemon, the results wouldn't be nearly as subtle and fragrant. Meyer lemons are widely available in supermarkets and produce markets.**

Per serving (1 slice): Calories 406; Fat 25g; Saturated Fat 4g; Sodium 322mg; Protein 5g; Fiber 1g

Bittersweet Chocolate Cake

MAKES 2 (8-INCH) CAKES / PREP: 25 MINUTES / COOK: 40 TO 45 MINUTES

Chocolate cake may just be the best of all cakes, especially when enclosed in a thick layer of chocolate frosting. With milk or coffee on the side, it's a great party treat. For even more sinful results, mix some chocolate chips into the batter.

For the cake

Vegetable oil or cooking spray

1 cup Quinoa Flour (page 37) or store bought

½ cup brown rice flour

⅓ cup unsweetened cocoa powder

1 tablespoon baking powder

¼ teaspoon salt

1½ cups sugar

¾ cup unsalted butter, at room temperature

4 eggs, lightly beaten

⅓ cup milk

¼ cup very strong black coffee, cooled

1 teaspoon vanilla extract

2 cups cooked quinoa

For the frosting

1 cup semisweet or bittersweet chocolate chips

1½ sticks unsalted butter, at room temperature

½ teaspoon vanilla extract

1 cup confectioners' sugar, sifted

½ ounce bittersweet chocolate, shaved

To make the cake Preheat the oven to 350°F.

Lightly grease two 8-inch round or square cake pans. Line the bottoms of the pans with parchment paper.

In a medium bowl, whisk together the Quinoa Flour, brown rice flour, cocoa powder, baking powder, and salt. Set aside.

In a large bowl, cream the sugar with the butter. Mix in the eggs, milk, coffee, and vanilla extract.

Slowly whisk the dry ingredients into the wet until the batter is fluffy and even. Stir in the quinoa. Add a bit more flour if the batter seems too thin, or add more milk if it seems too thick.

Divide the batter between the cake pans. Tap the pans against the counter a few times to get rid of any air bubbles. Bake until a toothpick inserted into the middle of each layer comes out clean and the centers spring back when lightly touched, 40 to 45 minutes. Let the cakes cool in the pans for 30 minutes.

To make the frosting In a large microwave-safe bowl, melt the chocolate chips, butter, and vanilla on high for 30 seconds. Whisk the mixture until smooth; if the chips aren't entirely melted, microwave them for another 15 seconds and whisk some more. When the chocolate mixture is smooth, whisk in the confectioners' sugar until the frosting is completely blended and airy. For best results, spread the still-warm frosting on the cooled cake.

Run a knife around the edges of the cake pans. Place one layer onto a serving plate and spread about ¾ cup of frosting evenly over the top of the layer. Carefully place the second cake layer on top of the first, aligning the edges of the layers.

Spread the remaining frosting over the top and around the sides of the cake, sprinkle the chocolate shavings over the cake, and serve.

To store, refrigerate or freeze in an airtight container. The cake will keep for 3 days in the refrigerator and 2 months in the freezer.

Per serving (1 slice): Calories 634; Fat 33g; Saturated Fat 19g; Sodium 243mg; Protein 8.5g; Fiber 5g

German Plum Tart

MAKES 1 TART / PREP: 40 MINUTES, PLUS 30 MINUTES TO CHILL
AND 30 MINUTES TO WARM UP / COOK: 45 MINUTES

This traditional Bavarian tart, the *Zwetschgendatschi,* is all about damson plums, also known as Italian prune plums. They are dark purple, almost black elongated plums with yellow flesh. Tart and sweet at the same time, they're a perfect ingredient for an elegant, sophisticated dessert. You can make this tart with other apples or another not-too-juicy fruit.

¾ cup Quinoa Flour (page 37) or store bought, plus more for dusting

¼ cup brown rice flour

½ cup cornstarch

⅓ cup sugar, divided

½ teaspoon salt

¼ teaspoon ground cinnamon

¾ cup unsalted butter, cold, cut into chunks

1 egg yolk

1 teaspoon vanilla extract

Vegetable oil or cooking spray

3 pounds damson plums

Over a large bowl, sift together the Quinoa Flour, brown rice flour, and cornstarch. Whisk in ¼ cup of sugar and the salt and cinnamon. Cut in the butter until the mixture resembles a coarse cornmeal.

In a small bowl, whisk together the egg yolk and vanilla extract. Form the flour mixture into a mound, and make a hollow in the top. Add the egg yolk a little at a time, kneading it in as you go, until the dough just begins to come together.

Place the dough on a clean, lightly floured work surface. Being careful not to overwork the dough, gently knead it until all the ingredients are integrated. If the dough doesn't come together, sprinkle it with several drops of milk or water and knead a little more. Form the dough into a 6-inch disk, wrap it in plastic, and refrigerate it for a minimum of 30 minutes and as long as overnight.

To make the tart, take the dough out of the refrigerator to warm up for about 30 minutes.

Preheat the oven to 350°F.

Grease an 8-inch fluted tart pan or 9-inch pie pan with vegetable oil.

Stone and quarter the plums, and set them aside in a bowl.

Using floured hands, break the dough up into small pieces and press each piece evenly across the bottom of the pan, making sure to smooth out any cracks. Press the dough at least ¼ inch up the sides of the pan. Reserve any leftover dough.

Working from the outer edge of the crust in toward the center, lay the plums out in a spiral, overlapping the slices by about ¼ inch. When you reach the center of the crust, place any remaining plums on spots where the dough shows through. Crumble any reserved dough over the top of the tart. Sprinkle the remaining sugar over the plums.

Bake the tart until the pastry is golden brown around the edges and the plums are tender and their juices are running and bubbling, about 45 minutes.

Let the tart cool at least until the plum juices firm up. Cut the tart into wedges and serve. If you like, top the servings with whipped cream.

To store, refrigerate or freeze in an airtight container. The tart will keep for 2 days in the refrigerator and 1 month in the freezer.

Per serving (1 slice): Calories 227; Fat 13g; Saturated Fat 8g; Sodium 181mg; Protein 2g; Fiber 2g

Peach Crisp
with Quinoa-Flake Topping

KIDS, LARGE GROUPS, SINGLETONS, VEGANS, MAKE AHEAD

MAKES 1 COBBLER / PREP: 10 MINUTES / COOK: 35 TO 40 MINUTES

A summer beauty, this dessert is a tummy-warmer all year round—if you can find the elusive good peach in the off-season. If you can't, swap in equally delicious fruits such as apples, cranberries, or persimmons. Topped with melting vanilla ice cream, a crisp is an especially beautiful thing.

4 cups sliced fresh peaches

1 cup plus 4 teaspoons Quinoa Flour (page 37) or store bought, divided

1 teaspoon cinnamon, divided

2 cups quinoa flakes

¼ cup brown sugar

½ teaspoon salt

⅓ cup plus ½ teaspoon extra-virgin coconut oil (see tip), divided

In a large bowl, toss the peaches with 4 teaspoons of Quinoa Flour and ½ teaspoon of cinnamon, coating them thoroughly.

In a large bowl, stir together the remaining 1 cup of flour, the quinoa flakes, sugar, remaining ½ teaspoon of cinnamon, and the salt. Add ⅓ cup of coconut oil, and toss until the ingredients are well combined. If you want larger chunks of crisp, use your hands to clump it to your preferred texture.

Preheat the oven to 350°F.

Grease a 9-inch baking dish with the remaining ½ teaspoon of coconut oil.

Add the fruit mixture to the baking dish, and sprinkle it with the topping.

Bake until the fruit is bubbling and the crisp is firm and golden brown, 35 to 40 minutes. Let the crisp cool for 15 minutes before serving.

To store, refrigerate or freeze it in an airtight container. The crisp will keep for 5 days in the refrigerator and 2 months in the freezer, though the topping will lose its crispiness.

Tip With a slightly sweet flavor, coconut oil is a good choice for dessert baking. Depending on the temperature of its surroundings, it may be solid, semi-solid, or liquid. You'll come across coconut oil in a lot of "healthy" recipes, in part because advocates claim it has health benefits ranging from improved immunity to reduced risk of cancer. Naysayers, however, point out that coconut oil is 92 percent saturated fat, higher than that of any other fat. None of that fat, though, is cholesterol. In short, the jury's still out on coconut oil. If you prefer, use another oil (except olive oil, which is too assertive) instead.

Per serving (1 slice): Calories 276; Fat 9g; Saturated Fat 5g; Sodium 107mg; Protein 7g; Fiber 4g

Toasted Quinoa Parfait
with Raspberry Coulis

KIDS, SINGLETONS, VEGANS

SERVES 4 / PREP: 20 MINUTES

When berries are in season, especially in June and July, you've got to seize the moment. Sure, you can get berries year-round, but they're at their very best fresh off the bush from your local produce stand or farmers' market. Made of nothing but berries and quinoa, this parfait is a perfect taste of summer.

For the coulis
4 cups fresh raspberries or 2 (10-ounce) bags frozen raspberries, thawed

For the parfait
¾ cup fresh blackberries
¾ cup fresh raspberries
¾ cup quartered fresh strawberries
2 cups Toasted Quinoa (page 36)
4 sprigs fresh mint

To make the coulis In a food processor or blender, purée the berries until smooth. Over a medium bowl, strain the purée through a fine-mesh sieve, pressing the coulis through with a spatula or spoon. Discard the seeds. This makes about 2 cups of coulis.

To make the parfaits In a medium bowl, toss together the blackberries, raspberries, and strawberries.

Spoon 3 tablespoons of coulis into each of 4 glass bowls or goblets. Top each with ⅓ cup of Toasted Quinoa. Layer another 3 tablespoons of coulis in each bowl, and sprinkle each with 2 tablespoons of toasted quinoa. Add ½ cup of berries to each parfait. If desired, drizzle more coulis over the berries. Garnish with a sprig of mint and serve.

To store, keep the coulis, berries, and quinoa in separate airtight containers. The items will keep for 3 days in the refrigerator. Do not freeze.

Per serving: Calories 388; Fat 6g; Saturated Fat 1g; Sodium 6mg; Protein 13g; Fiber 16g

Chocolate-Espresso Quinoa Pudding with Cocoa Nibs

KIDS, SINGLETONS, VEGETARIANS, MAKE AHEAD

SERVES 4 / PREP: 5 MINUTES / COOK: 30 MINUTES

Quinoa and chocolate are natural companions. Your taste buds will agree once they experience this pudding, a silky delight set off by the crunchiness of cocoa nibs. If you prefer, top your pudding with shaved dark chocolate; you can also turn the pudding vegan by substituting almond milk (or another nondairy milk) for the cow's milk.

⅓ cup unsweetened cocoa powder
¼ cup espresso or very strong coffee
3 cups milk
¼ cup water
⅓ cup sugar
1½ teaspoons vanilla extract
¼ teaspoon ground cinnamon
1 cup dry quinoa, rinsed
⅛ teaspoon salt
¼ cup cocoa nibs (see tip)

In a small bowl, whisk the cocoa powder into the espresso until smooth. Set aside.

In a medium saucepan over medium-high heat, mix together the milk, water, sugar, vanilla extract, and cinnamon. Bring the liquid to a boil, and stir in the quinoa and salt. Reduce the heat to medium-low, cover the pot ¾ of the way, and simmer the quinoa for about 25 minutes, stirring often. If the pudding becomes too dry before the quinoa is done, add 2 or 3 tablespoons of milk and continue cooking, covered.

Stir the cocoa-coffee mixture into the pudding. Remove the pudding from the heat, and let it cool to room temperature or chill it in the refrigerator. It will thicken as it cools.

Serve topped with cocoa nibs.

To store, refrigerate it in an airtight container. The pudding will keep for 4 days. Do not freeze.

Tip **Cocoa nibs are a byproduct of chocolate processing. When roasted cocoa beans are cracked open, little pieces called nibs are left behind. Crunchy and a bit bitter, they'll bring a little something special to your chocolate dishes. If you can't find them at your supermarket, you can get them at health food and gourmet stores, and, of course, online.**

Per serving: Calories 360; Fat 11g; Saturated Fat 5g; Sodium 162mg; Protein 14g; Fiber 6g

Pistachio–Quinoa Milk "Ice Cream"

KIDS, SINGLETONS, VEGETARIANS, MAKE AHEAD

MAKES 5 CUPS / PREP: 10 MINUTES, PLUS 3 HOURS TO FREEZE

Don't have an ice cream maker? No problem: You can whip up this rich pistachio ice cream with nothing more than a blender and your freezer. No cooking or specialty equipment required.

2 cups coarsely chopped unsalted pistachios, divided
1 cup sugar, divided
1¾ cups Quinoa Milk (page 78), cold
1½ cups cooked quinoa, cooled
¾ teaspoon almond extract
4 cups ice cubes
1 cup half-and-half, cold

Place a heavy baking dish in the freezer to chill.

In a food processor or blender, finely grind 1 cup of chopped pistachios with ½ cup of sugar. Blend in the remaining ½ cup of sugar and the Quinoa Milk, quinoa, and almond extract. Chill the food processor bowl or blender carafe in the freezer for 15 minutes. Add the ice cubes, and blend until the mixture is very smooth. Quickly stir in the half-and-half and the remaining 1 cup of chopped pistachios.

Pour the mixture into the chilled baking dish, and put it in the freezer. After 1 hour, give it a stir. Freeze and stir twice more, for a total of 3 hours in the freezer. If the ice cream is still soft at that point, freeze it for another half hour and stir again. Continue until the ice cream is firm enough for you, and serve.

Store the ice cream in an airtight container in the freezer. It will keep for 1 month.

Per serving (1 cup): Calories 598; Fat 30g; Saturated Fat 6g; Sodium 28mg; Protein 15g; Fiber 6g

Banana—Coconut Ice Pops

KIDS, ONE POT, VEGANS, MAKE AHEAD

MAKES 12 ICE POPS / PREP: 10 MINUTES, PLUS 5 HOURS TO FREEZE

Boy, does quinoa milk come in handy. This recipe proves you can have a creamy frozen treat without dairy or gluten. You can easily expand your ice pop horizons to some classic flavor combinations by adding peanut butter or cocoa powder.

3 very ripe bananas
1½ cups Quinoa Milk (page 78)
½ cup coconut cream
¼ cup confectioners' sugar
1 teaspoon vanilla extract

In a blender or food processor, purée the bananas until they are smooth. Blend in the Quinoa Milk, coconut cream, sugar, and vanilla until they are fully incorporated and the mixture is smooth.

Pour the mixture into ice pop molds or 5-ounce paper cups. Freeze them until the ice pops are solid throughout, about 5 hours. If you are using cups, freeze them for about 1 hour, until the ice pops are firm but not frozen, and insert a popsicle stick into each.

To unmold the ice pops, dip the mold in warm water for 10 to 30 seconds, or peel off the paper cups. Serve.

To store, wrap the ice pops individually in plastic wrap and put them in an airtight container. They will keep for 3 months.

Per serving (1 pop): Calories 76; Fat 3g; Saturated Fat 2g; Sodium 2mg; Protein 1g; Fiber 1g

The Dirty Dozen & the Clean Fifteen

A nonprofit and environmental watchdog organization called Environmental Working Group (EWG) looks at data supplied by the US Department of Agriculture (USDA) and the Food and Drug Administration (FDA) about pesticide residues and compiles a list each year of the best and worst pesticide loads found in commercial crops. You can refer to the Dirty Dozen list to know which fruits and vegetables you should always buy organic. The Clean Fifteen list lets you know which produce is considered safe enough when grown conventionally to allow you to skip the organics. This does not mean that the Clean Fifteen produce is pesticide-free, though, so wash these fruits and vegetables thoroughly.

These lists change every year, so make sure you look up the most recent before you fill your shopping cart. You'll find the most recent lists as well as a guide to pesticides in produce at EWG.org/FoodNews.

2015 Dirty Dozen

Apples	Peaches
Celery	Potatoes
Cherry tomatoes	Snap peas
	Spinach
Cucumbers	Strawberries
Grapes	Sweet bell peppers
Nectarines	

In addition to the Dirty Dozen, the EWG added two foods contaminated with highly toxic organo-phosphate insecticides:

Hot peppers	Kale/Collard greens

2015 Clean Fifteen

Asparagus	Mangoes
Avocados	Onions
Cabbage	Papayas
Cantaloupe	Pineapples
Cauliflower	Sweet corn
Eggplant	Sweet peas (frozen)
Grapefruit	Sweet potatoes
Kiwis	

Conversion Tables

VOLUME EQUIVALENTS (LIQUID)

US STANDARD	US STANDARD (OUNCES)	METRIC (APPROXIMATE)
2 tablespoons	1 fl. oz.	30 mL
¼ cup	2 fl. oz.	60 mL
½ cup	4 fl. oz.	120 mL
1 cup	8 fl. oz.	240 mL
1½ cups	12 fl. oz.	355 mL
2 cups or 1 pint	16 fl. oz.	475 mL
4 cups or 1 quart	32 fl. oz.	1 L
1 gallon	128 fl. oz.	4 L

OVEN TEMPERATURES

FAHRENHEIT (F)	CELSIUS (C) (APPROXIMATE)
250°	120°
300°	150°
325°	165°
350°	180°
375°	190°
400°	200°
425°	220°
450°	230°

VOLUME EQUIVALENTS (DRY)

US STANDARD	METRIC (APPROXIMATE)
⅛ teaspoon	0.5 mL
¼ teaspoon	1 mL
½ teaspoon	2 mL
¾ teaspoon	4 mL
1 teaspoon	5 mL
1 tablespoon	15 mL
¼ cup	59 mL
⅓ cup	79 mL
½ cup	118 mL
⅔ cup	156 mL
¾ cup	177 mL
1 cup	235 mL
2 cups or 1 pint	475 mL
3 cups	700 mL
4 cups or 1 quart	1 L

WEIGHT EQUIVALENTS

US STANDARD	METRIC (APPROXIMATE)
½ ounce	15 g
1 ounce	30 g
2 ounces	60 g
4 ounces	115 g
8 ounces	225 g
12 ounces	340 g
16 ounces or 1 pound	455 g

Glossary

AMARANTH: A tiny gluten-free seed similar to quinoa. Very rich in complete protein. Used much like grain. First cultivated by the pre-Columbian Aztecs of present-day Mexico.

ANCIENT GRAIN: An ill-defined marketing term referring to many lesser-known whole grains such as millet and teff. Not necessarily more "ancient" than conventional grains such as wheat. Categorized by some as superfoods and believed by some to be better for health than conventional grains. Often used to describe quinoa and amaranth, which are not grains.

ANTI-INFLAMMATORY: Describes one health benefit of antioxidants, which some say alleviate chronic inflammation in the body.

ANTIOXIDANTS (ALSO KNOWN AS POLYPHENOLS): Naturally occurring substances in the body that slow or prevent the production of disease-causing free radicals. Said to reduce the incidence of cancer, diminish inflammation, and support immune function. Includes vitamins C, E, and A. Quinoa is high in various antioxidants.

CELIAC DISEASE: A genetically transmitted autoimmune disorder that causes the body to attack the small intestine when gluten is ingested. Symptoms include diarrhea, fatigue, joint pain, and migraines. Results in intestinal damage.

COCONUT MILK: An ingredient in many culinary applications, especially Southeast Asian cooking. Made by boiling coconut flesh with water. Resembles cow's milk, but sweeter. Not to be confused with the much thicker coconut cream or clear, drinkable coconut water.

COMPLETE PROTEIN: A protein that contains all nine of the essential amino acids needed in a healthy diet. Quinoa contains complete protein.

FREE RADICALS: Damaged cells that destructively link to molecules in healthy cells, injuring or killing those cells. Can harm DNA in healthy cells, increasing the likelihood of diseases such as cancer.

GLUTEN: Composite term for two proteins, gliadin and glutenin, found in cereal grains such as wheat, rye, and barley. Very important in traditional baking. Creates elasticity in dough, allowing it to rise, and serves as a "glue" that helps grain-based foods hold together. Can give food a chewy texture.

GLUTEN-FREE: Term that describes ingredients and foods that contain no gluten. Examples include quinoa, corn, and rice.

GLUTEN-FREE FLOUR: Flour used in place of wheat flour and other flours containing gluten. Does not have the sticky properties of gluten flours, so it can be problematic in baking. Examples include quinoa flour, brown rice flour, tapioca flour, almond flour, and blended gluten-free flour.

GLUTEN INTOLERANCE or GLUTEN SENSITIVITY: Medically referred to as non-celiac gluten sensitivity. Gluten ingested by sufferers causes many celiac disease symptoms but does not damage the intestines.

GRAIN (ALSO KNOWN AS CEREAL GRAIN): The edible seeds of grasses. Includes wheat, barley, corn, and rice.

JULIENNE (V): To cut a vegetable or herb into very thin strips.

ON THE BIAS: Describes an angled crosswise cut, such as a cut made against the grain of meat or fish.

OXIDATION: The normal chemical reaction between oxygen and the body's cells. Damages 1 to 2 percent of cells, which become disease-causing free radicals. The process is slowed or prevented by antioxidants.

PEPITAS: Pumpkin seeds. Common in South American cooking.

PINE NUTS (ALSO KNOWN AS PIGNOLI NUTS): The edible seeds of certain varieties of pine trees. Common in Mediterranean cooking.

PSEUDOGRAIN (ALSO KNOWN AS PSEUDOCEREAL): A non-grain food that serves the purpose of grain. Examples include seeds such as quinoa and buckwheat and, in flour, nuts such as almonds and roots such as cassava (the source of tapioca).

QUINOA: The seed of the quinoa plant, a relative of spinach and beets. Native to the Andes Mountains of South America. Has a subtle nutty flavor and slight chewiness. High in protein and antioxidants. Common varieties are white, red, and black, sometimes blended to create tricolor rainbow quinoa.

QUINOA FLAKES: Uncooked quinoa granules that are rolled into a thin, flat shape. Can be used much like rolled oats.

QUINOA FLOUR: Uncooked, finely ground quinoa. Gluten-free substitute for wheat flour in non-yeast baked goods and other cooking applications, often in combination with other flours. Can be made from toasted or untoasted quinoa.

QUINOA MILK: A beverage made by blending cooked quinoa with water and straining out the solids.

QUINOA PASTA: Gluten-free noodles made from quinoa flour. Shapes include spaghetti, linguine, macaroni, and penne. Usually incorporates grains such as rice or corn. Some quinoa pasta contains significantly more grain than quinoa.

SAPONINS: The bitter natural substance that coats quinoa seeds in the field. Mostly removed by processing before quinoa is packaged for sale. Additional rinsing is recommended at home to remove remaining saponins.

SAUCEPAN: A pot.

SAUTÉ: To cook food quickly, stirring or tossing constantly, in a sauté pan over medium-high or high heat, using a small amount of oil or other fat. Results in browning.

SAUTÉ PAN: A wide pan with straight or slightly sloping sides somewhat higher than the sides of a frying pan. Used for sautéing. May substitute a frying pan in many cases.

SEED: In culinary terms, the edible fruit of non-grass plants, such as vines and broad-leaf plants. Includes quinoa, sesame seeds, buckwheat, and amaranth.

SUPERFOOD: A non-scientific term for foods containing high levels of nutrients, such as antioxidants, vitamins, and protein. Claimed to reduce the risk of chronic disease and to alleviate existing disease. Lists of superfoods vary because of the ill-defined criteria.

TAMARI: A soy-based Japanese sauce similar to common soy sauce. Generally darker in color, richer in flavor, and less salty. Unlike soy sauce, it contains little to no wheat.

TAPIOCA FLOUR (ALSO KNOWN AS TAPIOCA STARCH): Gluten-free flour made from the cassava root. Frequently combined with quinoa flour to add structure, as gluten does, to baked goods.

TOASTED QUINOA: Uncooked quinoa browned without oil in a sauté pan. May alternatively roast quinoa in the oven.

TURMERIC: A spice used extensively in the cuisine of India and Southeast Asia. Piquant flavor and mild peppery aroma. Imparts bright yellow color to food; sometimes used for color alone. Less expensive substitute for saffron.

VEGAN (N): A person who does not eat animals or animal products such as milk and eggs and also refrains from wearing or using animal products such as leather.

VINAIGRETTE: A sauce or dressing made of a vegetable oil, such as olive oil, and an acidic ingredient such as vinegar or citrus juice. May be flavored with ingredients such as mustard, herbs, spices, or fruit.

References

AncientHarvest.com. "Recipes." Accessed January 6, 2015. ancientharvest.com/quinoa-recipes.

Anies, San. "Quinoa Superfood" website. Accessed January 6, 2015. www.quinoasuperfood.com.

Blazes, Marian. "Quinoa." Accessed January 6, 2015. southamericanfood.about.com/od/glossaryofterms/g/quinoanew.htm.

Celiac.org. "Gluten-Free Diet." Accessed January 6, 2015. celiac.org/live-gluten-free/glutenfreediet.

Food and Agriculture Organization of the United Nations. *International Cookbook for Quinoa: Tradition and Innovation*. Rome, Italy: Food and Agriculture Organization of the United Nations, 2014.

Forberg, Cheryl. *Cooking with Quinoa for Dummies*. Hoboken, New Jersey: John Wiley & Sons, 2013.

Green, Patricia, and Carolyn Hemming. "Patricia & Carolyn" website. Accessed January 6, 2015. http://patriciaandcarolyn.com/.

Green, Patricia, and Carolyn Hemming. *Quinoa 365: The Everyday Superfood*. Vancouver, British Columbia, Canada: Whitecap Books Ltd, 2010.

Gruss, Teri. "How to Use Quinoa in Gluten-Free Recipes." Accessed January 6, 2015. glutenfreecooking.about.com/od/glutenfreeingredien2/p/quinoainglutenfreerecipes.htm.

Mikuy, Allin, and Sumak Mikuy. *Traditional High Andean Cuisine* (English Edition). Santiago de Chile, Chile: Food and Agriculture Organization of the United Nations, 2013.

NorQuin Staff. "NorQuin: Canadian Grown Quinoa" website. Accessed January 6, 2015. www.quinoa.com.

Polisi, Wendy. "Cooking Quinoa" website. Accessed January 6, 2015. www.cookingquinoa.net.

Pujol, Layla. "Ecuadorian Recipes." Accessed January 6, 2015. laylita.com/recipes/ecuadorian-recipes.

Rimmer, Alyssa. "Simply Quinoa" website. Accessed January 6, 2015. www.simplyquinoa.com.

Shulman, Martha Rose. "Recipes for Health: Quinoa." Accessed January 6, 2015. topics.nytimes.com/top/news/health/series/recipes_for_health/quinoa/index.html.

Slow Food Editore Staff. *Quinoa in the Kitchen*. Bra, Cuneo, Italy: Slow Food, 2013.

The World's Healthiest Foods. "Quinoa." Accessed January 6, 2015. www.whfoods.com/genpage.php?tname=foodspice&dbid=142.

Whole Grains Council. "Quinoa: March Grain of the Month." Accessed January 6, 2015. wholegrainscouncil.org/whole-grains-101/quinoa-march-grain-of-the-month.

Resources

allrecipes.com
Dozens of quinoa recipes.
allrecipes.com/recipes/ingredients/
whole-grains/quinoa.

amazon.com
Source for quinoa, quinoa products, and quinoa cookbooks.
amazon.com/gp/search/ref=sr_pg_1?
rh=i%3Aaps%2Ck%3Aquinoa&keywords=
quinoa&ie=UTF8&qid=1424104876.

Ancient Harvest website
Quinoa recipes from a major maker of quinoa products.
ancientharvest.com/quinoa-recipes.

Celiac Disease Foundation
Website includes information about celiac disease and living gluten-free, including recipes.
celiac.org.

cookingquinoa.net
Scores of quinoa recipes, plus links to quinoa cookbooks.
www.cookingquinoa.net.

foodnetwork.com
Dozens of quinoa recipes.
www.foodnetwork.com/topics/
quinoa.page-13.html.

Gluten Intolerance Group
Website includes listings of certified gluten-free products and restaurants offering gluten-free dishes.
www.gluten.net.

National Foundation for Celiac Awareness
Website includes information about celiac disease and gluten-free food, including recipes.
www.celiaccentral.org.

NorQuin: Canadian Grown Quinoa website
Quinoa recipes and information about quinoa from a major maker of quinoa products.
www.quinoa.com.

Patricia & Carolyn website
Quinoa recipes and information about quinoa from "The Quinoa Sisters."
patriciaandcarolyn.com.

Quinoa Superfood website
Quinoa recipes and information about quinoa.
www.quinoasuperfood.com.

Simply Quinoa website
Quinoa recipes and information about quinoa.
www.simplyquinoa.com.

Recipe Index

Index